Also by Jeff Koehler

Spain: Recipes and Traditions
Morocco: A Culinary Journey
Rice, Pasta, Couscous: The Heart of the Mediterranean Kitchen
La Paella: Deliciously Authentic Rice Dishes from Spain's Mediterranean
Coast

Darjeeling

Darjeeling

*The Colorful History and Precarious Fate of the World's
Greatest Tea*

JEFF KOEHLER

BLOOMSBURY

NEW YORK · LONDON · NEW DELHI · SYDNEY

Bloomsbury USA
An imprint of Bloomsbury Publishing Plc

1385 Broadway	50 Bedford Square
New York	London
NY 10018	WC1B 3DP
USA	UK

www.bloomsbury.com

BLOOMSBURY and the Diana logo are trademarks of Bloomsbury Publishing Plc

First published 2015

ISBN: HB: 978-1-62040-512-3
        PB: 978-1-62040-513-0
        ePub: 978-1-62040-514-7

Library of Congress Cataloging-in-Publication Data

Koehler, Jeff.
Darjeeling : the story of the world's greatest tea in four harvests / Jeff Koehler.—
First U.S. edition.
pages cm
Includes bibliographical references and index.
ISBN 978-1-62040-512-3 (hardcover) – ISBN 9781620405130 (paperback) –
ISBN 978-1-62040-514-7 (ebook)
1. Tea trade—India—Darjeeling (District)—History. 2. Tea—India--Darjeeling
(District)—History. I. Title. HD9198.I42K64 2015
338.1'7372—dc23
2014033312

2 4 6 8 10 9 7 5 3 1

Typeset by RefineCatch Limited, Bungay, Suffolk
Printed and bound in the U.S.A. by Thomson-Shore Inc., Dexter, Michigan

To Tod Nelson, for years of friendship and reading early drafts

Contents

Two Leaves and a Bud

The rows of ceiling fans struggled to cool the raked Kolkata auction room. Their collective whir barely covered the cawing of large crows on the trees outside or the incessant honking horns from black-and-canary-yellow Ambassador taxis moving through the perpetually slow traffic. Nearly two inches of rain had fallen on Friday, and after a relatively dry weekend, drenching monsoon showers returned on Monday, July 14, 2003. It was approaching ninety degrees Fahrenheit, and the humidity stood at over 90 percent. Parts of the city remained submerged knee-deep in water. Dark, spongy clouds hung overhead. Only the lightest of breezes moved in the thick air.

Tea buyers, agents, exporters, blenders, and "packeteers" had gathered for Sale No. 28 of Darjeeling tea[1] on the second floor of Nilhat House, a boxy and bright midcentury midrise shoehorned into the old city center. The building houses J. Thomas & Co., India's oldest and largest firm of tea brokers and auctioneers.

Darjeeling is known for its single-estate teas, unblended and unflavored. With characteristic brightness frequently likened to newly minted coins, fragrant aromas, and sophisticated, complex flavors—delicate, even flowery (more stem than petal, as one expert blender put it), with hints of apricots and peaches, muscat grapes, and toasty nuts—it's the world's premium tea, the "champagne of tea."

That day at the weekly event, the auctioneer Kavi Seth thought they might see unusually high prices with the exceptional quality of some of the tea on offer—specifically a lot from Makaibari, one of Darjeeling's oldest gardens. Since the early 1980s, Makaibari had been under control of Rajah

Banerjee, the charismatic, fourth-generation owner, who converted it into an organic oasis with more than half the estate under deep forest cover. He sought exceptional leaf quality through healthy soil and viewed the farm as a complete, self-contained organism. Some buyers considered it to be the finest, purest Darjeeling tea available—with a cosmic edge. Banerjee farms observed wider lunar patterns and planetary rhythms, and the lot in question up for auction that day, christened Silver Tips Imperial, had been picked under a full moon. "If Darjeeling is the champagne of teas," *Time* magazine proclaimed in 2008, "Makaibari is the Krug or Henri Giraud."[2]

Seth started with J. Thomas in 1985, had been intimately involved with Darjeeling tea for a decade, and had been in charge of the catalog and auction of Darjeeling teas for the previous two years. While he had tasted tens of thousands of Darjeeling teas, Seth recognized something extraordinary in the Makaibari lot. A decade later he still vividly recalls its "special flavor and quality." Seth did two things to build excitement. First, he spread the word among buyers. Second, quite extraordinarily, he listed it last in the catalog. Normally the standout teas are toward the beginning and then mixed around. But this would be the day's final lot and force buyers to stick around until the very end.

In the crowded auction room, Seth worked through hundreds of lots of teas, coming, at last, in late afternoon, to the anticipated Makaibari offering.

That midsummer, Darjeeling tea was fetching on average 150.25 rupees per kilo, then worth about $3.25, at the weekly auction, with leaf grades—the highest level—averaging Rs 295.[3] (By contrast, the year's all-India average for 2003 was Rs 77.25.)*

Yet Seth opened the bidding at Rs 3,000.

Buyers, perhaps drained from the anticipation and tension, the warm room, and humidity outside, and keenly aware of the significant amount of money they were committing to laying out, slowly countered one another with slightly higher offers under the auctioneer's nudging.

Then a new buyer jumped into the bidding. Representing a European firm, he was keen to secure the lot of five small chests of tea. A current surged through the room, and bidding rallied.

Sitting at a dais in the front of the room, the auctioneer took offers and counteroffers as the amount spiraled aggressively upward by the hundreds of rupees, speeding past Rs 8,000, Rs 10,000, and Rs 12,000. Soon it

---

* For general values, Rs 55 equals US$1—the average of the last decade or so. Historic exchange rates are also used. Prices are accurate into 2014.

approached—and quickly shot by—the standing world record of Rs 13,001 for tea sold at wholesale auction that had been set in 1992 by a tea from another Darjeeling estate, Castleton, which abuts Makaibari. A murmur charged through the audience—and then a hush. Everyone was aware of being part of something special. Seth thought he would see a good price that afternoon for the lot, but he hadn't imagined it would go this high.

Darjeeling tea is often sold not just by single estate like wines, but also by *flush*, or harvesting season, a term nearly exclusive to tea from the far northeast of India. The fresh shoots from each bush are picked—or, more properly, *plucked*—every week or so from mid-March to mid-November, as they gradually progress through a quartet of distinct seasons, beginning with first flush in spring and ending with autumn flush. While Darjeeling tea's unique brightness and aromatic flavors set it apart from other similar types of tea, each of the four periods produces a tea with distinctive characteristics.

Makaibari's stock selling that day had been picked during the prime early-summer second flush, when Darjeeling tea is at its most vibrant. Tea from this flush has a sublime body and pronounced muscatel tones, with a mellowed, intense fruitiness and bright coppery color. "At its best, Second Flush Darjeeling is unquestionably the most complex black tea the world produces," wrote James Norwood Pratt, one of North America's foremost tea authorities, "with an everlasting aftertaste it shares with no other."[4] Upward the price climbed, past Rs 14,000, Rs 15,000, and Rs 16,000, demolishing the auction world record. Past Rs 17,000.

An agent for Godfrey Phillips India, bidding on behalf of a couple of international clients, agreed to Rs 18,000 per kilo ($390.70). The amount was 120 times more than Darjeeling tea's average and almost 250 times the country's average for tea at auction. A million rupees—ten *lakhs*, as they say in India—for the small lot containing fifty-five kilograms (about 120 pounds) of tea. That's the equivalent of two tea-stuffed suitcases going for more than $10,000 each wholesale.

The European representative desperately wanted the invoice but had reached his authorized limit. He frantically tried to call on his cell phone for the go-ahead to bid higher.

Seth asked for takers for a higher bid.

The European buyer couldn't pick up a signal. No one else said a word. The crowded room smelled of sweat and tension and humidity. Fans whirled overhead.

Seth asked a last time.

In the silent room the agent struggled to get a signal and make his urgent call.

"Knocking to Godfrey Phillips at eighteen thousand," Seth finally said, smacking the table with the side of the wooden head of his Raj-era gavel cupped flat in his palm.

Cheers erupted in the auction room and a ringing round of applause. Seth thanked the buyers and participants—and their appreciation of the tea's quality. Two of the five chests were destined for Upton Tea Imports in Holliston, Massachusetts, one for Japan, and two to an associate of Makaibari's.[5] The garden had just set a new record for tea sold at whole-sale auction.

"It was a landmark event," Seth said by telephone from Kolkata. "The record still stands. We are unlikely to see it broken for many, many years."

Today tea is grown in forty-five countries around the world and is the second most commonly drunk beverage after water. It's a $90 billion global market.[6] Until just a few years ago, India was the world's largest producer of tea. Although overtaken by China, it still produces about a billion kilograms—more than two billion pounds—a year.

Tea can generally be classified in six distinct types: black, oolong, green, yellow, white, and pu-erh. All come from the same plant. The difference lies in processing. Nearly all of India's is black tea, which means that the leaves have been withered and fermented and certain characteristic flavors allowed to develop. (Green tea is neither withered nor fermented, and oolong is only semifermented.) Yet the wide geographic and climatic range of India's tea-growing areas, from lowland jungle to Himalayan foothills, means that it produces a variety of distinctive black teas.

A framed Tea Board of India map leans against the wall of Mittal Stores, a cramped, sixty-year-old tea shop in New Delhi's quiet Sunder Nagar market. Bordered by a braid of blue tea buds and colored in the saturated gold and green tones of 1970s Kodachrome 64 slide film, on the map the country sits raised, like an old-fashioned wooden puzzle piece lifted from its base, in three-dimensional thickness but strangely flat. Green-shaded areas, those with tea estates, stretch across the northeast limb of the country, the spine of hills that rise up in the south, and a handful of other spots in the north. Each place gives a little different character to the final cup, from the full-bodied teas of Assam to those from Nilgiri, which can be wonderfully brisk and aromatic yet carry a certain freshness.

Darjeeling has only eighty-seven tea estates. Together they have just 19,500 hectares (48,000 acres) under tea. That's not much; Queen Elizabeth II's Balmoral Estate measures the same amount. They produce only a fraction of the world's tea, and less than a single percent of India's total. Yet the tea from that limited crop is the indisputable jewel in India's tea-producing crown, its most iconic brew, and the flag-bearer of Indian teas abroad. Here, ecology, history, tradition, culture, and terroir come together to create a sublime product with an unduplicable essence.

"It has complexity with a certain level of intensity," noted Vikram Mittal on a recent autumn morning in his busy shop. He sipped a small cup of first flush Jungpana, an estate reached by hundreds of steps and considered by many in the industry to be currently producing the best tea in the district. "Complexity and flavor. An aftertaste that stays, that fills the mouth. A whole experience." Mittal, in his early fifties, thin, with frameless glasses perched on his sharp nose and a graying mustache, retains the enthusiasm and sense of wonder of a young science teacher. "There is complexity with a certain level of intensity. There is that complex aftertaste, that feeling you get afterward," he said in his quiet voice. "You can see it when you taste it with other teas. When you only drink Darjeeling, it seems nothing special. In the beginning I thought it was a bit of hype. But when I started tasting it with other teas . . ." He finished his cup of Jungpana and shook his head slightly, still amazed, after all these years, after thousands and thousands of teas, by the flavors that Darjeeling's hills can produce.

"You can't *create* a flavor," said Sanjay Kapur of Darjeeling's fine teas in his Aap Ki Pasand tea boutique, across town from Mittal Stores in Old Delhi. "It's natural."

Specifically, Darjeeling tea is *orthodox* black tea. The leaves are withered, rolled, fermented, and fired in the traditional method. Orthodox now implies premium teas that have been hand-plucked and hand-processed.

But more than 90 percent of the world's (and the majority of India's) black teas are produced by a method called CTC (cut, tear, curl). In the mid-twentieth century, with the growing popularity of tea bags, a new way to process leaves was developed that made it more convenient for filling the small sachets as well as brewing a quicker, stronger liquor—the name for the infused liquid. Instead of rolling and twisting the leaves, a machine chops and cuts them into small pieces with blades revolving at different speeds. The result is chocolate-brown granules of tea, even and pebbly rather than wiry and twisted like orthodox leaves. While CTC teas are easier and less expensive to produce, they don't have a wide spectrum of flavors. Tasters look for color and strength, something known in the industry as "good liquoring." The best way to assess is by adding a dash of milk to the cupped liquor. The drops disappear into the dark brew before blooming up and turning the tea a flat, slate brown.

"Darjeeling tea is a different ball game altogether," said Kapur.

Darjeeling has poise rather than the bounce of other Indian black teas, patience over velocity, and, like the finest female vocalists, can carry body as well as subtlety and grace. Its quiet, unadulterated elegance lingers on the palate.

India is a tea-drinking country. But it hasn't always been that way, or even for very long.

At Independence in 1947, all but 51 million kilograms, or 20 percent of its total production of 252 million kilograms (555 million pounds), was for national consumption.[7] The drink had imperial associations and was even considered unhealthy by some. "The leaves contain tannin which is harmful to the body," Mahatma Gandhi wrote in his 1948 book *Key to Health*. "Tannin is generally used in the tanneries to harden leather. When taken internally it produces a similar effect upon the mucous lining of the stomach and intestine. This impairs digestion and causes dyspepsia."[8] Not until the 1960s, with the availability of inexpensive CTC tea, which was well suited to being boiled with milk and plenty of sugar and even spices, did vast numbers of roadside tea stalls appear and the drink become popular within the country. Extremely popular. India consumes more tea that anywhere else in the world, and the drink has become equally a symbol for Indians as for the British. Today about 800 million kilograms (1.75 billion pounds)—80 percent of its total production—is for the local market, a 15,000 increase since Independence.

But such statistics don't apply to Darjeeling. Around three-fourths of Darjeeling tea is exported to some forty-three countries.

Darjeeling tea is the choice of the global connoisseur—and the well-heeled. At the upmarket Parisian tea purveyor Mariage Frères, arguably the world's greatest tea store, with six hundred varieties of tea from thirty producing countries in heavy tins lining the walls, the most expensive in the shop (excepting some gimmicky green teas crafted with gold) is a summer-flush Darjeeling. At the poshest places for afternoon tea in London—the Dorchester, the Langham, Claridge's in Mayfair, and even the Ritz, with five sittings a day, booked months in advance, jacket and tie required for gentlemen—Darjeeling teas are highlighted on the menu and recommended by tea sommeliers.

Perhaps most tellingly, it fills, insiders whisper, the most selective, discerning teapots of all: those in Buckingham Palace.

Darjeeling tea's story is romantic. Like all romances, it has a strong element of improbability, even randomness, to its beginnings, with false starts, near misses, and plenty of luck along the way to the plant's finding its perfect home. The story is rich in history, intrigue, and empire, in adventurers and unlikely successes, in the looming Himalayas and drenching monsoons, in culture, mythology, and religions, in ecology, and even opium. All these elements have contributed to making Darjeeling's tea unique.

But Darjeeling's tea estates are also based on a system of farming that has become untenable. The future—the present, even—of India's most famous export is under serious threat.

How will Darjeeling tea—one of the Raj's greatest legacies—and even Darjeeling itself, a symbol of that era, survive in these high-tech times? Can such traditions resist the riptide of India's strident economic and cultural changes, its modern ambitions? Can a product that requires such tedious, highly skilled, and lowly paid manual labor continue to exist with the rising role of education and technology? The aspirations of many workers in Darjeeling making less than $2 a day have awoken, inspired, no doubt, by dreams of software firms and Bangalore call centers (or even, more realistically, of being a Mumbai security guard or Delhi housemaid). In just a handful of years, worker absenteeism has shot up from negligible to as high as 40 percent on some estates. Simply put, few want to pluck tea anymore.

Especially when it takes a staggering *twenty-two thousand* selectively hand-picked shoots—just the tender first two leaves and a still-curled bud—to produce a single kilo of Darjeeling tea.

And that kilo of tea can sell for more than many months of wages.

This is far from the industry's only pressing challenge, though. Can Darjeeling's tea gardens, part of India's living heritage, survive the area's separatist unrest, which is pushing violently for independent statehood

with protests that shut down the hills for weeks at a time? Or the unprecedented pressure on its fragile ecosystem and changes in climate? The
monsoons have become stronger and less predictable and are often
bookended by severe droughts. Temperatures have risen. Hail the size of
baseballs can pile up three feet deep in a single storm. Soil erosion is a
severe issue, and landsides a yearly problem, sweeping away fields, roads,
and bridges, even small villages and swaths of tea estates. Even stable land
is problematic. The soil is depleted, many tea bushes are old and dying,
with little replanting in the last decades. Recent harvests have yielded
only half of what they once did. "Counterfeit" Darjeeling tea, produced
elsewhere and mislabeled, has flooded the market.

So this is the story of how Darjeeling came to produce the highest-
quality tea leaves anywhere in the world, and how it spiraled into decline
by the beginning of the twenty-first century. It's also about the radical
measures being taken to counter the multitude of challenges and save
India's most exclusive and iconic brew. The most revolutionary among
them is not based on technological advances or automation but ancient
practices grounded in three-thousand-year-old Hindu scriptures.

Tea is more than merely a drink—it's a soother and an energizer, a
marker of time and a measure of it, present at the most quotidian moments
of daily life and at the most special. It seeps into life, and sustains it.

And at its source, the world's most celebrated tea is more than just
any crop—it's the history and politics of India and Britain, the legacy of
colonialism, the rise of global commerce and worker aspirations, the
perils of climate change, and much, much more, writ large, and brewed
into one glorious cup of amber liquid.

First Flush

(late February to mid-April)

*B*rass bells wound with garlands of orange marigolds hang from the entrance arch for the faithful to ring as they enter the tree-filled temple complex atop Observatory Hill. Clean chimes reverberate in the quiet, chilly dawn from Darjeeling's highest spot. Printed prayer flags in bold, solid colors—red, green, yellow, white, blue—strung on hemp ropes between poles, pillars, and tree trunks stir in the spring breeze. A troop of pale-faced monkeys, whose connection to the holiness of temples means that they are left unmolested, roam and maraud, stealing shoes that have been removed by the faithful while they kneel, pray, and light incense and small clay lamps filled with ghee (clarified butter) to one of a pantheon of gods as morning sunlight gradually slides up the surrounding slopes.

The short, early spring rains have passed, and gleamings of verdant freshness are in the Darjeeling hills. Giant ferns blanket the mountainsides. Pink magnolias and camellias bloom, the first of the pinkish-red rhododendrons.

The tea bushes, stimulated by the moisture after a winter of dormancy, begin to flush new shoots so quickly that they need to be picked every four to five days. As the light filters through the darting clouds, workers pluck the young leaves: slender and lightly serrated, lacquered green in color, sprightly.

The finished tea comes out of the dryer grayish green. Steeped, it produces a pale-gold to almost-green-toned liquor that's grassy with fresh-cut-field aromas and a floralness in its bouquet, intensely fruity in the mouth, with a hint—no more—of tartness. The season is still cool and breezy in the high hills, and that freshness carries on into the cup.

"First flush is a spring tea," said Glenburn Tea Estate's young manager and resident tea maker, Sanjay Sharma, in the garden's well-lit tasting room.

"The cup's light, it's bright, it's fresh, it's green, it's brisk," Sanjay recited in *rapid-fire singsong, touching the tips of his fingers with each adjective. "It has that hint of astringency, so that lends a little crispness to the cup, it's fresh on the palate."*

Standing at the white-tiled counter, he considered the cup he was describing. Looking more like a safari guide than a tea planter, Sanjay wore polished leather Timberland boots with white socks rolled at the calves, khaki shorts, a pressed white polo shirt, and a zipper photo vest with an inch-thick Swiss Army knife snapped into a top pocket. He had a quick grin and ready one-liners, whiskery chin-beard, and an Errol Flynn mustache that gave him a slightly caddish look only somewhat offset by his rimless glasses. His left hand, partly covered with a patchy scar from a childhood cobra bite, fingered the white tasting cup emblazoned with Glenburn's name in elaborate Victorian cursive. "Also it's the time when we have all the citrus plants or trees blossoming, so it's got a very fruity kind of citrusy-ness note to it." It has, he said, "everything synonymous with springtime."

Darjeeling tea is "self-drinking," meaning not only that blending it with another tea is not required—a standard practice among most of the world's black teas—but also that it doesn't need milk or sugar or even, because of the slight astringency, lemon. While the bold and brisk black teas from other regions in India are often prepared as sweet, milky masala chai, spiced by ginger, cardamom, and cinnamon, and slurped scalding hot from a glass held nimbly between thumb and middle finger, Darjeeling's flavors are delicate, easily buried by such additions, and washed out by more than a few drops of milk.

First flush teas are the most delicate Darjeelings of all.

Commanding top prices, they are highly anticipated by aficionados, especially in Europe, where certain boutiques and tea rooms celebrate their arrival with pomp generally given over to Beaujolais wine. DARJEELING NOUVEAU announces a round sign in the window of the legendary Parisian maison de thé, Mariage Frères, and in a banner across the top of its Web site, of the year's first offerings. "Arrivage spécial par avion," it says, Grands Crus and Première Récolte from a highly selective choice of gardens: "Aloobari, Happy Valley, Ambootia, Namring, Castleton, North Tukvar, Nurbong, Bloomfield, Moondakotee." This is akin to listing Bordeaux's most prestigious châteaux.

Sanjay took a sip and yielded to the tea's gentle, composed embrace in silence.

"Springtime in a teacup," he calls it.

CHAPTER I

Into the Hills

Darjeeling is isolated. Located in the far north of the country among high mountain peaks, it's jammed like a thumb between once-forbidden Himalayan kingdoms: Nepal to the west, Bhutan to the east, and Sikkim (and then Tibet) to the north. The closest airport is Bagdogra, outside Siliguri, a hot, flat city down at the edge of the northeastern plains where the Himalayas begin their abrupt crest. From Delhi, Bagdogra is a two-hour flight east, paralleling the snowy, sinewy range; from Kolkata less, but still a solid hour flight straight north.

In March and April—dreaded April, "herald of horrors," E. M. Forster called it, when the sun returns "with power but without beauty"[1]—as winter lurches into summer, the flat landscape is parched. The browns turn bronze and sandy as the plane travels east. From above, through the hovering, dusty haze, the landscape takes on the sepia tone of an old American West photograph, and the ambling, channeled Ganges glints like a dulled scissor blade on its lazy arc to the Bay of Bengal. Walking down the narrow stairs from the airplane and across the tarmac, with fresh tar painted in broad strokes along its weathered cracks, to Bagdogra's low, white terminal, the sharp glare makes disembarking passengers wince, and the heat smacks with the unsettling force of an open palm.

While fields of tea are immediately around the airport—flat expanses broken by sal trees with tall, straight trunks—the famed estates of Darjeeling are on the slopes that rise through the shimmering, hot air to the north.

Darjeeling is just fifty miles away by road. But it takes about four hours to reach.

From the airport, seven or eight slow miles bring one to Siliguri, as traffic braids around potholes, bicycles and cycle rickshaws, goats, rusted buses, high-riding military trucks, and pale cows with coffin-shaped skulls. Schoolgirls with pigtails tied in colored ribbons walk along the uneven lip of the blacktop. Boys in boiled white shirts, their uniform jackets dangling jauntily by a thumb over the shoulder, follow behind. Long-stemmed leaves on pipal trees dangle downward, heart-shaped pendulums that rustle like muffled wind chimes with the slightest breeze. Rusted corrugated-tin roofs cover the small houses. Once the monsoon rains arrive in heady, uneven bursts, they turn the houses into reverberating echo chambers—and the road to muck. But in early spring, it's sweltering and dusty, and the relief of rain only a distant dream.

Once across the Balasan River, the route turns north up the Rohini Road toward the crumpled eruption of hills just discernible in the haze. In June 2010, landslides wiped out the main Hill Cart Road in a trio of places, and it has yet to be repaired. For the first half of the journey, the main route now cuts up a parallel valley to the west instead.

After passing through a cluster of small shops selling sodas and *paan*, school satchels and wicker tables, the road opens up and runs flat and straight at the foothills as it cuts between two tea estates—Longview on the left, the lower sections of Rohini on the right. Goats graze in the scrub, and a troop of macaques—pale brown fur, pinkish faces—squat patiently at the edge of the road as if waiting for a bus. A traffic sign cautions against elephants crossing; a handful of brilliant-white, erect egrets stand in sprouting fields; and browned, plate-size leaves, curled like old leather *chappals*, get swept along the blacktop behind trucks.

The lurch upward is sudden, and the flatness quickly turns steep and tropical. Passing through a handful of terraced rice fields, rippling green with tender, springtime shoots, the road begins to switchback, looping around clusters of bamboo stout as flagpoles and broad as a man's thigh, patches of wild bananas, and thick-buttressed trees with knobby boles. Blue, blunt-nosed trucks barrel downhill with processed first flush teas under the cinched canvas tarps and return carrying everything else to the out-of-the-way part of India. Uphill traffic has the right of way on the tightest stretches.

With its close position to the Bay of Bengal and the monsoon winds whose moisture condenses and causes heavy rainfall when they come against the mountain range, this is the most humid part of the entire Himalayan chain. "The abrupt juxtaposition of so many different biotopes of life zones—ranging from almost plains level"—Siliguri is a mere four hundred feet above sea level—"to over 6000 m [20,000 feet], and from tropical heat to arctic cold—all telescoped within a straight-line distance of hardly more than 80 km [50 miles]," wrote one of India's greatest naturalists, Sálim Ali, "has given to the eastern Himalayas a flora and fauna which for richness and variety is perhaps unequalled in the world."[2] Mark Twain, traveling to Darjeeling in the 1890s, was impressed by the journey—"so wild and interesting and exciting and enchanting"—but even more by the variety of roadside fauna. "As for the vegetation, it is a museum," he wrote of his ascent to the hill station in *Following the Equator*. "The jungle seemed to contain samples of every rare and curious tree and bush that we had ever seen or heard of. It is from that museum, I think, that the globe must have been supplied with the trees and vines and shrubs that it holds precious."[3]

At Kurseong (4,864 feet)—roughly the halfway point to Darjeeling— the Rohini Road feeds into Hill Cart Road, and the air, subtly, begins to freshen. Ahead, tiers of alpine greens; but looking back, the dust of the plains hangs in the air below as if the road spirals up from nothing but glare.

A grassy pull-off lies a switchback or two before the junction. A pair of weathered steel benches on a knoll overlooks a trio of converging valleys. The greenness feels excessive.

Along the steep, surrounding hillsides are some of Darjeeling's most celebrated tea estates, including Makaibari, Castleton, and Ambootia. Small groups of women can often be spotted on their slopes. They stand half-hidden between the linear rows of waist-high tea bushes, deep, conical wicker baskets on their backs, moving, almost unperceptibly, in their seemingly Sisyphean task of plucking new shoots along the grand sweep of tea-covered vista.

"From Kursiong a very steep zigzag leads up the mountain, through a magnificent forest of chestnut, walnut, oaks, and laurels," wrote the eminent British botanist Joseph Dalton Hooker on his mid-April 1848 journey up to a barely settled Darjeeling to collect plants in the region. "It is difficult to conceive a grander mass of vegetation:—the straight shafts of the timber-trees shooting aloft, some naked and clean, with grey, pale, or brown bark; others literally clothed for yards with a continuous garment of epiphytes, one mass of blossoms, especially the white Orchids, which bloom in a profuse manner, whitening their trunks like snow."[4]

That description remains much the same 165 years on. At least on Hill Cart Road's upper side. Below, patches of tea now cover much of the land, which falls sharply away toward the valley's base with a clutch of estates whose borders interlock like hand-cut jigsaw pieces: Monteviot, Edenvale, Margaret's Hope, Oaks, Singell, Rington, Dilaram, Balasun, Kaley Valley, Pussimbing.

The road cleaves through dense, tall evergreen forests with lichen-covered oaks and rhododendrons and runs for long stretches under a canopy of cool, shading foliage. Great bands of liana thick as cables sag among branches, and mosses and blooming climbers run up century-old brick retaining walls like vertical flower beds. Traffic is heavy from morning until dark, and drivers obey the signs that read HONK AT EVERY CURVE. Square stones set directly into the tarmac stud the road for traction. With the rains still a few months away, water trucks park at meager streams and siphon water into large, black plastic tanks to sell to hotels and Darjeeling residents. From telephone poles, leaf-green and white political flags flap and shimmy. Landslides and smaller landslips scar the hills and expose entrails of sheer rock like clawed gashes.

The road crests at Ghoom, elevation 7,407 feet. It passes an open-sided Darjeeling Himalayan Railway station—steam escapes from one of the coal-fired engines of the "toy train" that still plies a section of the narrow-gauge rail line; waiting passengers wear hats and coats in the chilly air—and then beneath an important nineteenth-century Buddhist monastery with gently curving rooftop corners and a hedge of sacred flags. From here, it's a gentle half-dozen-mile descent into Darjeeling.

The city soon comes into sight clinging to the steep ridges and shelves of the hillsides. The setting is dramatic. In Hooker's description:

> Dorjiling station occupies a narrow ridge, which divides into two spurs, and descends steeply to the bed of the great Rungeet river, up whose course the eye is carried to the base of the great snowy mountains. The ridge itself is very narrow at the top, along which most of the houses are perched, while others occupy positions on its flanks, where narrow *locations* on the east, and broader ones on the west, are cleared from wood. The valleys on either side are at least 6000 feet deep, forest-clad to the bottom, with very few and small level spots, and no absolute precipice; from their flanks project innumerable little spurs, occupied by native clearings.[5]

Beyond the city, the heavily forested Himalayan foothills layer off in waves toward an uninterrupted jumble of silvery-white peaks that stretch across the horizon and include the magnificent Kanchenjunga. The name means Five Treasures of Snow, after the five peaks that dominate the skyline like a collection of sails with their wide snowfields, glaciers, and blunt, angular whiteness. At 28,169 feet, it's the world's third-tallest peak behind Everest and K2. Kanchenjunga's proximity and the feeling of its hovering over Darjeeling is wholly unexpected.

Modern Darjeeling has spilled beyond its confines to sprawl farther along the ridges in a denser and more crowded clutter, and bulky cement structures have replaced most of the old wooden buildings, but the first view from the front seat is much the same as it has been for many decades.

So is the feeling of it as a frontier town when entering the crowded lower bazaar with its eclectic gathering of people—mountain peoples, with their coppery, Himalayan features—from surrounding hills and the strong sense of movement. Jeeps—so-called, but actually similar-looking Mahindra Boleros as well as Tata Sumos, beefy Mahindra Scorpios, and the odd vintage Land Rover patched together with few original parts—are continually being loaded or unloaded with passengers and bundles secured with rope.

The journey up from Siliguri is arduous and exhausting. Most people immediately look for a cup of tea. But one notable Darjeeling hotel, acknowledging the frazzling drive, hands arriving guests small snifters of local cherry brandy instead.

The pitched landscape is steeped with the religious, the sacred, and the picturesque. The tea's essence, uniqueness, and greatness begins in this terroir—naturally, but also spiritually.

The name Darjeeling comes from Dorji Ling, where the thunderbolt of the Hindu deity Lord Indra—King of the Heavens, God of War, God of Rain and Storms—fell. The spot it landed is known as Observatory Hill, the highest place in Darjeeling. In the late-eighteenth century, Nepalese troops destroyed the Buddhist monastery that stood atop it, and today a complex of shrines and small temples mark the location that is holy to Buddhists and also Hindus. Prayer flags flutter in the wind, gradually shred, and carry threads of goodwill off to distant lands.

Arcing some 1,550 miles southeast across the top of the Indian subcontinent, the Himalayan mountain range guards the fountain that makes India a fertile, prosperous, and holy land. According to Hindu mythology, the Himalayas—the name means "house of snow" in Sanskrit, the ancient Indic language of Hindu scriptures and epic poems—is the abode of Lord Shiva and the place from which all water flows. Most important is the River Ganges. Known as Mother Ganges to Hindus, it represents the nectar of immortality and is a symbol of fertility. "In our legends it is said that the goddess Ganga's descent from the heavens would have split the earth had Lord Shiva not tamed her torrent by tying it into his ash-smeared locks," wrote the novelist Amitav Ghosh. Lord Shiva's hair, wound into a shell-like curl, is the source of the sacred river, which sprouts from his matted locks, "a heavenly braid," Ghosh called it, "an immense rope of water, unfurling through a wide and thirsty plain" before untangling into the sea in "hundreds, maybe thousands, of tangled strands."[6]

The Himalayas give not just water, then, but life.

From these mountains, locals believe, the breath of God blows cool air down over the Darjeeling hills and brings mist and fog and moisture that nurtures the neat rows of tabled, jade-green tea bushes that follow the steep contours of the valleys around this Victorian hill town.

The tea bushes seem a natural, integrated part of the surrounding hills, but they are not indigenous. Tea was only planted on these slopes just over a century and a half ago, a few years after the town began to take shape, at the tail end of a lengthy and improbable journey.

Tea came to Darjeeling as something of an afterthought, something almost accidental. The area was never really considered as a place for planting seeds or saplings. Even the venerable and much-respected Joseph Hooker opined that Darjeeling was too high with too little sun and too much moisture to grow tea.[7]

How wrong he was.

CHAPTER 2

Journey from the East

According to an ancient legend, tea was discovered by Bodhidharma (c. A.D. 460–534), the wandering, devout Buddhist monk born near the modern southern Indian city of Chennai (Madras) who founded the Zen (or Ch'an) school of Buddhism. In the fifth year of a seven-year sleepless contemplation of Buddha, he began to feel drowsy. To keep from falling asleep, he cut off his eyelids and threw them to the ground. (Or, as Sanjay Kapur tells the story, "Bodhidharma was so angry when he fell asleep he cut off his eyelids!") In the spot where they landed, tea bushes grew.

Another, gentler version of the legend says that during the fifth year of a seven-year, sleepless promotion of Buddhism around China, Bodhidharma began to feel drowsy. From a nearby tree, he plucked a few leaves and chewed them, and his tiredness disappeared. The bush was wild tea.

Or, one day, while he was boiling a kettle of water to purify it for drinking, a gust of wind blew a leaf into the pot. When Bodhidharma drank the liquid, he began to feel alert and lively.

Tea's actual history predates Bodhidharma. It goes back at least twenty-five hundred years to the mountains around Yunnan, in south-western China,[1] where it was initially blended with herbs, seeds, and forest leaves.[2] During the Zhou Dynasty (1046–256 B.C.), tea leaves began to be boiled and drunk without the addition of other herbs—that is, drunk as *tea* rather than a medicinal brew.[3] As China gradually unified into a single state, and techniques for processing and brewing the leaves were refined, tea drinking became imbued with artistic, religious, and cultural notes. In the Tang Dynasty (A.D. 618–907), the apogee of ancient Chinese prosperity and refinement, the drink garnered ritual, etiquette, and specific utensils.

During this period of unparalleled splendor, merchants commissioned the gifted Lu Yü (733–804) to write the first book dedicated solely to tea, *Ch'a Ching* (*The Classic of Tea*). Biographical sketches generally tell a Moses-like story of an abandoned infant found beside a river in a basket by the abbot of the Dragon Cloud Monastery.[4] Raised by monks who grew and processed tea, Lu Yü eventually rebelled against monastic life, left before being ordained, and joined a theatrical troupe, becoming a popular circus clown and playwright.[5] He then worked as a government official before settling into life as a scholar, poet, and tea expert.

Around 780, he penned his brief but comprehensive masterpiece on tea. It contains such precise details on tea's origins, cultivation, processing, and preparation that a thousand years later the British drew upon it when they started producing tea themselves. Yet it is not written in the language of a technical manual, but with a poet's imagery and inventive use of metaphor, as this celebrated passage on something as elementary as boiling water for tea reveals:

> When the water is boiling, it must look like fishes' eyes and give off but the hint of a sound. When at the edges it chatters like a bubbling spring and looks like pearls innumerable strung together, it has reached the second stage. When it leaps like breakers majestic and resounds like a swelling wave, it is at its peak. Any more and the water will be boiled out and should not be used.[6]

Throughout, he infused the practical with the spiritual and emphasized the ritualized details of tea making. Tea drinking should be treated with reverence and be accompanied by beauty but also restraint: "Moderation is the very essence of tea. Tea does not lend itself to extravagance."[7]

In the final decades of his life, Lu Yü, renowned and celebrated, withdrew from society and lived in solitude as a hermit. Upon his death, he metamorphosed into the god of tea. According to a tenth-century encyclopedia, tea merchants worshipped statues of Lu Yü in order to be blessed with good sales.[8]

But when their tea didn't sell well, the merchants would pour boiling water over the statue.[9]

• • •

Tea spread from China outward across eastern Asia, retaining its spiritual ties. This was particularly true in Japan, where a monk named Myoan Eisai (1141–1215) is often considered the father of Japanese tea.

Eisai took two trips to China and introduced the Rinzai sect of Zen Buddhism to his country. On his second trip, in 1191, he carried back tea seeds, which were planted successfully, including at a temple compound in the forested Uji Hills between Kyoto and Nara. While tea had been planted as far back as the eighth century in Japan, it did not become widespread until after Eisai's reintroduction.

Its popularity stemmed in part from the healthy, medicinal proper-ties that Eisai lauded in his book *Kissa Yojoki*, which means something like "drinking tea for health." "Tea is the ultimate mental and medical remedy and has the ability to make one's life more full and complete," Eisai boldly asserted in the first line of the book.

That included spiritual health, too. Tea, Alan Watts noted in *The Way of Zen*, "so clarifies and invigorates the mind that it has been said, 'The taste of Zen [*ch'an*] and the taste of tea [*ch'a*] are the same.'"[10] Zen monks used tea as a mediation stimulant,[11] and the drink became paramount in aiding long periods of deep concentration. "If Christianity is wine and Islam coffee," Watts wrote, "Buddhism is most certainly tea."[12]

"Tea began as a medicine and grew into a beverage," opens Kakuzo Okakura's *The Book of Tea* (1906). "In China, in the eighth century, it entered the realm of poetry as one of the polite amusements. The fifteenth century saw Japan ennoble it into a religion of aestheticism—Teaism."[13] The influential art critic and scholar wrote his book in English in order to celebrate the oriental uniqueness of Japan. He used tea as a symbol and, in doing so, introduced the Japanese tea ceremony to the West. The cult of teaism celebrates, Okakura wrote, "the beautiful among the sordid facts of everyday existence" and "inculcates purity and harmony, the mystery of mutual charity, the romanticism of the social order."[14]

From the formalities of Zen came the highly ritualized tea ceremony know as *cha-no-yu* (literally "tea hot water"). Okakura's in-depth descrip-tions of the three elements of the tea room—tea, pot, and place—are heightened by moments of poetic flight that Lu Yü would have appreci-ated. The author liberally quotes his Chinese predecessor on boiling water and even takes a brave, lyrical stab at describing it himself: "The singing kettle, as it boils over the brazier, sounds like some cicada pouring forth his woes to departing summer."[15] And elsewhere:

> The kettle sings well, for pieces of iron are so arranged in the bottom as to produce a peculiar melody in which one may hear the echoes of a cataract muffled by clouds, of a distant sea breaking among the rocks, a rainstorm sweeping through a bamboo forest, or of the soughing of pines on some faraway hill.[16]

During these ceremonies, Japanese tea masters were not infusing standard rolled tea leaves, but rather *matcha*, tea that had been steamed, dried, and crushed into a fine powder, which was then whipped with a delicate brush of split bamboo in exquisite teacups. The ancient poets of the southern Chinese dynasties, Okakura wrote, referred to the luminous green brew as the "froth of the liquid jade."[17]

Tea arrived in Europe in 1580 when a Portuguese trader brought a chest of it along with other Chinese luxury goods—silks, spices, porcelain, lacquered objects. The Dutch and British followed, with the first tea reaching The Hague in 1610 and London about the same time. By 1635 it was fashionable in the Dutch court and soon after the French one. Garway's Coffee House in London was serving it alongside coffee, drinking chocolate, and sherbet—as well as sherry, punch, and ale—in 1657.[18] Two years later, the great and gossipy observer of people Samuel Pepys recorded his first "Cupp of Tee" in his diary. Within a decade, it had reached the American colonies.

"There is a subtle charm in the taste of tea which makes it irresistible and capable of idealisation," Okakura noted of its widespread appeal. "It has not the arrogance of wine, the self-consciousness of coffee, nor the simpering innocence of cocoa."[19]

Nor, in England, initially at least, refinement.

Generally ill-packaged for the humid, months-long sea journey from China, and carried in a ship's hull among stinking cargo, tea, in those early London days, was taxed in liquid form. That meant coffeehouses brewed a big batch in the morning, stored it in wooden kegs like ale until the tax inspector assessed it, then served the tea, reheating it as needed throughout the day. It's not hard to imagine the woody, tongue-coating tannins of the drink by midafternoon, or even midday. The taste drastically improved once the Crown started taxing it in dried-leaf form and tea was brewed on demand.

But even then, few early references appear saying that the drink tasted delicious or good or even, quite simply, fine. Certainly, it was bitter.* And if it was bitter, then it had to be healthy. At the beginning of Europe's affair with tea, references accent the drink's medicinal benefits. The first known mention of tea in Europe is found in the second volume of the Venetian writer and geographer Giovanni Battista Ramusio's collection of travel narratives, *Navigationi et Viaggi* (1559). Along with accounts of Marco Polo's journeys, it included a firsthand report by an Arab traveler to China that refers to an "herb, whether dry or fresh" that the Chinese "boil well in water" and then drink.

> One or two cups of this decoction taken on an empty stomach removes fever, headache, stomachache, pain in the side or in the joints, and it should be taken as hot as you can bear it. He said, besides, that it was good for no end of other ailments which he could not remember, but gout was one of them. And if it happens that one feels incommoded in the stomach from having eaten too much, one has but to take a little of this decoction, and in a short time all will be digested.[20]

A year later, the Dominican missionary Father Gaspar da Cruz, the first to preach the Catholic doctrine in China, returned to Portugal and wrote that when guests "come to any man's house of quality," they are offered "a kind of drinke called *ch'a*, which is somewhat bitter, red, and medicinall, which they are wont to make with a certayne concoction of herbes."[21]

In an early reference by the German Johan Albrecht de Mandelslo (1616–44) European merchants in the Mughal port of Surat in India partake: "At our ordinary meetings every day, we took only *Thé*, which is commonly used all over the Indies, not only among those of the country, but also among the Dutch and English, who take it as a drug that cleanses

---

* George Orwell—culinary proletarian, heroically, even perversely, aesthetic, and a rare vocal supporter of World War II cauldrons of the brew—thought so. "Tea is meant to be bitter," the India-born author wrote, extolling the beverage's virtues, "just as beer is meant to be bitter." ("If you sweeten it, you are no longer tasting the tea, you are merely tasting the sugar," Orwell pointed out. As the eighteenth-century English novelist and playwright Henry Fielding put it, "Love and scandal are the best sweeteners of tea.")

the stomach, and digests the superfluous humours, by a temperate heat particular thereto."[22]

Salesmen and admen were quick to pick up on such travelers' reports. Tea's first advertisement in England ran in the broadsheet *Mercurius Politicus* in September 1658: "That excellent, and by all Physitians approved, *China* Drink, called by the Chineans *Tcha*, by other Nations *Tay* alias *Tee*, is sold at the Sultaness-head, a Cophee-house in Sweetings Rents by the Royal Exchange, London."[23] In 1660, coffeehouse proprietor Thomas Garway ran a much lengthier ad—some thirteen hundred words long—that took this physicians' endorsement significantly further. It extolled tea's virtues in a list of dozens of disparate benefits from stimulating the appetite ("particularly for Men of a Corpulent Body, and such as are great eaters of Flesh") to "removeth the Obstructions of the Spleen" and "cleareth the Sight." Not surprisingly, it also took aim at that ultimate advertising target, man's virility, claiming in the very first line of the ad that tea "maketh the Body active and lusty." (Lust gained a certain uplift, no doubt, by tea's ability to "cleanseth and purifyeth adult Humours and hot Liver.")[24]

Tea was, moreover, nonalcoholic, a not inconsequential point at a time when ale was being drunk for breakfast. The eighteenth-century poet William Cowper called tea "the cups, / That cheer but not inebriate,"[25] an ideal slogan for the temperance movement that rose to prominence in the mid-nineteenth century.

But such virtues didn't necessarily make it immediately fashionable among the society ladies and upper classes in England, nor did its exclusivity from the prohibitively high price. It became chic with Charles II's marriage to the Portuguese princess and tea addict Catherine of Braganza in 1662. Along with the ports of Bombay and Tangier and the free right to trade in Brazil and the East Indies, her dowry included a chest of tea.

The drink was new to the country, and so, too, to the English language. According to the *Oxford English Dictionary*, the first use of the word *tea*—or rather, its early variant, *chaa*—dates back to the 1598 translation of Jan Huyghen van Linschoten's *Discours of Voyages into ye Easte & West Indies*, which referred to the drink as being "made with the powder of a certaine hearbe called Chaa."[26] The spelling quickly ran through various forms—tay, tey, té, thé, the, teee, thea—before finally landing on its more familiar form, tea. Much of Western Europe derived their word from the term for tea in Amoy (now Xiamen) following the Dutch (*thee*), who traded it to them from their early base of Bantam, Java: *thee*

(German), *te* (Danish and Swedish), *té* (Spanish), *tè* (Italian), and *thé* (French).

The Hindi and Bengali terms for tea (*chai* and *cha*, respectively) derive from the second source for the word, the Cantonese *ch'a* (pronounced *chah*). So does Japanese (*cha*), Arabic (*shai* or *chai*), Persian (*chay*), and Russian (*chai*). Portugal (*chá*) is a Western European exception, but then they first obtained tea from Canton (today called Guangzhou).

The modern English pronunciation of tea took longer to catch up. When coffeehouse habitué Alexander Pope wrote *The Rape of the Lock* in 1714, he rhymed *tea* with *away* and *obey*. Fifty years later, the vowel had tightened, and the rake, rebel, and poet Charles Churchill wrote this sprightly couplet about reading tea leaves:

Matrons, who toss the cup, and see
The grounds of fate in grounds of tea[27]

By the time Churchill penned his verse, the price of tea had dropped from the dearly unaffordable to the merely expensive, and soon the drink moved from being a luxury of the aristocracy and upper class to a necessity of the working class. The British were enjoying a two- (or three- or four-) cups-a-day habit. Samuel Johnson declared himself "a hardened and shameless tea-drinker, who has, for twenty years, diluted his meals with only the infusion of this fascinating plant; whose kettle has scarcely time to cool; who with tea amuses the evening, with tea solaces the midnight, and, with tea, welcomes the morning."[28]

Certainly, one habit set the British apart from Chinese and Japanese tea drinkers: they were adding milk. Was it to avoid staining their fine bone-china cups? To soften tea's astringency? Help digestion? Garway's famed advertisement assured customers that tea prepared with water and milk "strengtheneth the inward parts, and prevents Consumptions, and powerfully assuageth the pains of the Bowels, or griping of the Guts and Looseness."[29] Maybe even, initially, it was simply fashion, following the French fad begun by the witty, prolific seventeenth-century letter writer Marquise de Sévigné, who advised her daughter to drink it with milk *and* sugar.[30]

Even though Britain struggled with the expense of importing tea, a burden passed on to those drinking, by the mid-eighteenth century, it was unquestionably the favorite drink in the British Isles. Its popularity never waned, nor did its status or significance.

Preparing tea had its own rituals, but they were never permeated with religious or philosophical elements as in China and Japan. "Despite its popularity, then, tea never became in the West what it had meant and still means to the East," wrote Lu Yü's fine English translator, Francis Ross Carpenter, in the introduction to *The Classic of Tea*. "If it was an extrinsic detail in the culture of the West, it was intrinsic to that of the East. The culture and the drink lived symbiotically, tea acquiring its mystique from the culture as it added new meanings and dimensions to life within the culture."[31]

Yet in Britain tea gained a relevance unsurpassed in the rest of Europe, and the British drew as much pleasure and even dependence from the drink as those in any place in Asia.

CHAPTER 3

The Company

In 1817, England imported a staggering 36,234,380 pounds of tea[1]—with a population of just 10 million. But where was it getting all of it? By time the teenage Queen Victoria became monarch in 1837, Britain ruled a patchwork of dominions that spread around the globe. Yet tea did not come from any of them.

Just as incredibly, for more than two centuries a single company held the exclusive right to bring it to Britain.

On the last day of 1600, Queen Elizabeth I granted a royal charter for fifteen years to a group of merchants for all of the trading rights to India and the Far East, which meant the vast territory east of Africa's Cape of Good Hope and west of South America's Straits of Magellan. The Company of Merchants of London Trading into the East Indies was the first of many incarnations of what was soon known by the more familiar East India Company. Or the Honourable Company. Or John Company. Or, colloquially in India, Company Bahadur (from the Hindi word for "brave"). Or, simply, the Company, with—always—a capital *C*.

At first it wasn't looking for tea, but spices: pepper, cloves, mace, nutmeg. Flavorings to enhance food, in some cases, to preserve it, and, frequently, to cover the taste of spoiling meats drove merchants to forge distant trade routes and search the farthest known, and even unknown, reaches of the globe.

Within two months of the charter's being signed, Captain James Lancaster sailed not for India but for the East Indies—roughly the modern-day Indonesian archipelago—with a small fleet of four ships and 480 men. Two and a half years later, with an outbreak of the plague having carried away nearly 20 percent of London's population and James I now on the throne, Lancaster returned carrying 1 million pounds of peppercorns from Sumatra in the hold of his flagship, the *Red Dragon*. Yet the journey was only a qualified success and the Company's future was not immediately assured. While all four ships made it home—an impressive feat—the expedition cost the lives of 182 men, two-fifths of the crew.[2]

Unable to get ahold of cloves, Lancaster settled for a less valuable choice. Dumping five hundred tons of black pepper on the market drove down its value by about half, and the Company's warehouses were overstocked in the spice for the next half dozen years.[3]

The Company, though, raised funds and quickly dispatched a series of further trading missions to the East Indies. With the third venture, when a haul of cloves alone turned more than a 200 percent profit,[4] stakeholders began making healthy returns on their investments. In 1609 the Crown extended the Company's monopoly. Growth was quick. By 1620, it had two hundred "factors"—agents or representatives—in more than a dozen trading posts[5] that stretched from the Red Sea to Makassar on the southwestern tip of Sulawasi, Indonesia, near the Spice Islands. It also counted some thirty to forty "tall ships"—the type later known as Indiamen, with their high, raised poop and weapons—which the Company christened with names such as *Peppercorn, Clove*, and the particularly optimistic *Trades Increase*.[6]

Soon, but not by choice, the Company turned its attention to India. The Dutch had arrived first in the Spice Islands, and the Dutch East India Company, while smaller, exerted enough influence during the early decades of the spice trade to muscle the British out of the region and force them to set up elsewhere.[7]

In August 1608 an East India Company ship landed on the northwest coast of India at Surat, the principal Mughal port. While his ship returned to England, Captain William Hawkins headed inland to meet the Mughal emperor, Nuruddin Salim Jahangir, who ruled from the distant and splendid Agra. Hawkins, who spoke Turkish—not Persian, the language of the court, but Jahangir's native tongue—made such a good impression that the Mughal ruler insisted he marry "a whyte mayden" from the palace, an Armenian. Once Hawkins was assured that she was a Christian, he did so, and, as Hawkins later wrote, "so ever after I lived content and without feare."[8]

Yet a decade and succession of further envoys would pass before the Company was granted the right to reside and build some "factories," or trading stations, where goods such as pepper could be bought when the price was low and stored until ships arrived to haul them back to Europe.

Over the next decades, as the Company continued to grow—not in a steadily ascending curve of imports, exports, and revenues, but in fits and starts, of boom years followed by ones with lost or pirated cargo—it garnered broader diplomatic and political support in London as well as presence on the Indian coast. Oliver Cromwell renewed the Company's charter in 1657, during the short-lived republican Commonwealth of England, and extended its power to fortify and colonize any of its establishments, and to bring settlers, goods, and ammunition to them. In 1661, within a year of the House of Stuart's being restored to the throne, the Company, granted Charles II, "shall and may, from henceforth for ever . . . into the said East-Indies . . . Trade or Traffick."

The Company completed 404 voyages to the East Indies in the three decades between 1658 to 1688.[9] By the end of the seventeenth century, it had established and fortified three main coastal bases in India: the presidencies of Calcutta in the northeast; Madras, some 850 miles to its south; and, on the west coast, Bombay (today called Mumbai). Bombay was not conquered but rented for £10 in gold a year from the cash-strapped Charles II, who had received it in his wife's dowry. These, although just a trio of spots along the considerable coastline, with a vast interior between them, were a solid start.

The following century was relatively peaceful and focused on trade. Business was steady and so were dividends. "Though commercially astute, the Company's servants were not trained for politics or war," wrote the celebrated Delhi-born novelist Ahmed Ali.[10] At first they kept away from those twin distractions. But by the mid-eighteenth century, that changed. The Company's expanding riverside Fort William in Calcutta made the young nawab of Bengal, Siraj-ud-Daulah, suspicious. "You are merchants, what need have you of a fortress?" he demanded.[11] When the British ignored him, the nawab marched on the city and, in 1756, managed to briefly occupy it. While unable to expel them from Bengal, the nawab drew British public fury with the infamous Black Hole incident, in which a large (and still-disputed) number of British were jammed into the fort's small prison and, by morning, nearly all of them had suffocated.

In 1757, a Company force of a thousand British soldiers and two thousand sepoys—Indians, largely from the country's traditional warrior or soldier castes, trained and uniformed into a disciplined army—led by Robert Clive retaliated and defeated the nawab and his much larger (though largely unpaid and disgruntled) army of fifty thousand soldiers and five hundred war elephants[12] in the mango groves of Plassey outside Calcutta to claim the richest and most fertile province in the empire. It was a massive catch. The eminent Raj scholar Lawrence James speculates that Bengal had a population of perhaps 40 million, or about four times that of Britain.[13] On the nawab's throne, the Company placed Mir Jafar—a leader who had switched sides with his soldiers to join Clive—and dictated to him the terms of the treaty, which provided, not surprisingly, a windfall. The Company made a tidy £2.5 million. The British officers took over £1.25 million, with Clive getting £234,000 of the bonanza,[14] plus a piece of property in Calcutta that brought him £27,000 a year in rent. Clive sailed home in 1759 some £300,000 richer. It was the greatest fortune ever made by an Englishman in India, and an especially staggering amount for a man who had gone out to India at nineteen on a modest salary of £5 per year—a trip he had to pay for himself as well as cover the expenses during the journey. At thirty-three, Clive had suddenly become one of the richest men in Britain.[15]

The Company soon reaped even larger rewards. In 1765, it dramatically improved its financial stake when it was awarded the *diwani* of Bengal, Bihar, and Orissa, gaining, in exchange for a tribute to the emperor in Agra, rights to collect tax revenues. (The tribute part of the deal did not last long. Warren Hastings, India's first governor-general, soon canceled it.)

The significance of Plassey only became fully evident in hindsight. If Surat was the kernel of the British rule in India, Bengal and its tax revenues became the solid foundation toward gradual rule of the entire subcontinent. The East India Company's private army ballooned over the next half century from 18,000 to 154,000 by 1805, "far beyond the needs of self-defense," as one modern historian put it.[16] Or of merchants. As the Mughal Empire slowly declined, the East India Company moved into its place.

The Company began by looking for nutmeg, clove, cinnamon, and pepper and, in doing so, grew into the most powerful commercial company ever to exist. It established global cities such as Calcutta and Bombay as well as Singapore and Hong Kong and shaped and governed much of the Indian subcontinent. At one time, it employed a third of the British workforce, controlled about half of world trade, and had the largest merchant navy in the world. It moved from a mercantile organization—the standard-bearer of what Karl Marx labeled Britain's "moneyocracy"—to being the main political and military power in South Asia. Ahmed Ali likened the new character of the Company, once well versed in both politics and war, "to that of war lords."[17]

But if spices were the Company's initial commercial impetus, tea became the locus of its financial success, and the cornerstone of its trade strategies.

The Company began by importing tea from China using intermediaries. Its first chest, in 1664, was shipped via Bantam, Java, and classified alongside "rarities of birds, beasts or other curiosities . . . fit to present to His Majesty,"[18] Charles II, though most likely destined for his tea-drinking Portuguese wife. A similar negligible amount followed two years later. In 1669, the East India Company brought its first significant order of 143½ pounds from Bantam. A load of nearly five thousand pounds of tea in 1678 flooded the market for the next few years.[19]

As imports increased, the Company soon wanted to buy directly from the Chinese. In 1689, it made its first purchase of tea from the port of Amoy.[20] Initially limited, quantities shot up within a few decades and surpassed 1 million pounds by the early 1720s. In 1750, the East India Company's annual imports of tea equaled nearly 5 million pounds, and in 1766 hit 6 million.[21] Because of the high taxes levied on tea in Britain, another 4 to 7 million pounds was being smuggled in illegally.[22] Dutch and French ships carried some of the contraband that made its way to the English coastline via the Channel Islands, but it was also transported on the Company's own vessels by officers using their allotted cargo space.

A significant amount was sent on to the American colonies, which by 1760 were brewing tea from more than 1 million pounds of leaves a year.[23] Taxes on the tea became the focus of colonial anger, which culminated in the 1773 Boston Tea Party, when protesters dumped some ninety thousand pounds of tea into the harbor. This led to rebellion and ultimately to the colonies' declaring independence in the face of corporate and governmental greed.

Even with the taxes and high transport costs, tea was the Company's most important commodity. At the end of the eighteenth century it was more profitable than all other goods combined, accounting for 60 percent of the company's total trade. (It had also become the most profitable item on a London grocer's shelf.)[24] British demand seemed insatiable. In 1800, the East India Company sold a staggering 25,378,816 pounds of it.[25] During the 1809–10 trading season, tea accounted for sales worth nearly £3.5 million. That same season, spices totaled just £150,000, or about 4 percent of tea's amount. In 1817, tea imports topped 36 million pounds.[26]

Paying the Chinese for so much tea was a significant—and growing—problem. The British had to buy it with silver, specifically Spanish silver reals minted in Mexico.[27] The Chinese wanted nothing else from the British. Notoriously xenophobic and self-sufficient with a highly developed manufacturing industry, the Middle Kingdom preferred its own goods over all others.[28] Aside from some cotton goods from India, namely the fine muslins and calicoes woven in Bengal, they wanted little else. The Chinese had no desire for woolens milled in the British Midlands or blue Wedgwood plates and only wanted so many clocks and other knickknacks, and, anyway, most imports sold for a loss.[29] "Strange and costly objects do not interest me," the Qianlong Emperor wrote to his counterpart, George III, after an early and unsuccessful British trade mission to China. "As your Ambassador can see for himself, we possess all things. I set no value on strange objects and have no use for your country's manufactures."[30]

Tea's trade imbalance deeply concerned the British government. It was draining the country's silver reserves. The British needed to find a Chinese demand or to create one.[31] At last they found a commodity that satisfied both criteria.

When Vasco da Gama reached the southern Indian city of Calicut on the Malabar Coast in 1498, he was greeted rather hostilely by Muslim merchants. "May the devil take thee! What brought you hither?" they wanted to know, the Portuguese explorer recorded in his journal,[32] to which he famously replied, "Christians and spices." When the English arrived a century later, they came searching mostly for spices. But they found another, more lucrative crop being cultivated on the subcontinent under the Mughals that would prove to be a tonic for Britain's one-way commerce with the Chinese and a means of halting the bullion drain: *Papaver somniferum.* Opium.

Opium most likely arrived with Arab traders, perhaps by the middle of the ninth century, and was being grown on the subcontinent by the end of the fifteenth century.[33] (The Hindi *aphim* and Sanskrit *ahifen*, which also means snake venom, derive from the Arabic *afyun*.) In the 1590s, Abu'l-Fazl, intimate adviser to Akbar—the great Mughal leader who ruled over much of South Asia—and gifted historian to his reign (1556–1605), described the opium production in Fatehphur, Allahabad, and Ghazipur in northern India. Opium was, Fazl wrote, a controlled monopoly of the state.[34]

When William Hastings was appointed the first governor-general in 1773, he publically opposed the trade. "The drug is not a necessity of life but a pernicious article of luxury which ought not to be permitted. I shall stamp it out," he told his new bosses.[35] He brought the opium trade in Bengal, Bihar, and Orissa under Company control, but quickly changed his tune about stopping it.

Just as the Mughals had, the British saw the trade as a natural right. "Thus the State Monopoly in Opium and the policy which is practically that pursued at the present day, was a hereditary gift to the British successors of the great Mogul Empires," a Department of Revenue and Agriculture publication stated in the late-nineteenth century.[36] The Company simply expanded distribution from the national market in India to China and increased production. The first shipment of Indian opium arrived in the port of Canton the same year Hastings took office.

Nineteenth-century India had two key areas of opium production. Patna, in Bihar along the Ganges, was the capital of India's main opium industry. Here it was grown and manufactured under the aegis of the East India Company. An important factory was located in Patna, as well as another large one in Ghazipur, to the east of Benares. The second area was in a collection of independent, princely states located largely in the Punjab and collectively referred to as Malwa, which initially shipped from the Gujarati port of Cambray (now Khambhat). The British held the monopoly on the country's trade and did all they could to thwart competition from Malwa, mainly by encircling the area and charging exorbitant rates to transit across their land. The Chinese considered Malwa opium to have a "higher touch," according to an 1839 report of the Official Records of the Colonial Office, "but not so mellow, nor so pleasant in flavor as the Patna opium."[37]

Along the Gangetic plain, Company agents forced peasants to stop farming traditional food crops, such as winter vegetables, wheat, and dal, and plant only poppies. In the dry, cool weather of late autumn, they scattered opium seeds around their fields. By the new year, plants stood a few feet high and were beginning to bloom. As the heat of the plains intensified in February and March, the pale-pink and blanched-crimson-colored petals fell, and the bulbous seed capsules grew globular and waxy.

When the pods were turning from yellow to pale green—that is, quite mature but not fully ripe—workers lanced them using a set of sharp blades mounted in a wood handle. Milky, latexlike sap seeped out from the vertical slits overnight and, in the air, turned a gummy brown. Workers returned at dawn to scrape the resin off the capsules with a curved trowel and place the raw opium into an earthen pot hanging at their waists. The pods remained viable for just a dozen or so days until reaching full maturity, during which time lancing and scraping were repeated a handful of times.

Brought to the factory, the raw opium was processed, molded into spherical cakes six inches in diameter and weighing just over three pounds, and stacked on towering shelves to dry and harden. In autumn, once the rains had passed, the balls were weighed and valued, wrapped in a lattice of pressed opium petals, and packed into mango-wood chests that held about 120 pounds of the drug. These were then shipped a few hundred miles downstream to Calcutta to be sold at auction.

While the Company controlled every aspect of the production and even placed its seal on the opium as an imprimatur of quality, once it was sold to independent merchants who operated under Company license, it was no longer the Company's concern.[38] It officially turned its head on what happened after that. Private traders organized transport to Canton, the only port open for foreigners to trade.

But opium was illegal in China. The ships passed through the archipelago at the mouth of the Pearl River Delta, with Macao and its small community of Portuguese on the port side and forest-covered Hong Kong on the starboard, and anchored at Whampoa, still about ten miles shy of Canton, to off-load their cargo. Lithe boats with many oarsman evocatively called "fast crabs" and "scrambling dragons" carried the opium chests swiftly to shore for distribution, up the coastline, and into the interior on caravans of donkeys and camels.

"As tea and opium could not be bartered directly, opium was sold for silver, which in turn paid for tea," explained tea scholar John Griffiths. "This suited Western merchants very well, for it saved them a long journey in pirate-infested waters with cargoes of silver."[39]

To cover the cost of a steadily increasing demand for tea (and silver), opium had to made "a 'commodity,'" wrote the Australian historian Carl Trocki, "to organize its production with a force of cheap and malleable labor, on land that was already controlled for as cheap a price as possible. It would be necessary to create centralized control over collection and processing of the product. It was also necessary to gain access to the market where it could be consumed on a mass basis." The British accomplished that.

But they also had to increase demand. Or, as Trocki put it, "It was necessary to create an opium epidemic in Asia."[40]

They eventually accomplished that, too.

Opium had been used in China for centuries, but its lethal form of consumption by smoking had only gained a foothold from Dutch traders who laced their tobacco with a pinch of opium and arsenic. Eventually the tobacco and other additives fell away, and by the mid-eighteenth century, opium was smoked alone in long, tubelike pipes. With streamlined production and increased flow of the drug out of India, there were, by the end of the 1830s, upward of 12 million opium smokers in China,[41] perhaps 2 million of them addicts.* Addiction riddled every level of society, from the highest officials in the central government on down. The British realized the effects of their contraband and actively undermined efforts to slow, much less stop, the problem. The Chinese court even made a personal, ethical appeal to the twenty-year-old Queen Victoria. It was ignored. But how could it be otherwise?

For the East India Company, the opium trade was crucial to its solvency and yielded it some £2 million a year. By the early 1800s, it was the leading source of revenue for the Company. But it was also the second-largest one for the government of British India after land taxes, regularly contributing more than 15 percent of the total.[42] And taxes on tea back in Britain, which the opium effectively purchased, were adding at least £3 million annually to the coffers of the Exchequer, nearly 10 percent of the revenue from the whole of England.[43] That amount covered half of the expenses of the mighty Royal Navy, which dominated the globe's seas.[44]

The opium trade was too important to stop—or allow to be stopped.

However, that is exactly what the Chinese emperor—officially, "Son of Heaven and Lord of Ten Thousand Years"—tried to do. He appointed a special emissary to Canton, the morally upright Lin Zexu. (His

---

* In Britain, the legendary soldier Robert Clive was one of the most famous casualties of opium, and his suicide at forty-nine is blamed on his addiction to the drug and years of steadily increasing dosages for a stomach ailment.

nickname was Blue Sky, referring to his supposedly clear and incorruptible nature.)[45] Lin made sixteen hundred arrests, closed the channel that led to Canton, effectively blockading the port, and publically destroyed some twenty thousand chests of opium held in foreign warehouses. It took workers three weeks to dissolve 3 million pounds of the drug in pits and watch it be swept out to sea by the currents.[46]

In response, Britain launched a war to force the Chinese to open their ports to the trade. The First Opium War (1839–42) was a prolonged, intermittent, and lopsided affair, with Britain's superior weapons crushing the emperor's far more numerous troops, who carried muskets, flintlocks, pikes, and bows and arrows. Lin, scapegoat for the humiliating defeat, was recalled to Peking and sentenced to death. "You have been no better than a wooden doll," the emperor told him.[47]*

The Treaty of Nanking, ending the First Opium War, resulted in the opening of five ports for foreign trade: Canton, Amoy, Foochow (Fuzhou), Ningpo (Ninbo), and Shanghai. As well, China ceded Hong Kong, then a minor outpost, where British citizens were exempt from Chinese jurisdiction and would be held accountable by their own laws rather than local ones. It also included an indemnity payment to Britain of $21 million, about half of China's total tax revenues for the year, to cover war costs and compensation to traders for the destroyed opium. China, though, refused to legalize opium, and Henry Pottinger, who negotiated the treaty for the British, did not insist. Opium is not mentioned anywhere in the document.

While tea imports to Britain jumped from 32 million pounds in 1834 to 56.5 million pounds by 1846,[48] the terms of the treaty, and their protracted implementation, did not appease the British for long. With several of the key points disputed, they launched the Second Opium War in 1856. They handily won this, too, and burned down the vast and sumptuous imperial Summer Palace in spiteful vengeance. Not unexpectedly, the new treaty reached further with British demands. The victors demanded all ports be opened, British goods be exempt from import duties, foreigners be allowed to travel across the country, missionaries given free and unrestricted right to spread Christianity, and the establishment of a full embassy in

---

* Lin had his sentence commuted to exile in the farthest northwestern hinterlands of Xinjiang. He returned some years later, though, forgiven and with his reputation somewhat resurrected; today he is a national hero and symbol of Chinese resistance to European imperialism.

Peking (Beijing) with a British diplomat in residence. Another large indemnity payment was also stipulated—and continued access to China's tea. "It secures us a few round millions of dollars and no end of very refreshing tea," the *Illustrated London News* happily reported.[49]

And this time, opium was to be completely legalized.

On the eve of the First Opium War, some forty thousand chests of the drug—about 5.5 million pounds—had been shipped to China;[50] within two decades after the Second Opium War, the opium trade had more than doubled. Imports hit 93,000 chests in 1872 and 112,000 chests—nearly 16 million pounds—a decade later.[51]

By the time the British had launched the First Opium War in 1839, though, the East India Company had begun intensively searching for other sources of *their* national addiction: tea. Under public pressure demanding cheaper tea, the Crown broke the Company's long-running monopoly on importing it in 1833. The first non-Company consignment of tea shipped out of China was by Jardine, Matheson & Co., the largest and most famous of the opium merchants.*

The East India Company scrambled to find a place where it could dictate not just the price but all aspects of production. After decades of ignoring rumors and reports that tea had been found growing in India, the Company could no longer wait.

---

* It and its Scottish founders were models for James Clavell in his novels *Tai-Pan* and *Noble House*. Today, Jardine Matheson is a highly respected Fortune Global 500 company.

CHAPTER 4

An Indian Tea Industry

The northeastern section of India hangs like a limb between Bangladesh, Bhutan, China, and Myanmar (Burma), a lazy-T-shaped expanse connected to the rest of the country by a slender 125-mile-long strip of land called the Siliguri Corridor. (Colloquially, and more evocatively, it's known as the Chicken's Neck). Stretching to the foothills of the eastern Himalayas, Assam—now the area's central state and, until recently, the name for the entire region—is largely at low elevation, hot, and tropical. The mighty Brahmaputra River cleaves Assam in half with a four-hundred-mile-long valley as it slithers southwest toward the Bay of Bengal. Altering its path and shifting its braided strands from year to year, the river widens to a dozen miles in places.

In 1823, Robert Bruce, a Scottish adventurer, explorer, and businessman, was trading along the upper Brahmaputra Valley when he came across indigenous tea growing in the dense jungle. Local Singpho tribes pickled the leaves and ate them with oil and garlic and sometimes dried fish, much in the manner of the Burmese dish *lahpet*, which is still popular today. The Singphos also made a primitive tea with the leaves.

Bruce befriended a Singpho chief named Bisa Gam and made arrangements to get some tea seeds and plants. But then two events interceded. In 1824, the First Anglo-Burmese War opened in response to Assam's being largely overrun by invading Burmese. That same year, Bruce—by then a major in the Bengal Artillery—died. His story ends abruptly, and the thread gets taken up by his younger brother, Charles Alexander (C. A.) Bruce, who was commanding a flotilla of gunboats in the area.[1]

The younger Bruce, evidently tipped off by his sibling before he died, got ahold of the tea samples. Exactly how is not clear. One version says Gam delivered the samples to C. A.[2] Another claims that Gam came to pay respects,[3] found Bruce's younger brother, and passed him the tea. A third relates that C. A. retraced his brother's steps and met with the chief, who presented the younger Bruce with several hundred plants.[4]

With Britain's unquenchable thirst for tea, C. A. Bruce suspected the impact of this discovery could be immense. He sent the samples on to the East India Company's man in Assam, who, in June 1825, forwarded the packet of leaves and seeds to the Company's botanic garden for verification.[5]

The Calcutta botanic garden was the Empire's nursery. It had been established in Sibpur, across the Hooghly River and just around the downstream bend from Calcutta, in 1787 by Colonel Robert Kyd. Using his own private garden as the foundation, Kyd conceived the new initiative "not for the purpose of collecting rare plants (although they also have their use) as things of curiosity or furnishing articles for the gratification of luxury," he explained in his initial request for funding, "but for establishing a stock for the disseminating [of] such articles as may prove beneficial to the Inhabitants [of India], as well as the natives of Great Britain and which ultimately may tend to the extension of the national Commerce and Riches."[6]

Coming on the heels of the 1770 famine that killed some 10 million Bengalis, about a quarter of the population, Kyd meant to improve Indian agriculture with better food crops. This was the moral imperative for the gardens. But Kyd also appealed to the Company's mercantile character in his brief. He planned to introduce items that could make a profit: teak plantations for shipbuilding, rubber, indigo for dye, spices, tobacco, cotton, and sugar. And medicinal ones, too, such as cinchona. Its bark was used for quinine, the only known treatment for malaria, a significant obstacle in conquering and ruling many tropical areas—including vast parts of India—and in expanding Britain's dominion. Botanical science was part of the Empire—with an eye on commerce.

By the nineteenth century, botanic gardens in India had also been established in Saharanpur, Bombay, Madras, and Poona (Pune), with the one in Calcutta as the subcontinent's nerve center.* Under Kyd's successor, William Roxburgh—the first salaried man to take charge and often called the Father of Indian Botany—it developed into a top-notch institution. Along with splendid gardens and beds, it had a herbarium with dried species for taxonomical reference, a vast library that held key works from around the globe, and the domed-toped, octagonal Palm House, with pink- and white-flowering climbers growing up over the ironwork to shade the palms inside.

At its helm when the packet of indigenous tea samples from Assam arrived was Dr. Nathaniel Wallich. Even in a time of unlikely success stories, he was something of a surprise to be the East India Company's chief botanist in India.

Born Nathanael Wulff Wallich, the son of a Jewish merchant in Denmark, he studied medicine at the Danish Academy of Surgeons in Copenhagen. At twenty-one, with limited prospects in the academic world of Lutheran Denmark, he took a position as a surgeon in the Danish "factory" at Serampore, near Calcutta. He arrived in late autumn of 1807. The timing was terrible. Denmark had allied with France during the Napoleonic Wars, a coalition enemy of Britain's, and the East India Company annexed the settlement in 1808. Wallich became a prisoner of war.[7]

But Roxburgh, then superintendent of the Botanic Garden, recognized the Dane's skills and not only successfully petitioned for Wallich's release, but also to have him join the East India Company as his assistant. Wallich rose swiftly. In 1815, at age twenty-nine, he became the temporary superintendent of the garden, and then, two years later, was made permanent. Under his tenure, it grew greatly in size and number of workers, employing upward of three hundred gardeners and laborers. Wallich held his post until retiring to London in 1846. Such longevity was nearly unknown in British India, especially among botanists and plant collectors, who tended to die in their thirties—or younger—from the hazards of climate and endemic diseases amplified by spending months at a time in the field.

---

*Originally known as the East India Company's Garden or Company Bagan (garden) or Calcutta Garden, it became the Royal Botanic Garden in the early 1860s when the Crown assumed the assets of the defunct East India Company. Its current name is Acharya Jagadish Chandra Bose Indian Botanic Garden, in honor of the physicist-turned-plant biologist.

An early and vocal advocate in protecting the forests in India and Burma,[8] Wallich was also an assiduous and generous collector. In 1828, on convalescence leave in England, he took along thirty crates that contained between eight thousand and ten thousand species[9] gathered over the previous quarter century and passed them out. The haul was dubbed the "Wallichian herbarium" and is considered one of largest ever brought—or distributed—in Europe.[10] Institutions shared the spoils, but so did private collectors. Some of these individuals became wealthy from the gifts, while Wallich remained, as he put it himself, "as poor as a church rat."[11] Not that poverty stopped his largess. Back in India, he was even more lavishly open handed. Between 1836 and 1840, the botanic garden, under his leadership, distributed 190,000 plants to more than two thousand institutions and individuals in India and abroad, to parks and native princes, civil servants, and even European collectors.[12]

His future generosity aide, Wallich made a key mistake that summer of 1825. The leaves and seeds that Bruce had sent came from the camellia family, Wallich concluded, but they were not *Camellia sinensis*—tea. He did nothing to pursue the lead.

Was it an authentic error? The botanical authorities in Calcutta were deeply reluctant to acknowledge that tea existed in India, suggested Harold Mann. It was "always apparently the part of the botanists to doubt and deny, rather than to encourage the idea that tea was present in the country."[13]

The Company simply had little reason to put its energy or money into exploring the possibility. At the time Bruce's packet arrived, the East India Company still held a monopoly on bringing Chinese tea to Britain.

The revoking of that monopoly in 1833 jolted the Company from complacency, and in February of the following year it hurriedly formed the Tea Committee under the governor-general, Lord William Bentinck.

Aristocratic, liberal, and wealthy, Bentinck was handsome, with large, languorous eyes, full lips, and a Lord Byron–esque dashing appeal. An Anglicist heavily influenced by both the evangelical and liberal movements,[14] he arrived in India with experience both political (he had been governor of Madras) and military (he had led troops in Sicily against the French and in Genoa). His term as governor-general (1828–35) was marked by sweeping social and economic reforms, and moves to Westernize Indian society. Abolishing sati—or suttee, where a widow immolates herself on the funeral pyre of her husband—and suppressing the *thuggees*, robber bands who ritually murdered their victims, were two famous achievements. More far-reaching was his role in anglicizing the Indian judicial system—he made English the court language—and education. A member of the Governor-General's Council, Thomas Babington Macaulay, wrote his infamous 1835 "Minute on Education" on establishing in India English-language schooling to create "a class of persons Indian in blood and colour, but English in tastes, in opinions, in morals and in intellect."

Under Bentinck, the Tea Committee comprised thirteen members, including two natives and Dr. Wallich.[15] It immediately dispatched its secretary, George James Gordon, to China to acquire tea seeds and plants for transplanting on Indian soil. Gordon was also to recruit "a select rather than a numerous body of planters; men qualified to conduct every operation connected with the production of good tea, from the selection of a proper site for a plantation, to the gathering of the leaf, its preparation and packing."[16]

In June 1834, Gordon sailed from Calcutta on the opium clipper *Water Witch* to Macau. Foreign traders in Canton were not allowed to reside on the mainland year-round, and the Chinese government required them to spend from April to October in the nearby Portuguese enclave. Gordon enlisted a notorious German Protestant preacher, the Reverend Karl Gützlaff, to be his guide and interpreter to the interior. A talented linguist fluent in several Chinese dialects, Gützlaff, a tailor's son who had arrived in East Asia in the 1820s, helped translate the Bible into Chinese (and also Thai) and actively distributed Christian literature (considered contraband).

Gützlaff, though, was known for pushing opium as well as Bibles— or pushing Bibles *with* opium. He worked for Jardine, Matheson & Co. as a translator for ship captains trying to open new markets along the southern-China coast. Along with receiving a commission for his work as spokesman, salesman, and interpreter, Gützlaff used the opportunity to hand out chapters of the Bible that he had translated himself.[17]

While Gordon was in China, the Tea Committee in Calcutta was exploring possibilities for growing tea in India. Somewhere between the Himalayas in the north and Cape Comorin at the very southern end of the subcontinent had to be a suitable site for planting tea stock, Bentinck argued in a speech, and he sent out an official circular inquiring about feasible spots.

One response, from a Captain Jenkins, came from a place that fell outside the anticipated locales and ideal geographical and climatic characteristics: Assam. Jenkins was intimately familiar with the region, which had been annexed by the Company at the end of the war with Burma a decade before. He included a letter sent to him from a Lieutenant Charlton with information on Assam as not only a good place to grow tea but where locals were actually already making it:

> I have not had an opportunity of making any experiments on the leaves; they are devoid of smell in their green state, but acquire the fragrance and flavour of Chinese tea when dried. The Singphos and the Kamptees are in the habit of drinking an infusion of the leaves, which I have lately understood they prepare by pulling them into small pieces, taking out the stalks and fibers, boiling and then squeezing them into a ball, which they dry in the sun and retain for use.[18]

About six months after his initial letter, Charlton sent a packet of seeds, leaves, fruit, blossoms, and even some prepared tea leaves made by the hill tribes to Jenkins, who relayed them to the Company's botanic garden in Calcutta to confirm that it was indeed tea.

Wallich had a second chance, and this time he didn't balk.

On December 24, 1834, the Tea Committee informed Bentinck "with feelings of the highest possible satisfaction" that "the tea shrub is beyond all doubt indigenous in Upper Assam." The committee was, it said, "now enabled to state with certainty, that not only is it a genuine tea, but that no doubt can be entertained of its being the identical tea of China."[19]

The committee was right—to an extent.

Tea comes from the *Camellia sinensis* plant, classified in 1753 by the Swedish botanist Carolus Linnaeus. *Sinensis* means "from China." The genus *Camellia*—from the flowering Theaceae family—was named in memory of a seventeenth-century Jesuit missionary and botanist in the Philippines, Georg Joseph Kamel, who made important early descriptions and drawings of plants (although curiously not of camellias). This sturdy evergreen plant grows as a shrub or a tree. Its young, lightly serrated leaves are bright green; they darken to a leathery and shiny forest green. In fall, small, white flowers with a half dozen petals and a density of stamens blossom. The fruit is a smooth-skinned, greenish-brown drupe that ripens to a saddle brown and into the size of a hazelnut with the seed inside.

Camellia sinensis has are two main varieties. The first is *Camellia sinensis sinensis*, known as China leaf or China *jat* (variety). If left unpruned, it can grow to be twelve or fifteen feet tall. Mature leaves are matted feeling and measure roughly two inches in length. The life span of a shrub is around one hundred years. The second variety is *Camellia sinensis assamica*, more technically a tree rather than a bush. This is what Wallich received from Assam. While its life span is generally less than half of its Chinese counterpart, when left wild it grows much taller, reaching forty-five to sixty feet, with a large trunk and robust branches. The leaves of the Assam variety are larger and coarser than China ones but also glossier.

The Tea Committee considered their finding momentous, however speculative it still was. "We have no hesitation in declaring this discovery . . . to be by far the most important and valuable that has ever been made on matters connected with the agricultural or commercial resources of this empire,"[20] Wallich and the Tea Committee informed the governor-general on Christmas Eve.

Wallich, as the committee's acting secretary, argued strongly that with tea growing in Upper Assam, the efforts to obtain stock in China were no longer necessary nor justifiable. "The Assam plant exists in sufficient abundance to produce seeds for all the purposes of the Committee, with this great advantage, that they can be procured in a state of perfect freshness," Wallich wrote in a missive to the governor-general, "finally, taking into consideration the great expenses necessarily incurred in obtaining supplies of seeds from China, which are now ascertained to be no longer required."[21]

At the same time, he dispatched a letter to Gordon himself that was even more direct:

> It is, therefore, useless and unnecessary to import from China, at a great expense and great risk, what may be had, as it were, on the spot, to any extent almost in point of quantity, and in a state of perfect freshness and strength for vegetating, your continuance in China, so far as regards supplies of seed, is, therefore, useless and unnecessary.[22]

Gordon was immediately recalled.

Yet Wallich's position was not shared by all; he was most vocally refuted by a London-born botanist twenty-five years his junior named William Griffith. The Londoner logically argued that plants, selectively cultivated for generations, would produce better than wild Indian ones, and that Chinese stock planted in Assam would be superior to indigenous ones.[23] He also scoffed at the idea that they could quickly compete with China's industry.[24]

Waffling on a decisive course of action, the Tea Committee hedged its bets, made another hasty reversal, and sent Gordon back to China. He was again to gather seeds and plants, but the emphasis of his brief this time was to recruit Chinese who knew how to make tea.

Gordon's China trips did yield not only some tea stock but also a handful of Chinese "tea manufacturers" from around Canton to help with cultivation and processing. But few of the plants and seeds survived the journey to Calcutta and then on to various experimental tea gardens being set up in Assam, the south, and the northwest Himalayan foothills for replanting. And the ones that did live were dogged by suspicion of their quality. Gordon had gathered the first batch in the Bohea Hills, but the following two were procured in his absence by emissaries.

Griffith had been right that higher-quality Chinese stock was needed, but wrong to assume that it could grow well in the tropical conditions of low-lying Assam. The few Chinese plants that did make it struggled in the hot, humid climate. Instead, the native Assam leaves flourished.

While Gordon flitted back and forth between India and China, work progressed in Upper Assam. The handful of Chinese tea manufacturers that Gordon had recruited worked assiduously with local laborers under the leadership of Bruce. In 1835 the first tea garden was opened at Sadiya (now Suddeya), near the confluence of the Brahmaputra and Kundil Rivers. It received the first seeds and seedlings from China, but these soon died. The site was wrongly chosen, the soil poor for tea, and Bruce recommended abandoning it the following year. He replanted sixty miles away on higher ground at Jaypur.*

---

*A wise decision. River water soon flowed freely over the original site, while the Jaypur garden still exists today.

Like his brother Robert, C. A. Bruce was a tireless traveler. He spent large chunks of time looking for patches of wild tea growing around Assam. With the local chief, he would arrange the purchase of leaves, or even the land. "He was essentially an explorer, peculiarly equipped by long residence in Assam to understand the climate and the people," wrote tea's most thorough historian, William Ukers, "and possessed of an amazing store of good health and fine animal spirits, combined with tact and resourcefulness."[25] Locals, though, suspicious of Bruce's travels along their bush pathways, were often cagey in revealing much about their tea bushes. "All their country abounds with the plant," Bruce wrote, "but they are very jealous and will give no information where it is to be found."[26] According to a Tea Committee letter to the governor-general, Bruce often successfully bypassed this evasiveness by proffering "a little opium" along with a "few soft words."[27] Bruce knew "how to pioneer a jungle, and make it give up its hidden treasures."[28] By 1839, 120 such areas with colonies of indigenous tea had been found.[29]

The early Assamese tea centers that Bruce, his Chinese advisers, and workers set up around the valley were not, as they are today, formal "gardens" or "plantations." The jungle and weeds around colonies of indigenous tea bushes were cleared, and the leaves pruned to encourage new growth. Appropriately, they were called tea forests.

Even this kind of farming was difficult. The hill tribes were not universally friendly, the area was sparsely populated, and finding labor was a huge challenge. The British regarded the local Nagas as dependable in head-hunting but less so in cultivating crops.[30] The work was difficult. A Victorian tea planter described in awe an extended line of men clearing the jungle for tea: "cleaving their way steadily and surely through the dense undergrowth and bamboo jungle, dexterously swinging their peculiarly-shaped daos (half axe, half sword) in unison and in time with the barbarous refrain of some war song which they continually chant in their wild and unintelligible jargon . . ."[31]

The early days of the industry were a massive struggle. Workers suffered malaria, cholera, jungle fever, and blackwater fever (named for the color the illness turns the urine). Tigers, leopards, and snakes patrolled the forests. Labor shortages seemed almost insurmountable. Wild elephants had to be caught, tamed, and trained to remove trees, clear roads, and transport tea.

In 1838, the Bengal Military Orphan Press published Bruce's short monograph, *An Account of the Manufacture of the Black Tea as Now*

Practised at Suddeya in Upper Assam, by the Chinamen Sent Thither for That Purpose. With Some Observations on the Culture of the Plant in China, and Its Growth in Assam. Reading it shows how the early planters were still almost blindly groping their way in learning. Bruce packed all that he knew about tea planting and processing into a mere nineteen pages, including a page explaining the plates. The booklet is comprised largely of techniques garnered from the handful of Chinese manufacturers and includes "A Dialogue between Mr C. A. Bruce and the China Black-Tea Makers" with exchanges such as

> How do you plant the Tea seeds? "I dig a hole about four fingers deep and eight inches in diameter, and put as many seeds as I can hold in both hands into it, then cover it up."[32]

and

> After you have made the Tea in China, how long is it before it is fit to drink? "About one year; if drank before that, it will taste unpleasantly and of the fire, and will affect the head."[33]

Bruce also offered some observations on the native tea plant in Assam and details on the Singpho method of processing tea.

> They pluck the young and tender leaves and dry them a little in the sun; some put them out into the dew and then again into the sun three successive days, others only after a little drying put them into hot pans, turn them about until quite hot, and then place them into the hollow of a bamboo, and drive the whole down with a stick, holding and turning the bamboo over the fire all the time, until it is full, then tie the end up with leaves, and hang the bamboo up in some smoky place in the hut; thus prepared the Tea will keep good for years.[34]

But about how their tea actually tasted, he made no mention in his monograph.

William Griffith offered a comparable description of native tea making in his private journal, kept while traveling with Bruce, Wallich, and another Company scientist through Upper Assam, looking for suitable sites for tea. In an entry dated January 16, 1836, Griffith wrote:

We halted after gathering a crop of leaves under a fine Dillenia, which was loaded with its fruit. Here the Singfos demonstrated the mode in which the tea is prepared among them. I must premise, however, that they use none but young leaves. They roasted or rather semi-roasted the leaves in a large iron vessel, which must be quite clean, stirring them up and rolling them in the hands during the roasting. When duly roasted, they expose them to the sun for three days; some to the dew alternately with the sun. It is then finally packed into bamboo chungas, into which it is tightly rammed.[35]

He also neglected to say anything about how the tea tasted.

Given the obstacles, Bruce and his crew made surprisingly quick progress. The first teas they processed in 1836 were promising, and in 1837 they had enough tea from indigenous Assam plants to send to officials in Calcutta. (The tea plants from China *jat* had not yet matured, although many had already perished.) By then, Lord Bentinck had quit his post in India because of poor health. The new governor-general, Lord Auckland, sampled the tea himself and pronounced it good quality.[36] The next batch was an improvement, and by the end of the year there was a sufficient amount to send to East India Company headquarters in London. Forty-six boxes made purely from Assam tea leaves were sent down the Brahmaputra River and from there by ship to Calcutta, arriving on the last day of January 1838. Moisture and dampness had spoiled most of the tea. Just a dozen boxes arrived in decent shape.

But that was enough. Repacked in specially soldered tin cases to keep the merchandise not only dry, but to keep it from absorbing the stench of other cargo, the tea was loaded onto the *Calcutta* and, in May 1838, sailed for England.[37]

The shipment landed at the East India Company's warehouses in November. The Company allowed excitement and speculation to build for a couple of months. At last, on January 10, 1839, more than a year after it had been processed, eight chests of Assam tea—some 350 pounds total—went up for auction under the round skylight of India House on Mincing Lane. The Company's experts had divided it into two qualities, with three lots classified as souchong (with larger leaves) and five lots as pekoe (smaller and slightly less coarse).

By the end of the auction, all eight lots had been knocked down to Captain Pidding, owner of Howqua's Mixture Tea. While tea was selling at auction for a couple of shillings a pound at the time, Pidding paid twenty-one shillings for the first lot, while the last—with almost sixty bids—cost him an extraordinary thirty-four shillings. But he recouped his enormous investment by repacking and selling the novelty tea in small bags.

"The general opinion of the collected tea brokers and dealers, with whom the room was crowded, was, that the Assam tea is not only valuable as a curiosity," went one typical positive notice in the press, "but that the tea itself is of very superior quality, being of a pleasant flavor, and of such strength that some asserted that the fifth water from it was as strong as the first."[38]

Another shipment arrived at the end of the year, and a second sale of Assam tea took place on March 17, 1840, and while prices dropped somewhat, industry insiders—Twinings & Co. of London among them—deemed it an improvement that contained plenty of potential.[39] That wild tea grew in Assam, could be cultivated and processed, and would sell on the market had been proven. It was clearly commercially possible. Incredibly, it had all happened within a stunningly short half dozen years since Bentinck had formed the Tea Committee.

To actualize that promise, tap its potential, and bring it to the vast marketplace, two companies formed immediately and simultaneously—one in London, one in Calcutta—that soon combined into the Assam Company. It was a rival of sorts to the East India Company, whose plans had long been to leave the tea plantation business once it had progressed out of the experimental phase. The East India Company retained just a few small gardens,[40] and the government supported the Assam Company by offering it land. But extremely high production costs, mismanagement, and lack of tea-farming know-how nearly doomed the project at the outset. By the mid–1840s it was bankrupt and facing liquidation. The board admitted failure and discussed giving up the entire endeavor in Upper Assam.[41]

The gardens were still under the supervision of Bruce, who was now working for the new company. Like many of the early planters, he lacked an appropriate background for the job. As a contemporary report stated of the onetime gunboat commander, he "does not seem to have possessed any knowledge of botany or horticulture, or indeed any special qualification for the post."[42] Not surprisingly, the Assam Company sacked him.

In 1847 new heads took over management, improved cultivation and the company's financial structure, and quickly turned it around. In 1852 the company offered a small dividend. This grew steadily over the next few years and by 1856 had reached 8 percent.[43] From the hard work and successes of India's tea pioneers sprang an entire industry as the secrets of tea production were gradually unveiled. Commercial aspirations and imaginations were unleashed, and production began to compete with China's. One of Bruce's goals in planting tea in Assam was not just "to enrich our own dominions" but also to "pull down the haughty pride of China."[44]

Given the rivalry in this competitiveness, comments in the newspapers were at times dismissive, possessive, patriotic, or aggrandizing. "We have also beaten the Chinese in their porcelain ware . . . and so shall it be with her tea," brayed the *Illustrated London News* on August 15, 1857, as it reported on finding a place on the subcontinent with the right climate, soil, and abundance of labor.

> May not the day arrive when we may be independent of the saucy Chinaman, and, instead of sending our ships to Canton for our tea, we shall send them to Calcutta for the rich and well-flavoured teas of Assam, Chachar, Darjeeling-Kumaon, and other tea-growing districts, now springing up along the broad front of our splendid mountains?[45]

Sauciness aside, the article was prescient. Within three decades—by 1888—Britain was importing more tea from India than China.* It was an "imperial dream come true."[46]

By then the undertaking was long out of its pioneering days, and the foundations for one of the country's greatest industries well established. The success of the Assam Company had quickly spawned rivals.† Other

---

* One of Bentinck's most significant achievements was pushing for the development of a tea industry on Indian soil. Yet it is never mentioned among his accomplishments. Full biographies on the man, including Demetrius Boulger's *Lord William Bentinck* (1892) and John Rosselli's *Lord William Bentinck: The Making of a Liberal Imperialist, 1774–1839* (1974), make not a single reference to his role in tea or the Tea Committee, even though the industry is one of the Raj's most profitable and lasting legacies.

† The Assam Company still exists today as a large, publicly traded company that, along with producing tea, has expanded into oil and gas exploration and transportation.

companies formed and established gardens, as did some wealthy individuals. They leased or purchased property from the government, cleared it, and planted tea. The amount of tea being cultivated was rapidly increasing, and as it matured, so did yields. By the time the newly opened railway linked some of the tea-covered hills with the Brahmaputra River in 1882, Assam produced 12.7 million pounds of tea.[47] By 1891 it had reached some 49.5 million pounds.[48] But these numbers were still meager. Eight years later, the Brahmaputra Valley produced 75,287,500 pounds,[49] and by 1913, plantations in Assam produced a staggering 199,722,000 pounds[50]— enough to brew somewhere between 35 and 45 *billion* cups of tea.

Today Assam alone produces about 500 million kilograms—over 1 billion pounds—of tea a year.

But quantity and quality are not synonymous. Assam's tropically grown teas are malty, a hint woody, at times pungent, frequently a touch rough, and always strong and bracing. The British realized this back in the 1840s, as the Assam industry was just getting under way. Tea would make a profitable commodity. "It flourishes best in a jungle atmosphere of heat and humidity," said the recent head of India's largest tea company. "It is an easy plant to grow. But to get a good-quality tea is extremely difficult."[51]

From the beginning of their experimenting with growing tea in India, the British also wanted to produce teas that had the delicate floral aromas of those from the hills of China: light and bright, rather than husky and earthy. The teas of Assam had plenty of body but little finesse.

For this, the British needed better plant stock from China—and to find a way to get it back to places in India more similar to their original geography without perishing. Even if they achieved this seemingly impossible task, they also needed to learn how to better cultivate the plant. From horticulture to processing, the British still had little idea how to produce tea. Lu Yü's thousand-year-old book-cum-manual remained a main source of information, supplemented with a scattering of monographs such as Bruce's and travelogues such as Griffith's, and some details from the handful of Chinese workers in Assam.

China jealously guarded its tea and production secrets and would not give them up easily. The East India Company would have to send a shrewd plant hunter to travel to the forbidden interior regions where the best teas grew and smuggle them out.

CHAPTER 5

China Leaf

The East India Company's agent was Robert Fortune, a curator at the Chelsea Physic Garden in London. Unlike many of his colleagues, Fortune was neither titled nor wealthy nor even well connected. He was born in Edrom, in rural, southeast Scotland, a few miles from the border with England, and on his birth entry his father's occupation is listed as "hedger."[1] Having little formal education, Fortune began as an apprentice and then obtained a qualification in horticulture (though not medicine like most botanists). Skilled and ambitious, he worked in positions at the botanic garden at Edinburgh and then gardens of London's Horticultural Society[2] (now the Royal Horticultural Society). He lacked the financial self-sufficiency generally expected for such gentlemanly expeditions, even those taken at the behest of others. But as a talented botanist, experienced in the delicate process of sending plants back to Europe, and, quite exceptionally, widely traveled in China, he was the perfect man for the job.

Fortune had not long returned from a lengthy trip in China. Six months to the day after the signing of the 1841 Treaty of Nanking, following the First Opium War, the Horticultural Society had dispatched the thirty–year-old on a flora-gathering mission. Surely, the parts in his subsequent book, *Three Years' Wanderings in the Northern Provinces of China*, about traveling into prohibited areas of the Middle Kingdom in disguise particularly caught the attention of the Company's board.

For this new mission, Fortune's brief was different—and difficult: to gather tea plants, as well as production secrets, for both green and black tea. The consensus of British botanists was that green and black tea came from different plants rather than different ways of processing the leaves; Fortune suspected otherwise. While five ports were then open to foreigners, the great tea-producing regions of the interior remained off-limits. Fortune knew that he could not rely on agents but had to go himself to be certain of the plants' sources, as well as to gather careful notes on soil and cultivation. Apart from a handful of Arab traders and Jesuit missionaries, few foreigners had ever penetrated so deeply into China or returned alive to tell of it.

Arriving in Hong Kong in August 1848, Fortune traveled immediately a thousand miles north to Shanghai and then inland to the picturesque, green-tea-producing areas around the Yellow Mountain region. A day out of Shanghai, he had his head shaved, donned Chinese robes, and had his servant sew on a braided hair tail that hung nearly to his heels.[3] Like this, Fortune became his alter ego, Sing Wa, a respected businessman from some country "beyond the great wall" that justified his height and pale skin, heavy accent, and inability to speak the local dialects, and perhaps the reason he lacked a certain intrinsic fluency with chopsticks. Traveling by boat and on a sedan chair carried by teams of locally hired "coolies," he reached his target and found tea growing luxuriantly on the hillside. He didn't collect tea himself, but obtained plants and seeds from nurseries.

Back in Shanghai, Fortune readied his first shipment for the Calcutta Botanic Garden. At that time, a major problem for plant hunters was getting species back to sponsoring gardens in good shape. With stowage at a premium and freshwater always in short supply, ships were reluctant to transport them. Salty sea spray and merciless tropical sun were enemies of a plant's survival, as were livestock on board, which would nibble on the tender shoots and flowers whenever possible.

To combat this, Fortune used Wardian cases, sealed glass boxes that had been recently developed by a physician in London's East End named Nathaniel Ward. Acting like mini-greenhouses, they allowed the plants plenty of light and a fairly stable temperature. By recycling moisture, the plants could stay alive for years within the closed environment.

Fortune packed the first batch of plants in the glazed cases. Tea seeds were particularly sensitive and, Fortune observed, only retained their vitality for a short period of time. Unsure as to the best approach, he tried several. "Some were packed in loose canvas bags," he wrote, "others were mixed with dry earth and put into boxes, and others again were put up in very small packages, in order to be quickly forwarded by post."[4]

Not until the following year (1849) did word reach him that the plants had arrived in Calcutta in good shape. The seeds, though, had failed to germinate. None of his methods, he wrote drily, "were attended with much success."[5] Although his travelogue, *A Journey to the Tea Countries of China; Including Sung-Lo and the Bohea Hills; with a Short Notice of the East India Company's Tea Plantations in the Himalaya Mountains*, does not record it as such, the loss must have been a deep blow.

By then, Fortune had long since headed back into the interior. This time he traveled southwest to the famed black-tea-producing hills up the Min River and into the Bohea Hills of Fujian Province. Again, Fortune was successful in obtaining stock. With this load he tried new ways to send the seeds.

> Having procured some fine mulberry-plants from the district where the best Chinese silk is produced, I planted them in a Ward's case in the usual way, and watered them well. In two or three days, when the soil was sufficiently dry, a large quantity of tea-seeds were scattered over its surface, and covered with earth about half an inch deep. The whole was now sprinkled with water, and fastened down with a few crossbars to keep the earth in its place. The case was then screwed down in the usual way, and made as tight as possible.[6]

When the cases arrived in Calcutta, the mulberry plants were in good condition, and, encouragingly, the tea seeds had germinated. "The young tea-plants were sprouting around the mulberries as thick as they could come up," wrote Dr. Hugh Falconer,[7] who had recently taken over from Wallich as superintendent of the botanic garden, upon their receipt.

Fortune continued to hone his techniques as he filled and sent on more Wardian cases to Falconer. They arrived in good shape and were sent on to experimental tea gardens newly established in the western Himalayan foothills.

Now confident in his system of getting the plants and seeds to India in good shape, Fortune gathered his final, grand batch, the one that he would accompany himself to Calcutta. When this was accomplished, Fortune set out to fulfill what he deemed the most difficult part of his commission. He needed to convince experienced Chinese tea manufacturers from the best tea districts to go to India and teach their techniques to the fledging industry.

It proved easier than expected. Using a well-connected agent who offered the Chinese experts handsomely paid three-year contracts along with the promise of certain freedom in their tea planting and power over both Indians and British workers,[8] Fortune engaged eight tea makers to emigrate illegally, even given the threat of torture and flogging not only to themselves but their families. He obtained a large assortment of tea-making implements.

Fortune filled fourteen Wardian cases with rows of young tea plants and sowed the tea seeds among them. He was left with a bushel of remaining seeds that he did not want to waste and layered them with earth under a collection of Chinese camellia plants for the botanic garden in two additional glass cases.

In mid-February 1851, Fortune, the Chinese recruits, the tools of their trade, and the tea-filled Wardian cases sailed from Shanghai to Hong Kong. There, the group boarded the *Lady Mary Wood*, a Peninsular & Oriental wooden steamship built ten years before and used on the Calcutta–Hong Kong service, for which the 160-foot steamer had carried a cargo of opium on its outbound run.[9]

The journey to Calcutta took a month. In mid-March, the *Lady Mary Wood* crossed the Bay of Bengal and entered the Hooghly River, the westernmost distributary of the Ganges. "Almost any pilot will tell you that his work is much more difficult than you imagine," begins a Rudyard Kipling story, "but the Pilots of the Hugli know that they have one hundred miles of the most dangerous river on earth running through their hands—the Hugli between Calcutta and the Bay of Bengal."[10] In addition to shifting shoals, silt beds, mud banks, heavy currents, and a seven-foot tidal bore, at the time of year when Fortune and company were making their way to Calcutta, early monsoon winds were beginning to blow up through the funnel-shaped bay. Eventually the *Lady Mary Wood* neared the Second City of the Empire, the City of Palaces: Calcutta.

Founded as a trading post by merchant-adventurer Job Charnock and the East India Company in 1690, Calcutta grew quickly—it had 120,000 people by 1750—and became the capital of British India in 1772. By the time Robert Fortune sailed up the Hooghly with his Wardian cases of tea, Calcutta was the largest colonial trade center in

Asia and a global city, the administrative and commercial center of India, and its cultural and intellectual hub.*

Spread along the eastern bank of the Hooghly, the city was safe-guarded by the beefy, irregularly octagonal riverside Fort William and administered by an army of East India Company scribes in the Writers' Building. Theaters and an opera house (1827) offered cultured entertainment, elite gentlemen's clubs—the stoutly white Bengal Club (1827) with its dancing-cobra emblem,† even a number of Masonic lodges—provided social status, and the Auckland Hotel (1841) added luxury.‡ A handful of churches preached familiar themes in familiar settings: St. John's Church (1787), modeled on London's St. Martin-in-the-Fields; the brilliant white St. Andrew's Kirk (1818), with its black weather vane topped by a crowing cock; and the newly consecrated St. Paul's Cathedral (1847). The city even had a golf course; founded in 1829, the Royal Calcutta Golf Club was the oldest outside the British Isles. There were, to be sure, also less salubrious ways to pass time. In the 1750s, Robert Clive, the celebrated soldier and first governor of Bengal, called it "one of the most wicked places in the Universe . . . Rapacious and Luxurious beyond concepcion [*sic*]."[11]

Fortune's exact destination, though, lay five miles downriver from the city itself: the Calcutta Botanic Garden.

He was met at the garden's riverside ghat (steps down to the river) by Dr. Falconer, a heavy-set northern Scot from the coastal village of Forres, with whom Fortune had been corresponding. Anxious to see how the tea had fared, the Wardian cases were unloaded. As Fortune later wrote:

> When the cases were opened in Calcutta the young tea-plants were found to be in good condition. The seeds which had been sown between the rows were also just beginning to germinate. These, of course, were left undisturbed, as there was room enough for them to grow; but it was necessary to take other measures with those in the camellia cases. On opening the

---

*In 2001 Calcutta changed its name to its Bengali equivalent, Kolkata, losing the longer, languid *u* to something sharper. The shift to its precolonial moniker was an effort to help preserve its Bengali identity.

† Its great rival, the Tollygunge Club, would be founded in 1895.

‡ In the 1860s, the Auckland Hotel was expanded and renamed the Great Eastern Hotel. Mark Twain stayed here and called it the finest hotel east of the Suez Canal.

latter, the whole mass of seeds, from the bottom to the top, was swelling, and germination had just commenced. The camellias, which had now arrived at their destination, were lifted gently out and potted, and appeared as if they had never left their native country. Fourteen new cases were got ready, filled with earth, and these germinating seeds were sown thickly over the surface, and covered with soil in the usual way. In a few days the young plants came sprouting through the soil; every seed seemed to have grown . . .[12]

Their journey far from over, the smuggled botanical jewels now had to be quickly taken from tropical Calcutta up to the Company's gardens in the Himalayas. Within ten days the collection of plants, tools, and Chinese tea makers were ready to move on. Fortune had already been gone for nearly three years by then, but instead of returning home to England and his family, he accompanied the tea and its entourage.

As the monsoon rains were still a few months off, and the Hooghly River too shallow upstream to travel by boat, the group was obliged to take a ship back down to the Bay of Bengal to access the main branch of the Ganges where it flowed into the sea. Under the brutal late-March sun, the ship slid away from Calcutta in the ebb tide, down the Hooghly, and into the tangled tidal fringes and deltaic channels of the Sundarbans, the swampy, intermittently submerged archipelagic maze of mangrove forest that fingers into the sea. Narrow-snooted gharial crocodiles, soft-shelled turtles, and stocky freshwater sharks swam in abundance. From the shoreline or perched in tipsy wooden canoes, bare-chested fishermen cast nets for freshwater eel, catfish, and carp, including the golden *mahseer*, with its large, thick scales the size of tea saucers. The ship joined the main channel of the Ganges and traveled three hundred miles north to the Rajmahal Hills, then followed the river's northwest arc to Allahabad, more than five hundred miles farther upstream. In the nineteenth century, thousands of "blind" Ganges River dolphins swam there, foraging in the muddy bed with their long, narrow beaks and large flippers, and Fortune would have seen schools of them rolling on the water and ducking and diving under the surface.

His travelogue, though, mentions none of this, nor of the opium growing along the river valley. While he passed through the main opium-producing belt of British India during the harvesting season and surely saw peasants lancing the plump, pale-green poppy capsules and scraping off the tarry sap with curved knives, the only references to opium in his book were to ruffian addicts he encountered in China—never of the drug's source. "All the towns on its banks have already been frequently described in accounts of India," he wrote instead. "I may, therefore, simply state that we passed in succession the large towns of Patna, Dinapoor, Ghazepoor, Benares, and Mirzapoor, and reached Allahabad on the 14th of April."[13]

Beyond Allahabad, the Ganges is strewn with shoals and rapids and not navigable by boat, so the entourage had to continue its journey by land. The twenty-eight Wardian cases plus the tea-processing implements filled nine bullock-pulled wagons. Throughout the 450-mile journey, fraught with danger, hardship, and, for the Scot, deep exoticism, he kept to his austere style. "In due time all arrived at their destination in perfect safety,"[14] he wrote, with impressive restraint, of the weeks plodding north-west toward the Himalayas as the heat of the plains grew fierce.

The destination was Saharanpur, a former Mughal garden laid out in the mid-eighteenth century in the lower foothills. "When the cases were opened, the tea-plants were found to be in a very healthy state," Fortune wrote. "No fewer than 12,838 plants were counted in the cases, and many more were germinating. Notwithstanding their long voyage from the north of China, and the frequent transshipment and changes by the way, they seemed as green and vigorous as if they had been all the while growing on the Chinese hills."[15]

Between these and the earlier batches, Fortune added, by his own estimation, nearly twenty thousand new tea plants from China into India.[16]

Having safely delivered his charges—both plants and tea makers—to their new homes, Fortune spent the remainder of the spring and summer touring the government's infant Himalayan tea plantations. At last, he began his long journey home. The first stage from the mountains to Calcutta took a month, visiting en route "the well-known cities of Delhi and Agra."[17] Fortune arrived in Calcutta at the end of August and stayed with Dr. Falconer at the botanic garden until a mail steamer was ready to depart for England.

"On the 5th of September I had the pleasure of seeing the *Victoria regia* flower for the first time in India," he wrote, referring to the giant water lily with leaves that can measure nearly six feet across and bear the weight of a young teenager. "It was growing luxuriantly in one of the ponds in the botanic garden, and no doubt will soon be a great ornament to Indian gardens. It will soon reign as the queen of flowers in every land, and, like our beloved sovereign whose name it bears, the sun will never set on its dominions."[18]

Those are the final lines of Fortune's book. It ends not on tea, the purpose of his journey, the obsession that drove the three-and-a-half-year undertaking, but rather an ornamental water lily gathered in the South American Amazon.

Fortune returned to the Far East thrice more—once in the service of the U.S. government to find tea that could grow in the southern states—and traveled to China as well as Japan, Indonesia, Taiwan, and the Philippines in search of plants. He is credited with introducing some 120 new species into Western gardens.

But little is known about Fortune himself outside the adventure- and plant-filled travelogues. As fascinating as these are to read, they are, for the most part, impersonal. Given his restraint in writing nothing of Agra or its sumptuous Taj Mahal to a society hungry for the exotic, it is no surprise that he was equally reticent of himself.

When Fortune died in 1880, his family—who are absent from his works—burned his diaries, letters, and personal effects. The few photos that remain show a stern-looking man with a high forehead and heavy lamb-chop whiskers. He looks remarkably similar throughout the years. In the final portrait, his forehead is higher and the whiskers friskier and fringed in white.

But the tea plants he smuggled from China carry on. From Saharanpur, they spread to various Himalayan plantations. And some of that exceptional stock eventually made its way to Darjeeling, where it would eventually produce the world's finest and most expensive teas.

Second Flush

(May through June)

*A*fter the first flush, a month or so of dormancy follows from mid-April to mid-May, called the banji period—a brief time when pluckers can only take two leaves but no bud—beset by sudden, sporadic, and intense showers, with sharp claps of thunder, power outages, and pulsating rain. The moisture spurs on the second flush, and the tea bushes again sprout new shoots and leaves.

Summers* in the Darjeeling hills are hot and dry, the sky generally cloudless but not vibrant: azure with a cataract of haze. While days are balmy, the nights remain fresh, offering relief from the sweltering plains below that can top 115 degrees Fahrenheit, even graze 120. Azaleas and orchids blossom, Himalayan golden eagles and griffon vultures wheel above on mountain updrafts, and down in the lower foothills, the breeding season for the hawk-cuckoo is under way. The size of a slender pigeon and known in Hindi as papiha, it's usually called the brainfever bird for its repetitive and progressively more urgent three-syllable call—brain-FE-ver—that runs up in shrill, spiraling crescendos and gets repeated all day, all night.

"The slumbering life forces come alive, the birds, the bees," Rajah Banerjee said one sunny morning in the Makaibari tasting room. "A midsummer night's dream!" Lanky as a cricket star, with a thick shock of pewter-colored hair that crests up in a swooping, offset front part like that of a slightly rebellious prep-schooler, he walks with the gait of a man who has spent many hours on a horse (and has the bad back of someone who has been thrown from one).

---

*Summer in Darjeeling is the premonsoon season, beginning sometime in April and running to July. The hottest month tends to be May.

On these warm days, workers pick leaves that are larger than first flush ones and have a slightly purplish bloom and high number of silvery tips. With summer kicking in, the tea changes. It is the preferred season for many enthusiasts. Describing this flush and the sublime teas it produces, the reedy timbre of Rajah's voice softens, his clipped syllables become drawn out, and he finishes, abruptly, with a broad, silent smile.

The fired leaves have a darker hue than those in the first flush, moving from spring tea's grayish greens to oxidized coppers and mahogany. The hot weather gives more color to the liquor, turning it a bright, deep amber, even tawny, tone. "The color of a newly minted copper penny," Banerjee said. In white sneakers and pant cuffs tucked into gym socks, he moved among the row of a dozen teas with a jaunty pride.

The body of a second flush tea is fuller but still relaxed, the flavors deeper and less grassy, a touch more prominent on the palate, yet roundly mellow with a sweetish, fruity, often peachy note. And, important for connoisseurs, Darjeeling tea's renowned muscatel flavor—a musky spice with sweet hints— is more pronounced. So pronounced that the season often carries the moniker "muscatel flush."

The year's opening harvest might garner excitement and attention, but this second one, famed for its concentrated signature flavors, fetches just as high prices.

*It also offers a special quirk of nature when an infestation of insects is actually beneficial. For a couple of weeks, tea jassids (*Empoasca flavescens*)— commonly called green flies in Darjeeling, even though they look more like mini-grasshoppers just one-tenth-inch long—come and feed on the leaves. "They suck out the moisture and the leaf shrivels downward," said Sujoy Sengupta at the Chamong Tee group's headquarters in Kolkata on a steamy, late-summer afternoon. Holding out a hand, he curled his fingers down into an arthritic claw. "It is called, in Nepali,* kakreko *patti. Patti is 'leaf,' and* kakreko *is 'curled,'" he explained, noting that this doesn't kill the leaf completely but stunts its growth, which further concentrates flavors. "This is the topmost quality of leaf."*

The pinpricks the tea jassids make as they feed start natural fermentation. Fine veins of brown appear on the edges, like the dark fissures in an old tea-stained porcelain tasting cup. There is a patina of death while the leaf surrounding it remains wholly alive and freshly green, a dichotomy that offers, for Banerjee, "symmetry for the senses."

CHAPTER 6

Darjeeling

Darjeeling as it exists today began as a strip of isolated, heavily forested ridges that the rajah of the Kingdom of Sikkim deeded to the East India Company. It was not part of a specific, long-term plan of British colonial expansion, but a more piecemeal and opportunistic move among Himalayan kingdoms. Similar small steps were being taken elsewhere as the disjointed puzzle of the subcontinent was being pulled together under a unified British rule and aligned princely states, and the map of India gradually became further shaded in British red.

In the 1780s, Gorkhas from Nepal marched into Sikkim and began wrestling away territory in the lower foothills and skirting flatlands, and eventually seized land as far east as the Teesta River. But when the Nepalese looked to take the rest of Sikkim, the British intervened with the 1814–16 Anglo-Gorkha (or Nepalese) War. The East India Company signed a treaty with Sikkim in 1817 and returned some four thousand square miles of reclaimed territory to the rajah and guaranteed his sovereignty over it. The British essentially wanted a forty-mile-wide buffer zone—Joseph Hooker fittingly called it a "fender"[1]—between Nepal and Bhutan to keep them apart for two reasons: to prevent them from fighting with each other, but also to prevent them from forming an alliance against the British, who controlled the bordering territory to the south.

The ruling family of Sikkim was largely Tibetan, while its subjects were mostly Lepchas and other tribes, a cause of internal friction. When the rajah had a Lepcha leader assassinated, many of the leader's followers fled west into Nepal. Aided by the Gorkhas, they commenced a series of raids on Sikkim.² The dispute drew the attention of the East India Company, which, following a treaty article, was bound to arbitrate any conflict between Sikkim and its neighbors. The Company dispatched Captain George Lloyd, a forty-year-old commander of a nearby army camp, and J. W. Grant, an explorer and the commercial resident of Malda (a village on the plains about halfway to Calcutta, now called English Bazar), who were familiar with the terrain.

During their 1829 trip, the two men spent six days at "the old Goorka station called Dorjeling," the first Europeans to do so. No doubt they were besotted by the spot's beauty and views. On seeing the chain of mountains that stand to the north of Darjeeling, "the observer is struck with the precision and sharpness of their outlines," wrote Joseph Hooker in his *Himalayan Journals*, "and still more with the wonderful play of colours on their snowy flanks, from the glowing hues reflected in orange, gold and ruby, from clouds illumined by the sinking or rising sun, to the ghastly pallor that succeeds with twilight, when the red seems to give place to its complementary colour, green."³

The governor-general of India, Lord Bentinck—not long in his position and still a few years away from forming the Tea Committee—pressed for more on the region's suitability as a sanitarium. The East India Company had begun establishing hill station retreats, with healthy mountain climates and clean air, for their men to recuperate from the heat and ill effects of the tropical climate. (Air was considered to be the source of numerous diseases, from cholera to malaria, whose name derives from the Italian *mal'aria*, "bad air.") Delhi and the Punjab had Shimla (Simla) and Mussoorie nearby, Madras had Ootacamund (affectionately known as Ooty) in the Nilgiri mountains, to the southeast of Bombay rose the hills of Poona, and soon the company would lease Mt. Abu in Rajasthan from its princely owner. But soldiers stationed in Calcutta and around Bengal had no convenient Company settlement to escape the heat.

After Lloyd and Grant wrote encouragingly of the area's potential in their report, Bentinck sent Grant back, along with the deputy surveyor-general of India, Captain James Herbert, a trained geologist with considerable Himalayan experience, to fully assess the site's suitability. Grant's 1830 report suggested Darjeeling was ideally situated for a sanitarium but also, importantly, offered a vantage point to keep watch on the Lepchas and Nepalese, control over a key pass to Nepal, and access to trade with Sikkim and Tibet.

A formal request was made to the Rajah of Sikkim for the land that same year. Lloyd assumed it would be easy to obtain cession, but the petition was denied.[4]

The Company instructed Lloyd to acquire it "on the first convenient occasion."[5] Another border dispute erupted in 1834, and the British went to mediate again. This time they wanted the Darjeeling tract in exchange. The rajah was reluctant and offered alternatives. Lloyd continued to insist, and finally the rajah relented. By then, though, the British had told their agent to stop negotiating. Lloyd ignored instructions, secured the land, and only later informed his superiors.

Dated February 1, 1835, the deed is brief:

> The Governor-General [Lord Bentinck] having expressed his desire for the possession of the hills of Darjeeling on account of its cool climate, for the purpose of enabling the servants of his Government, suffering from sickness, to avail themselves of its advantages, I, the Sikkimputtee Rajah, out of friendship for the said Governor-General, hereby present Darjeeling to the East India Company, that is, all the land south of the Great Ranjeet river, east of the Balasur, Kahail and Little Runjeet rivers, and west of the Rungno and Mahanadi rivers.[6]

What had been a request for land to house a sanitarium became a generous 138-square-mile tract, an unconditional gift. In exchange, the rajah received one rifle, one double-barreled shotgun, twenty yards of red broadcloth, and two pairs of shawls, one of superior quality, the other inferior. A few years later the government granted the rajah an allowance of Rs 3,000 per annum for compensation, then doubled it to Rs 6,000.

Once in East India Company hands, Lloyd returned to the site in November 1836, along with an assistant surgeon, to spend the winter and spring studying the area and its climate in detail. The Company hoped to avoid a fate similar to that of another hill station recently built in Assam at Cherrapunji, which turned out to be the wettest place on earth.*

---

*Quite literally. In 1860–61, Cherrapunji set a world record of 1,042 inches of rainfall in twelve months, a record that still stands. In July 1861 alone, the monsoon dumped 366 inches—over thirty feet!—of rain.

The men submitted their final report in June 1837, and the Company decided to proceed with the considerable challenge of establishing a town. The hills were steep and spurred, cleaved by precipitous valleys with few level spots, and largely covered with nearly impassable growth. "All is still forest and so thick that one can hardly crawl through it," wrote one settler in the early 1840s.[7] Everything had to be brought up from the plains on bullock carts, then carried by porters along the series of *chorbatos* (paths) that ran through the dense, primeval forests.[8] Tigers and leopards roamed the hills, with small bears, Himalayan wolves, and numerous species of highly venomous snakes. Malaria-carrying mosquitoes came out at dusk, monkeys pillaged the maize fields at night, and during the wet months leeches became endemic. Perhaps the biggest torment on the way to and from Darjeeling were tiny, robust black flies called *peepsa* (or *pipsa*; *Simulium indicum*), which managed to get through the finest mesh nets.[9] Their bites caused swelling, intolerable itching, and no small number of workers brought in from the plains to flee the area.

The Darjeeling tract, Lloyd wrote in an early report, had no villages and only twenty to thirty houses. Though sparsely inhabited, the land—home to the Lepcha people—was not *un*inhabited.

When the British arrived, the Lepcha still practiced a type of migratory agriculture called *jhum*. Just before the rainy season, they would burn a tract of forest, making room to plant and also releasing nutrients in the ash. Once rain fell, and the ash had soaked into the earth, they planted. After intensely farming a plot for three years, with the land exhausted from a rapid string of different crops, they abandoned the site and repeated the process elsewhere. Firing season made for spectacular displays, as Hooker—one of the first to document Lepcha agricultural traditions in detail—recorded:

> The voices of the birds and insects being hushed, nothing is audible but the harsh roar of the rivers, and occasionally, rising far above it, that of the forest fires. At night we were literally surrounded by them; some smoldering, like shale-heaps at a colliery, others fitfully bursting forth, whilst others again stalked along with a steadily increasing and enlarging flame, shooting out great tongues of fire, which spared nothing as they advanced with irresistible might. Their triumph is in

reaching a great bamboo clump, when the noise of the flames drowns that of the torrents, and as the great stem-joints burst from the expansion of confined air, the report is as that of a salvo from a park of artillery. At Dorjiling the blaze is visible, and the deadened reports of the bamboos bursting is heard throughout the night; but in the valley, and within a mile of the scene of destruction, the effect is the most grand, being heightened by the glare reflected from the masses of mist which hover above.[10]

Lepchas were short, with dark, coppery skin and Mongolian features. They went barefoot and mostly bareheaded (their hats, when they had them, were made of leaves and plaited slips of bamboo), and wore long, red-and-white-striped robes of untreated wool or cotton cloth, which wrapped around the body, pinned at the shoulder, and tied at the waist. Over their shoulders the men slung wooden sheaths that held a two-foot-long knife and a pouch of arrows for hunting birds. "They are constantly armed with a long, heavy, straight knife," which, Hooker wrote, "serves equally for plough, toothpick, table-knife, hatchet, hammer, and sword."[11] (To these tasks another early commentator added "hoe, spade, and nail parer.")[12] Hooker also noted the bamboo bow and quiver of arrows they carried along with a pouch holding aconite to poison their tips.[13]

Keen hunters and highly skilled trackers and herbalists, the Lepcha collected roots, leaves, and herbs from the forest, foraged for wild honey and fungi, and trapped fish in the streams. They grew oranges and tapioca, farmed cardamom under large trees on the steep slopes, and planted terraces of rice. Bamboo was key. Not only did the Lepcha utilize twenty-two different varieties of it that grew in the area,[14] but they believed God created bamboo along with their people.[15]

They called their land Mayel Lyang, Abode of the Gods. While, gradually over the centuries, the Lepcha largely adopted Buddhism, they never fully forwent some of their culture's more primitive spiritual elements. Early Lepchas observed a religion called Bon that worshipped nature in its physical forms—trees, forests, rivers, lakes, mountains—with God omnipresent in them. "Though the first man and woman were created out of pure snow from *Kingtsoomzaongboo Chyue* (Mt. Kanchenjunga), each clan, after the downfall of man, had its own lake and mountain," wrote Dennis Lepcha, a member and adviser to the Indigenous Lepcha Tribal Association. "Hence, after death, a Lepcha soul will rest in the lap of his ancestors who are residing in their respective clan's mountain and lake."[16] According to another Lepcha author, they "chant their hymns and prayers in the tune of birds, in the sound of winds, water-falls, rivers, etc."[17] Call it an ecotheology or ecosophy.

Lepcha is the name given by the Nepalese from *lep* (speech) and *cha* (unintelligible). This is somewhat paradoxical as the Lepcha language is unusually rich in the vocabulary of the natural world, with not only terms for every plant, leaf, moss, and mushroom of the forest, but also distinctive names for the stages of a plant's ripeness. No wonder they often prefer to call themselves Rongpas (ravine dwellers).

While today Lepchas live in Sikkim, eastern Nepal, southwestern Bhutan, and Tibet, most reside in West Bengal. Of the approximately 150,000 of them, more than 90 percent live in the Darjeeling hills.[18]

Though well versed in the ways and rhythms of the forests around Darjeeling—or perhaps because of it—the Lepchas were not interested in becoming laborers for the British in establishing a new sanitarium. Progress stuttered along. Lloyd must have felt that to turn this isolated mountain ridgeline, lacking communication with the rest of India and surrounded by unhelpful locals, into a hill station on par with Shimla or Ooty was a near impossible task. Indeed, by the summer of 1839, the powers in Calcutta were so unhappy with Lloyd's sluggish progress that they curtly dismissed him.[19] Lloyd returned to his military unit and in early 1840 sailed for China to participate in the First Opium War.[20]

But Lloyd's story in India—and Darjeeling—was far from over. He rose to the rank of lieutenant general, and by the time sepoys on the plains launched their rebellion in 1857, he was almost seventy, gout-ridden, and long-past retirement age.[21] He hesitated on disarming the sepoys in his brigade as those to the south were mutinying. While he had his luncheon aboard a steamer on the Ganges, three regiments in the Bengal Native Infantry—over two thousand men—fled with arms and ammunition and joined up with other rebels. Lloyd's response in sending out troops in pursuit was equally hesitant and bungled. At last 343 Europeans, 70 Sikhs, and a few gentlemen volunteers went out after them.[22] The white-uniformed men were ambushed by rebels in brilliant moonlight as they passed through a mango grove. It was a complete debacle—or turning point in the rebellion, depending on one's view-point. Relieved of his command for "culpable neglect,"[23] Lloyd retired to

Darjeeling, where he died an uncelebrated figure a few years later. His widow had to arrange the memorial plaque that read "discoverer of Darjeeling."*

The development of Darjeeling into a famous hill station—and home of the world's finest tea—is attributed almost solely to another East India Company man who arrived just weeks after Lloyd's unceremonious sacking.

In June 1839, a Scottish civil servant in the Indian Medical Service, Dr. Archibald Campbell, was transferred from Kathmandu to Darjeeling to take up the newly created superintendent post.[24] The Scot devoted himself with workaholic energy to building the new station. With planning by Lieutenant Robert Napier of the Royal Engineers (later commander in chief in India, eventually Field Marshal Lord Napier, and ultimately one of Britain's most celebrated soldiers), the settlement quickly began to take shape across the flanks and spurs of Darjeeling's Y-shaped ridge.

Although discouraged by Sikkim's unwillingness to supply laborers, within a dozen years Campbell had gotten built a good stretch of road through the tough terrain, at least seventy European houses, a sanatorium for troops, a hotel, a bazaar, and a jail, and he introduced a justice system and abolished forced labor.[25]

At the end of 1839, just a handful of Europeans resided in town. Until a rail link was established in the 1880s, the journey from Calcutta to Darjeeling took months by bullock cart to the base of the hills, and then by horse, foot, and *dooly*, a litter slung between long poles and carried by four bearers. The hazardous, uncomfortable trip was made only by the desperate or the determined.

Yet the population of the area jumped from less than a hundred people when Campbell arrived to ten thousand in a decade and to twenty-two thousand by 1869.[26] Most were Gorkhas from across the border in

---

*Although Lloyd's grave in the European cemetery was declared to be of national importance under the Ancient Monuments and Archaeological Sites and Remains Act of 1958, little public attention has been paid it. On June 6, 2011, the front page of the *Calcutta Telegraph* read, "Darjeeling discovers Lloyd after 146 yrs—Individuals for the first time pay homage to the man who 'found' the hill town." Even that was a muted affair. The grave has a five-foot-high obelisk marker. Its blue-tinted whitewashing is fading and streaked with mold. Flowers never appear at its base.

Nepal. A special commissioner from the East India Company who visited Darjeeling to check on its progress in the early 1850s stated in his report, "It is necessary to observe that whatever has been done here has been done by Dr Campbell alone."[27] (The Nepalese workers would surely have disagreed.)

Campbell—he was called both Archibald and Arthur—came from the blustery island of Islay, known for its smoky, peat-fired whisky. He studied medicine at the University of Glasgow and then the University of Edinburgh before joining the East India Company as an assistant surgeon in 1827. A year later, he was posted to a horse artillery unit in Meerut, northeast of Delhi. Five years on he took up an appointment as surgeon to the mission in Kathmandu, where he served under B. H. Hodgson.[28] Well-known for his deep love of the Himalayas, Hodgson wrote extensively on its flora and fauna, religion, and languages. Under him, Campbell's interest in the region grew, and like his mentor, he penned a number of scholarly articles on topics that ranged from the Lepcha to taming elephants in Assam. "He was a warm friend, of a remarkably generous and affectionate disposition," an obituary of Campbell later read; "he was liberal in his views of all matters, and averse to disputation, though tenacious of his opinions."[29]

Two years after arriving in Darjeeling, Campbell married a women fifteen years his junior[30] and fathered twelve children.[31] Along with the supervising tasks of his position—essentially managing the fiscal, criminal, and civil administration of the district—the energetic Scot also controlled the station funds, acted as postmaster, and was the marriage registrar.[32] He started a papermaking factory that lasted for a couple of years[33] and introduced various new crops, including cinchona for producing quinine to treat malaria. (Cinchona is Darjeeling's second most important crop today.)

And with undreamed-of consequences, Campbell was also the first to grow tea in Darjeeling.

In 1841, just two years after arriving, Campbell planted tea in the garden of his residence, known as Beachwood, with stock that came from the nurseries in the western Himalayan foothills. The trees came to bear in the second half of that decade, and the Company inspector reported in 1853 that both Chinese and Assam varieties were doing well in Campbell's garden. Civil Surgeon Dr. J. R. Withecombe and Major James Arden

Crommelin, a Calcutta-born member of the Royal Bengal Engineers, also had extensive plantings near Darjeeling town. Campbell stated in a report dated April 28, 1853 that some two thousand tea plants, ranging from twelve years old to seedlings of a few months, were growing at two thousand to seven thousand feet in elevation.[34] He requested that none other than Robert Fortune, once again back in China for the Company, personally come to Darjeeling and give his opinion on the "suitableness of the climate and soil of the Hills for the cultivation and manufacture of Tea."[35]

With governmental backing, Campbell established tea nurseries in Darjeeling and in Kurseong. While both types of leaf varieties were planted,[36] Chinese ones that had largely failed to flourish down in the jungle conditions of Assam were wildly, even unexpectedly, successful. Plants from stock Fortune had smuggled out of China thrived in Darjeeling's misty, high-elevation climate.

The Company began to propagate plants for individuals and small companies opening up land and clearing plots for tea gardens. Nepalese laborers stripped the Himalayan foothills of their virgin forest by cutting away and burning the underbrush, and severing the lateral roots of large trees so that they toppled over under their own weight. Rocks and roots were removed, the land hoed smooth and, in places, terraced, and saplings transplanted in straight, even lines along the contours of the hills. The first commercial gardens were planted out in 1852 at Tukvar by Captain Masson, Steinthal ("Stone Valley" in German) by a German missionary named Joachim Stölke, and Aloobari. More gardens quickly followed: Makaibari, Pandam, Ging, Ambootia, Takdah, Phubsering. The first factory opened on Makaibari on 1859.

Darjeeling was growing—but remained an enclave within the rajah of Sikkim's domain. It was only a matter of time for the British to be intimately drawn into the kingdom's internal affairs and conflicts, and to want to expand out of isolation.

The situation came to a head during Joseph Hooker's plant-hunting visit in the late 1840s. Attracted to the region's lavish and diverse flora—four thousand species of flowering plants and three hundred varieties of ferns grow in and around the forests of Darjeeling alone[37]—Hooker spent three years in the Darjeeling hills, Sikkim, and Nepal identifying and collecting. "In short, there is no quarter of the globe so rich in plants,"[38] he wrote in the preface of *The Flora of British India*, his magnum opus coming out of the trip. The seven-volume work, published between 1875 and 1897, totaling nearly six thousand pages and including some sixteen thousand species, contributed greatly to public knowledge of the region's rich floral biotope. But Hooker's travelogue of the journey, *Himalayan Journals: Notes of a Naturalist* (1854), dedicated to his close friend Charles Darwin, was an immense popular success. The book informed, inspired, and excited a public with its high-peaked Central Asian descriptions and adventures.

Hooker was a grandee in the heroic age of scientific exploration. After completing his medical studies in Glasgow, the twenty-two-year-old Scot joined Captain James Clark Ross's four-year-long expedition to Antarctica, which set off in 1839—the last of the epic voyages of exploration done under sail—as assistant surgeon and botanist on the *Erebus*. He had the opportunity not only to observe and collect at the southern pole, but at all the main areas of the southern hemisphere, from Tierra del Fuego to Tasmania and the Cape. Back in Britain, as Hooker began assembling his great work on the region's flora (published between 1844 and 1859 in six large quarto volumes), the urge to collect in rich, unexplored regions returned. When offered a chance to go to the Himalayas, he took it and traveled with official accreditation and a government grant.

Hooker, with tiny spectacles crowned by wild, worried brows, and with heavy side whiskers and a beard encircling his otherwise clean-shaven face, arrived in Darjeeling famous and also well connected. His father was director of Kew Gardens. (Hooker *fils* would succeed him at the august institution.) The young Joseph was a confidant, collaborator, and early reader of Darwin.* On the ship traveling out to India, Hooker became friends with the new governor-general, Lord Dalhousie.

For Hooker's first expedition into Sikkim, Superintendent Campbell himself obtained permission. On Hooker's second one, in 1849, which would take him through Sikkim to the frontier of Tibet, Campbell, unable to resist the opportunity to fulfill a decades'-old dream to see the mysterious and forbidden kingdom, joined his esteemed visitor.

That autumn the men, against protests of Sikkimese guards, crossed into Tibet. Once back in Sikkim territory, the two Scotchmen were

---

*Asked by Darwin in 1843 to work on his newly collected plant specimens from the *Beagle* voyage, Hooker went on to read and comment on Darwin's ideas on evolution that would form *On the Origin of Species*. Over a friendship that spanned forty years, the two exchanged fourteen hundred letters.

immediately placed under arrest. According to a contemporary newspaper account, Campbell was beaten, tightly bound with bamboo cords, and tortured. Officials interrogated Campbell and tried to force him to sign various documents promising that the British wouldn't exert their influence in Sikkim. Campbell refused. The men were then escorted to the Sikkimese capital, Tumlong. While Hooker remained free to collect along the way, guards restrained Campbell, who, exhausted after some days of walking, had his hands bound to the tail of a mule was and pulled the final distance.[39] The men remained locked up in Tumlong well into December. Eventually released, they arrived back in Darjeeling on Christmas Eve, six weeks after being seized.

Repercussions were swift. A punitive British force crossed into Sikkim and camped for a couple of weeks. The soldiers didn't fire a shot; they simply made their presence known. That was enough. The British stopped paying the rajah's annual allowance for Darjeeling and, more significantly, annexed the lower part of Sikkim, called the Terai. The name translates to "moist land," referring to its marshy grasslands and boggy forest. While Hooker called it "that low malarious belt which skirts the base of the Himalaya"[40] and a "fatal"[41] district, the 640-square-mile tract of land was the most fertile part of Sikkim's largely mountainous dominion.

For the Sikkimese, this turned their kingdom—bordered to the east and west by enemies and enclosed on the north by impenetrable Himalayan peaks—into a landlocked mountain hinterland cut off from all access to the plains below. They now had to pass through British territory to reach them.

But for the British, the move connected Darjeeling to the adjacent lands of British-controlled India.

Some Indian historians see Campbell's journey as a calculated attempt to provoke the Sikkimese leaders, with whom his relations had soured, thus handing the British justification to grab land. It also made irrelevant any lingering doubts surrounding the original deed to Darjeeling that Lloyd had coaxed from the rajah of Sikkim or the circumstances in which it was obtained.[42] If the wording actually meant the British had the right to more than merely reside on the tract, or even if the deed, as some suspected, had actually been written by the Sikkimese ruler himself (and not Lloyd), it was now immaterial.[43]

Darjeeling was not yet done expanding. Following their loss in the Anglo-Bhutan War (1863–65), Bhutan was forced to cede the Kalimpong tract, along with a section of foothill plains called the Dooars, to the Company in return for an annual payment. These were added to the district of Darjeeling, which then had its final—and present—shape, some 1,234 square miles.[44]

For the Company, the move on the Terai and Dooars proved both timely and propitious. With the tea industry in the Darjeeling hills and Assam growing quickly, it was already looking to expand. In 1860, the first experimental gardens were opened in the Terai, and in 1862—the year Campbell retired to London after twenty-two years in Darjeeling and thirty-five in Company service (without increase of pay or allowances)[45]—James White planted out Champta Tea Estate.[46] By 1872 the Terai had fourteen estates, and in 1874 more than two dozen.

Today, the Dooars and Terai together produce around 225 million kilograms (nearly 500 million pounds) of tea a year, about a quarter of India's total, and some twenty-five times more than Darjeeling. Full, creamy, and good liquoring, the tea is generally mellower than those from Assam, a hint sweeter, but also thinner in the cup, with a flavor that one Delhi tea merchant calls "ropy." The orthodox tea is dark, stylish, and twisty, while the CTC—most of the production—is grainy and hard. Dooars-Terai have a logo designed by the Tea Board of India, which shows the head of one of the area's elephants in a brownish-orange circle. Rarely does the tea retail abroad on its own, but rather is sought after for blending.

Having the Terai under British control directly benefited the Darjeeling tea industry. Work began on the wider, more gently sloped Hill Cart Road between Darjeeling and the plains and greater India. Its completion in 1866 was a turning point in the development of the town and its tea industry. That year, thirty-nine gardens in Darjeeling produced 433,000 pounds of tea.[47] By 1874 the number of tea gardens had ballooned to 113, and production had multiplied nearly ten times to nearly 4 million pounds.[48]

Once the Darjeeling Himalayan Railway opened in 1881, cutting travel time and transport costs significantly, and allowing heavy steam- and coal-driven machinery for processing tea to be pulled up the hill, Darjeeling tea found its final footing. In 1885 production past 9 million pounds.[49]

That was a fraction compared to Assam standards, or even those in the Dooars and Terai. But then Darjeeling was never about quantity. It has always been about quality.

CHAPTER 7

Terroir to Teacup

W hy *did* the China leaves thrive in Darjeeling? Why does the tea grown in these hills have such flavor—such *unique* flavor? And why can't other mountainous areas replicate it? "You plant the bush in Darjeeling and you get Darjeeling tea," one garden manager said. "You plant the same bush in south India and you get south-Indian tea."

To start, the steep, terraced terrain around Darjeeling is a perfect blend of climate, altitude, and the right soil. The weather combines sunshine—no more than five or six hours a day, and only for about 180 days a year—and humid mountain mists and clouds that protect the shoots and leaves from too much direct sunlight. The tea bush needs sun, but not all day long. Even more, it craves rain. At least fifty to sixty inches of rainfall per year is essential for good growth. Darjeeling receives an annual average of 126 and up to 160 inches. Abundant rain, but not swampiness. The steepness of the slopes offers excellent natural drainage.

The slightly acidic soil is rich and loamy with organic material from the surrounding forests, gritty, and generally contains the right proportion of clay. To demonstrate the ideal soil on Glenburn Tea Estate, Sanjay Sharma compressed in his fist a handful of fine, light-chocolate-colored earth from a pile near neat rows of young saplings. He held his arm straight out at shoulder height. "It should explode into dust, not little balls," he said. "If you get those balls, then too much clay, too heavy, and won't drain, yeah? If it won't hold together, there is too much sand." He opened his hand. The clod fell and exploded into pure dust. He smiled and bent down to brush off his polished leather Timberland boots.

In the cool, high elevation and thin air, the buds grow slowly, allowing flavors to develop and concentrate. The aromas of high-grown teas—
as opposed to mid-grown or low-grown—tend to be more expansive and
the flavors more intense.

The yield, though, is significantly less than that in warmer climes. A
tea bush in Darjeeling will produce only up to three and a half ounces of
finished tea per year, enough for about forty cups. Overall, Darjeeling's
gardens produce around four hundred kilograms (nine hundred pounds)
per hectare, just a third as the average in India. Such disparity comes
from other reasons, too. The China variety of bushes in Darjeeling have
smaller, slower-growing leaves than Assam bushes, the most common
type planted across the country. The season is shorter, too. In Darjeeling
the tea bushes go into hibernation for three or four months in the winter,
while in Assam, the humid, low-lying conditions offer almost year-round
harvesting.

The area's sharply pitched geography means that Darjeeling estates
vary greatly in elevation from top to bottom. Lingia Tea Estate reaches
from twenty-eight hundred to six thousand feet and yet covers a mere
220 hectares (544 acres). Tukvar is twice as large but stretches from
fifteen hundred to sixty-five hundred feet. With such range, each garden
contains a number of microclimates. They reach from tropical to temperate and even alpine forest, with hillsides that catch more of the sun's rays
as well as shadier, moister ones. The tea in the higher sections has more
delicate flavors, but lower yields. Ripening periods also differ. When
bushes on the upper reaches of an estate are just moving into the first
flush, the ones at the bottom might already be starting to produce second
flush teas. According to Hrishikesh "Rishi" Saria, who owns and manages
Gopaldhara and Rohini tea estates with his father, harvesting on the
lower-elevation Rohini starts one month earlier than on Gopaldhara,
whose fields run from fifty-five hundred to seven thousand feet, and ends
one month later.

Another geographical component contributes to Darjeeling tea's
unique taste. "In the south of India we have the right conditions and
more sunshine," said New Delhi tea merchant Vikram Mittal in his
cluttered Sunder Nagar shop. But Darjeeling is in proximity to the snow-
covered Himalayas. "It gives a 'crisping effect' to flavor," he said. The cold,
dry air that blows across the icy peaks wicks away the excess moisture,
reduces the relative humidity, and concentrates the flavor compounds.
North-facing gardens benefit most, especially in autumn.

• • •

But terroir is only the first part of the flavor equation. The remainder resides in the way the tea leaves are cultivated, selectively plucked, and then turned into made tea. Walking among workers in a garden's steep rows of tea bushes (grasping branches for support, to the amusement of the pluckers), visiting its small, on-site "factory" (more like a barn-size, well-lit workshop) that is the hub of every estate, or tasting the day's finished batches of tea, one point is immediately clear: the hands-on (and nose-in) element remains fundamental to Darjeeling's final, distinctive, and celebrated flavors.

"Darjeeling tea is special for the most important thing, the human element," said Sujoy Sengupta. Easygoing, wearing a short-sleeved shirt in his Kolkata office during the summer heat (while many of his colleagues wore ties), he spent a dozen years on some of Darjeeling's finest gardens before moving to the headquarters of the Chamong group.

"Plucking can only be done by hand," he said, as machines are unable to selectively chose the right shoots that Darjeeling tea requires. "Judging fermentation can only be done by nose." The process is tactile and intuitive. It's about feeling the leaves as they change in texture, about smelling them. And about making often spontaneous judgment calls. "You cannot just put the leaves in huge machines and expect to make excellent Darjeeling tea," he insisted. "The human touch is in every step."

That begins early in cultivation. Saplings are planted out in the field, usually in April or May. A tea bush will grow into an ungainly tree and needs to be shaped into a low, flat table if it is to be plucked. After reaching about three or four feet tall, it will start getting regular pruning. This tedious and laborious work is fundamental. Such cutting encourages lateral branching, and the young trees are trained to spread and create a solid frame and high density of plucking points. When properly shaped, new shoots will appear above the level surface of the table, which pluckers can easily reach, rather than at the center of the bush. Pruning also stimulates regular flushing of the bush.

Pluckers, who are always women, do not take all of a tea bush's leaves. The coarse leaves do not make quality teas. The women look for the tender, newer shoots that are smaller, a lighter, brighter green, and have a softer feel. They select only the first two leaves and a terminal bud at a time, a pluck called *dwi paat suiro* in Nepali. It is done by taking the stem between thumb and forefinger and twisting for a clean snap of the top shoot with the hand and wrist, rather than by breaking with the fingernail or clipping with sheers or any kind of blade. This is the classic

Darjeeling "fine-pluck." It requires ten thousand of these to produce a single pound of finished Darjeeling tea.

Plucking this apical part of a tea shoot stimulates growth of dormant leaves and buds. In seven days or so, new shoots appear above the plucking table as the fresh leaves and buds unfold, and the bush is picked again. This is called a plucking round. Seven days is the Darjeeling standard. Beyond that and the leaves' quality for made tea decreases.

Older tea sections on an estate have a single hedge layout with around eight thousand plants per hectare, but new plantings normally use a double-hedge formation containing up to eighteen thousand bushes per hectare, with upper reaches and steeper slopes closer to twelve thousand. In this style, saplings are placed two feet apart in parallel rows of tea bushes along the contours, with a four-foot gap for pluckers to move, and then two more parallel rows of bushes spaced two feet apart. Planted intermittently among the tea are shade trees. These lower the temperature and raise the humidity around them, create windbreaks, and also help replace the nitrogen in the soil. These are tall, high-branching species that won't interfere with plucking and have small leaves that won't cover the hedges when they fall.

Making their way between rows of tight, interlocked bushes, the women pluck with both hands and, when they cannot hold any more, toss the leaves into the conical basket on their backs. The woven bamboo basket measures about eighteen inches deep, eighteen inches across the top, and tapers down to a flat bottom just eight inches wide. Depending on personal preference, they use either a loosely woven one called *tokri* in Nepali or one with a tighter weave called *doko*. The baskets are suspended not by shoulder straps like a backpack but by a thick strap of bright cloth that stretches across the top of the forehead. During the day, pluckers dump their baskets twice: once before lunch and once at the end of the day. Apart from weighing progressively more, the leaves start to chemically change once plucked and need to be processed as soon as possible.

The precariously steep terrain that adds to the unfeasibility of mechanized harvesting also makes the meticulous plucking required even more difficult. The average worker produces just 396 pounds of finished tea a year, less than a quarter of the 1,644 pounds than her Assam counterpart manages.[1] (It takes five pounds of freshly plucked leaves for one pound of finished Darjeeling tea.)

Small villages are spread throughout the slopes of a garden, and women, working in groups of a dozen to twenty, generally pluck sections nearest their homes. Work starts at seven thirty A.M. There is an hour break for lunch. They walk back to their houses to prepare a quick meal or sit in a shady spot along the road and eat from a nested tiffin lunch box. Afternoon plucking lasts until four P.M. or so.

While plucking is a woman's job, supervising them is generally considered a man's. In 1990, the Makaibari plucker Maya Davi Chettrini became the first woman supervisor in Darjeeling. With strong, wiry arms, a buried but easily unearthed smile, and a bright vermilion *bindi* on her forehead, Chettrini exudes a clear sense of leadership and offers unshakable support to the women under her. She tells them which section to work, precisely which type of pluck is required—two-leaves-and-a-bud, one-leaf-and-a-bud, silver leaves (meaning bud only)—and the minimum daily picking levels. (Less, and they are docked; more and they receive a bonus.) There is no set district or even garden standard. The small leaves of the first flush mean a lower picking minimum than during the larger, more profusely flushing moments of the monsoon. A garden's—or section's—elevation can determine the amount, as do the style of pluck and leaf type, with the traditional China *jat* having smaller leaves than the Assam variety, which can also be found on most estates. The trend of women supervisors is slowly taking hold across the district.

The supervisor also makes certain that leaves are weighed and recorded correctly. Strategically located around the farm, weighment sheds are simple, open structures with corrugated-tin roofs, just enough to shelter from the sun, or the rain, and a place for the large, portable hanging scale with a hook to suspend the plucking basket.*

The weighed leaves get piled into the back of a pickup truck or a small tractor trailer, which heads up the narrow, steep, and precarious dirt estate roads to the tin-roofed factory to be processed on-site. As with wine and olive oil—but unlike with most other agricultural products—all production, from cultivation to processing, takes place on the estate.

Getting green leaves rapidly to the factory is key to the final quality of the tea. Some estates set up makeshift weighment stations closer to each day's picking areas to facilitate this. Glenburn has sunk a series of sturdy bamboo poles into the ground to create pairs of overlapping A-framed bases. When picking nearby, a bamboo pole is suspended over

---

*The sheds also occasionally shelter animals. During the first flush on Makaibari, pluckers discovered a nine-foot-long king cobra curled in the rafters of one station. One of the forest rangers who patrols Makaibari's woodlands caught it with his hands and carried it to the edge of a forested area of the estate to release it away from the houses.

the top to hang a heavy scale, looking something like a pioneer swing set. "They increase productivity time," Sharma said on a brief stop at one of these stations during his daily rounds of the garden in autumn. A woman held a tall ledger to record in her fine, neat hand the amount of each plucker. "And the leaf comes to factory faster."

Sharma picked up a handful of leaves from the pile dumped from the women's baskets after being weighed. "Tea making is about control," he said. "The moment you pluck a leaf the process starts. You set in motion a chain reaction." When the leaves are mounded up, they generate a lot of heat. A hand thrust into the center of the pile can feel the warmth created under the pressure. This can damage the leaves. "All the damage that needs to be done, *you* want to do to it," he added with a grin. The leaves in his hand were bright and tender as baby salad greens.

Once reaching the factory, the leaves will become finished tea within twenty-four hours.

The unique taste of Darjeeling tea comes, finally, in the manner of processing, where each step influences the final flavor of the liquor. Here, the art—and magic—of making tea comes, when the leaves begin to develop their unique flavors and aromas, almost mystically transforming into something far richer.

While the process has been simplified from Lu Yü's instructions thirteen centuries ago—machines instead of hands now do the rolling; fermented tea is essentially baked rather than pan-cooked—it continues true to ancient principles. In Darjeeling, tea makers remain stridently, adamantly orthodox in their processing, which, in fact, is called, simply, "orthodox." It contains just a handful of steps to turn green leaves into finished Darjeeling black tea: withering, rolling, fermenting, and drying before the tea gets sorted, graded, and packed.

The long building where the tea is processed is called a factory. But that name is misleading. Generally two or three stories high with pitched, corrugated-tin roofs and worn-smooth wood floors, they tend to be airy, somewhat lofty spaces, clean, and continuously swept of falling tea leaves with a long whisk broom called *phool jhadoo* (made with a spray of dried native grass flowers called *kuccho*). Factories are tidy rather than sterile, manual rather than automated. Even in celebrated gardens such as Makaibari, Castleton, Jungpana, and Lingia, the industrial equipment is a century old and still driven, or fired, by coal.

"It is nothing but a big kitchen," Makaibari's Rajah Banerjee said, and the key "was good housekeeping."

"You can't enhance quality of leaf in the factory, but you can destroy it," Rishi Saria said over a late breakfast in the Rohini bungalow. "It is very easy to destroy in factory."

The freshly picked leaves are taken to a factory's low-ceilinged withering loft and evenly and loosely spread, some eight inches or so deep, in long, narrow wooden troughs. Stretching seventy to eighty feet in length and just an arm's span wide, they have fine-wire-mesh bottoms through which air blows. Over fourteen to sixteen hours, about two-thirds of the moisture gets removed from the leaf. In the monsoon season, with wet leaves and humidity at nearly 100 percent, the air is first cool to wick away the surface moisture, then gets heated by a coal fire to help the withering.

During withering, the fresh leaves begin to wilt and turn, far from uniformly, into deeper olive-green shades edged and splotched with browns, like unraked leaves after a series of prefall windstorms. The leaves soften and become pliable and limp so that they can be rolled without breaking. By morning, the soft blanket of leaves in the troughs has wilted to barely knuckle deep.

Gathered into the hands, they exude a faint autumn fruitiness, smelling lightly of apples, say, or pears. "But smell is not important in withering," said B. B. Singh at Rohini. "It's *feel*."

Experienced workers can tell by touch when the correct wither has been reached. Indrey Sarki has been in charge of the withering for forty-three years at Makaibari and knows just by squeezing a handful of leaves when they have lost 50 or 60 or the optimal 65 percent of their moisture. One morning in the withering loft at the end of the second flush, when the monsoon rains had begun their continual drenching, Sarki took some leaves in a hand, bunched up his fist—the ball ought to initially hold together—and then opened it. "It should slowly open," he explained in Nepali as the cluster of leaves unfurled on his palm. His voice was low, barely audible over the rollicking hum of the rolling machines below. "If it is brittle, it is not a good sign. You won't get a good roll." The leaves will break instead. This is a particular challenge during the monsoon season when the air is warmed.

Sarki tossed the leaves back on the trough and walked on. They had sprung open too quickly and weren't ready yet.

• • •

Once fully withered, the leaves get gathered up and dropped down a square hatch in the upper floor or through a cloth chute to the rolling machines below. Nearly all of the factories use beefy models manufactured in Calcutta by Britannia, often eighty- or ninety-year-old machines that have layer upon layer of paint like a barge's hull. Workers in the first decades of the tea industry in Darjeeling rolled leaves back and forth against the hard surface of long wooden tables using their palms and forearms in a repetitive up-and-then-across motion. The Britannia machines mimic this somewhat. They have a central rotary piece that holds the leaves while the saucerlike table beneath it gyrates to twist and curl the leaves without breaking them. This is the most mechanized part of tea making.

A worker watches constantly to make sure that the leaves don't get too warm from the friction and to see when the roll is tight enough—not wound into a ball (like gunpowder green tea), but something much more open than that. Imagine taking a couple of leaves and rubbing them between the palms to get long, wiry, and twisty leaves.

Rolling takes from fifteen to ninety minutes depending on the flush, weather, and wither of the leaves, plus desired strength in the final tea. A longer roll or a harder one—more pressure on the leaves—will give more color and body to the liquor, more astringency, but less finesse and aroma.

"If the leaf is rough," the factory manager at Castleton said, "then more wither and harder rolling." This complements an old tea maker's adage: "The higher the wither, the harder the roll." But the first flush can't handle a hard roll. "It has a lot of juice," Castleton's deputy manager, Parminder Singh Bhoi, added. "A harder roll will break the leaf. If the leaf is fine, then already the flavor is there."

In rolling, the leaves become like curing tobacco in feel and turn from deep grayish green to coppery brown. They also become warm, evidence that changes are happening within the leaf.

That transformation is the beginning of fermentation. Or, more correctly, oxidization. Rolling initiates this process by rupturing the cells and releasing the natural juices of the leaves. When exposed to the air, they begin to oxidize.

Fermentation acts as a catalyst for the flavors and colors associated with Darjeeling tea. The tea develops the pungency, strength, and aroma that will be in the final cup.

This takes place on fermentation tables. At Goomtee and Bannockburn, these are portable sheets of steel no more than six feet long, carried like triage gurneys, and stacked on top of one another as needed in front of the rolling machines. Castleton has eight white, polished tables, roughly twenty-five feet long by about six feet wide in a well-lit side of the factory below windows that look out over a steep valley to the east of Kurseong and onto Mount Kanchenjunga. Nearby, Makaibari uses a set of concrete bunks with four tiers in a dim, partitioned corner of the factory. The tea goes on long, metal trays with lips like oversize baking sheets, which are carried by two men. The much larger Tukvar has well over a dozen similar bunk-bed-like tables, sturdy and given numerous whitewashings over the years, that hold the wide metal trays of fermenting tea. Marybong's setup is altogether different: Four waist-high stainless-steel tables some twenty paces long run across one end of the factory and are cared for by men in blue jumpsuits and baseball caps who, excluding their flip-flops and lack of grease stains, look like mechanics at a chain of oil-lube shops.

While the beds may vary, their purpose remains identical. On them, workers spread the leaves in a thin layer just a few inches deep so they can get plenty of the air required to oxidize. Except during the first flush, when fermentation is short, this step takes a couple of hours. As elsewhere in tea making, the constants are few, and a series of variables change from day to day—temperature, humidity, and leaf quality, as well as the desired strength of the final tea. Gauging exactly how long to ferment falls outside the realm of the intellect or even a reliable calculated equation, residing in instinct, experience, and the nose. As the leaves take on their distinctive coppery-brown color, managers or assistants repeatedly scoop handfuls of the leaves to check their progress by smelling them. The aromas have ripened, become sweeter, and exude hints of dried fruits and nuts: mellower as opposed to sharper; richer. "Smell is what decides fermentation," said Rohini's Singh, pressing a handful of fermenting autumn flush to his nose. This is the only way.

The flavor line climbs steeply like a wave, increasing to what Sarki calls "the first nose," decreases for two or three minutes, then goes up again to the "second nose," where it peaks before dropping off sharply. The goal is to find that topmost crest, the point when a particular batch of tea is at its best—and then fire the leaves immediately to stop the fermentation before their qualities begin to fade. "If it goes past the second nose, you can't get back flavor," Sarki said. "It's lost." While the leaves are fermenting, he sniffs them every ten or fifteen minutes, even more frequently toward the end.

Determining that moment is the most critical part of tea making. Every leaf on the bed does not ferment exactly the same, and a majority approach is used when gauging the overall progression of the batch. Underfermented, the finished tea will be brownish and brittle, the liquor less bright, thin, with less body; overfermented, it turns blackish, the tea loses its sheen, turns flat, and Darjeeling's refined lightness becomes heavier and stewy. At Makaibari, as with withering, Sarki makes the call. He's slight, with tiny, deep-set eyes, a reluctant smile, and a trademark soft, Nepalese *Dhaka topi* cloth cap in a woven black, red, and silver pattern. Born on Makaibari—his father was a laborer on the estate—he is the most senior man in the factory. But this isn't why he is responsible for this key decision. Sarki possesses an extraordinary olfactory gift, a once-in-a-generation talent, according to Rajah Banerjee. "He's a bloodhound."

The correct fermentation offers a balance of aroma, brightness, briskness, and strength. Compromises must be gauged and weighed, and a proper equilibrium found among those attributes for the final, desired cup. This depends on each garden and on each tea maker.

"When you are fermenting or oxidizing teas, there are the two aspects of the cup [you are looking for]," Sanjay Sharma explained one second flush morning in the Glenburn factory. Bright, glary light flooded in through the large windows, giving the wooden floor beams, polished from wear, the clean shine on an old dance hall. "Firstly, you've got the texture, the mouth feel." This is the body, the briskness. "And then you've got the aroma and flavor." He held his two index fingers together and moved them up and down in parallel. "It's a different set of compounds that are working, simultaneously, towards, say, flavor and texture." He began to move his hands as if juggling billiard balls. "But they don't always move together, you know?"

Sanjay talks quickly and peppers his sentences with *you know, yeah*, and *okay*. These seem less like questions—even rhetorical—than a way of letting the listener catch up.

"You might have a tea that you know has an exceptional nose, a good flavor. But it might be very thin in the cup," he continued. This is in part because aroma compounds develop earlier in the process. "And then you want that 'perfect cup.' You want that flavor *and* you want that body . . . it doesn't always happen, okay. So you have to decide what you want to highlight." It's about trade-offs. "The elusive 'perfect cup,'" he said later, almost wistfully. "It doesn't exist."

These natural products are not industrial. Nothing is certain in making them. The materials are continually changing, their reaction never fully predictable. "Making tea," Sanjay said one autumn evening on the verandah of Glenburn's old planter's bungalow, "is like calling your shots on a pool table."

Once leaves are judged to have reached their fermentation peak, workers quickly tip them into the dryer's hopper to inactivate the enzymes and microorganisms at work. By removing the moisture with heat, fermentation is stopped, and flavors get sealed in.

The dryers are boxy and oversize rectangular machines six or eight feet tall and twice as long that surely looked futuristic a century—even a half century—ago. A conveyor belt slowly zigzags from top to bottom for twenty to thirty minutes in about 240-degree-Fahrenheit air. Looking through one of the small, smoked-glass windows in the side of the dryer as the tea slides by under a red lightbulb feels more like peering into a darkroom than an oven. The last of the moisture gets wicked away—the final moisture content is only 2 percent—before the tea cascades into a trough at the bottom front of the dryer.

As with any baking, the duration can't be too long nor the temperature too hot, or the tea gets overly crisp or simply dried out. This gives the liquor an unpleasant baked flavor or even stronger burnt one. While it depends on the flush and the climate and even the elevation of the garden, times are specific. "It is precisely twenty-three minutes," a factory manager on Makaibari said during the first flush. "Not twenty-two, not twenty-four." At the end of the second flush, with larger leaves, stronger brews, and more humid conditions (the rains had just begun), the time had been increased to—precisely—twenty-six minutes. At Namring in the Teesta Valley, 2013 first flush teas fired at 230 degrees Fahrenheit for twenty minutes, but as the leaves became coarser and could handle a harder wither and a harder roll, both time and temperature gradually increased. Second flush ones got twenty-three minutes at 250 degrees Fahrenheit, and autumn ones twenty-five minutes at 255.

From the trough, the tea is lifted out using a white-bladed shovel with the type of wide, curved scoop used for clearing snow. A bin of still-warm and slightly brittle leaves exudes lovely, toasty, lightly caramelized aromas and carries a heightened smell of tea in the same way that warm loaves fresh from a baker's oven carry an intensified scent of bread.

When hot water is poured over the leaves in a teapot, they will release their vibrant and lively flavors of the flushing hills that were trapped by the burst of heat.

Or those of death? Always the contrarian opining to a different tune, Rajah Banerjee offered an alternative take in the Makaibari tasting room: "Fermentation is simply a process of death and decay. We are afraid of death—but love the flavor of it." Along with the green flies feasting on second flush leaves, for him this is another "where there is life, there is death" dichotomy. Firing the leaves in this deep state of oxidation, when fermenting flavors are at their ripest, he said with a mischievous expression, "kills the process of death and seals it."

The last stage in the factory is sorting and grading the tea. The four categories, in descending order of size, are whole leaf, broken leaf, fannings, and dust. The last two are used to fill tea bags. Most Darjeeling gardens aim for 60 or 70 percent leaf-grade tea.

Whole-leaf teas are graded using a string of letters—essentially, the more the better—that refer to the size of the processed leaf, rather than the quality or flavor of the tea. The highest level is FTGFOP, which stands for "Fine Tippy Golden Flowery Orange Pekoe." (*Tippy* means a generous amount of sought-after whole-leaf tips. *Orange pekoe* describes large-leafed tea.) Wits say, though, that the acronym means "Far Too Good for Ordinary People."

On occasion the acronym gets a prefix and/or a suffix. An *S* is added at the beginning for "superfine" and a 1 at the end to show the highest possible grade: SFTGFOP–1. These are exalted teas.

Sorting is usually done both mechanically and by hand. Vibrating machines bounce the leaves down a narrow, slightly pitched ramp as the tea falls through gaps into a series of bins by size. Hand sorting is similar, but more gentle (not to mention quieter), using flat, round trays.

Glenburn estate does all its sorting by hand. Using a set of metal trays with progressively smaller square perforations, a dozen women sit in a quiet, sunny corner of the factory and swirl and shake a handful of tea at a time. The smaller particles fall through the perforations while the women pick out any debris, stalks, or twigs. It's dusty, tedious work.

While men generally perform every other factory step, sorting is done strictly by women. "They have delicate hands," Vijay Dhancholia at Marybong explained. Other managers across Darjeeling give the identical answer.

Once sorted, tea is set aside by leaf type, even garden section, until there is enough to make an invoice, about 150 kilograms (330 pounds). Sometimes batches of similar types are blended to balance out the flavors. Once the invoice is complete, the tea gets packed.

Traditionally tea goes into wooden tea chests edged with tin and lined with foil to keep the leaves from absorbing odors or moisture. Measuring about twenty-four by sixteen by sixteen inches, they remain ideal for the finest, largest leaf-grade teas and protect against breakage during shipping. Most tea now, though, gets packed into hefty, foil-lined brown-paper sacks that hold about twenty-five kilograms (fifty-five pounds) of tea. This is often at the request of buyers, who find it easier to store them than unwieldy wooden boxes.

Hand-inking on the chests or sacks using stencils conveys all of the details of production, including leaf grade, date of processing, and total weight of the tea.

They also carry the official medallion-shaped logo of Darjeeling tea. Created in 1983, it's a bold green-and-white, stylized rendering of an Indian plucker in profile, with a round earring, nose stud, and Picasso-like almond-shaped eye, who is holding between thumb and forefinger, two leaves and a bud. The word DARJEELING curls around the gap to complete the circular design.

At the gardens, the chests and the sacks are loaded daily onto trucks and sent to warehouses down in Kolkata, the center of the tea industry. Still fresh leaves on a bush only the morning before, the tea is now destined for the cups and palates of distinguished tea drinkers around the world.

CHAPTER 8

A Decision for the Mouth to Make

Tasting tea has all of the complexities and subtleties of tasting wine. Even more so. The liquor gets sampled at varying temperatures as it cools. Dry tea leaves are looked over, felt, and smelled, as well as damp ones. (Somewhat confusing to the outsider, the infused leaves are called *the infusion*.) Harvesting and production take place daily for nine months, with the tea changing a little each day as the leaves progress through a daisy chain of four flushes.

While Darjeeling teas are tasted at various times by various people before reaching the customer, daily batch tastings in the factory of freshly processed teas are an integral part of the tea *making*—rather than the buying or selling. Tastings happen, without exception, six days a week. (With no plucking on Sunday, that means no processing or tasting on Mondays.) Done generally in the late morning but always by afternoon, when the natural light begins to fade, the ritual of sampling tea just fired that same day has changed little over the decades.

A medium-size garden might do ten to twenty batches in a day, depending on the flush (November, for instance, sees significantly less tea than July). A batch usually runs between 100 to 160 kilograms (220 to 350 pounds) of finished tea that has been withered, rolled, fermented, and fired together. From each batch, a small amount is tasted. Gardens are looking at quality and consider what to improve, adjusting to the continually shifting conditions of the weather and leaves.

"We do it to see what we can do better," said Vijay Dhancholia at Marybong. "It's for *tomorrow's* batches." While his heavy mustache has gone a touch gray and his hair begun to thin during almost forty years of working on tea estates in Darjeeling, his daily tastings remain unchanged and fundamental to his work as a tea maker. Each day, alongside the factory manager, he closely samples the batches that have been withered overnight and processed that morning.

Estates have a tasting room set aside. Marybong's is in a corner of the factory, like an attached, glassed-walled office. So is Glenburn's, though it's right at the entrance of the building. In Castleton's, various certifications, framed newspaper articles, and four world-record certificates it achieved between 1989 and 1992 hang on the wall above stacks of upturned tasting cups. Goomtee's tasting room is separated from the sorting room by a door and looks out over a deep cleft of hills. Jungpana's is a couple of steps away, among offices perched on a blunt precipice above the valley below. The tasting room at Makaibari is in the top of a small, two-story building facing the factory, whose shiny silver-and-green roof dominates the view and whose steady hum pierces the windows. At Thurbo it's a separate hut, with shiny white tiles and wood paneling giving it the feel of a bar in a slightly outdated European ski resort.

Each of these rooms is uncluttered, painted in white, and contains a long, white-tiled counter that is a touch over waist high so the taster need not unduly bend over. Above is a wall of north-facing windows that provide good, even light, the kind that portrait photographers look for, or those shooting food for cookbooks: steady, clean, and diffused, offering balanced, true colors. Such light is important since tasting tea is as much about using the eyes as the nose and mouth.

A half hour or so before the tasting begins, an assistant begins setting out small infusion pots and cups in a straight line along the counter, one pair for each of the day's batches. The white porcelain cups show off best a tea's color when "cupping" it, as professionals call tea tasting. The white rims have been worn down, revealing earthy, reddish clay beneath the glaze. But they are spotlessly clean, with no trace of residual odors. Faint cracks stained black from years of tea spread around the inside of the cups like a fine netting.

The infusion pots are white, ceramic, and individual-size and hold, if filled to the brim, 180 ml (¾ cup) of liquid. Most are small, handleless pitchers with short spouts and a fitted lid with an inset rim, Indian-made and bought in one of the wholesale shops on a side street near the Tea Board of India headquarters in Kolkata. The other style, made in Sri Lanka, is more expensive but smoother. Instead of a spout, these have five sharp, V-shaped notches like the jagged teeth of a Halloween pumpkin carved by a seven-year-old. The matching cups of both versions are almost perfectly spherical and also without handles, akin to small, white tea bowls.

A foil packet or a little, round metal tin behind each holds a small amount of dry leaf. Lying atop the leaves is a slip of paper that identifies by number and letter codes the batch, grade, leaf type, and amounts. These can be checked in a ledger to find out the section of origin in the garden and the precise timings of withering, rolling, fermentation, and firing.

With an electric silver kettle filled and heating, the assistant takes a portable, brass, handheld balance scale and begins working down the line of infusion pots like Lady Justice, measuring out a generous pinch of dry tea leaves in one tray so that it equals the weight of the other, which holds an old Indian twenty-five-paise coin weighing precisely 2.5 grams (just a touch over one twelfth of an ounce, or a smidge more than an American dime), the customary counterbalance across Darjeeling.

Once each of the pots has its exact measure of dry leaf and the kettle reaches a boil, the assistant pours 150 ml (⅔ cup) water over the leaves and then covers the pots with their ceramic lids. An hourglass timer is turned over, and the tea is left to infuse as the sand drains though the narrow waist. Five minutes is standard. Some tasters, although preferring to steep for three to four minutes when preparing a cup at home, always test at this length of time.

The differences between the batches of tea during a single day are slight at best—but important. Weight, time, and amounts must be precise. Consistency is everything.

One by one, the liquors are poured out into the small, white tea bowls, the lid held tight with the fingers and the pot then propped horizontally into the bowl. The size is perfect: the infusion pot lies snugly in the bowl with the lid firmly pinched shut as it completely drains, with the trapped leaves acting as a natural strainer.

Going back to the beginning of the row, the assistant places the pots upright and checks the liquors in the bowls to see if any leaves have escaped. As these would continue to strengthen the brew, the liquor gets drained into a clean cup if needed. Each cup now holds tea quite similar in tone.

By the time the tea has been cupped, the manager and assistant manager, and perhaps the factory or production managers, have gathered in the room.

Like his colleagues on gardens across Darjeeling, Dhancholia works from left to right in deft and brusque movements. He vigorously shakes the last of the liquid from the pitcher, spraying the wooden floor (and his shoes) with fine droplets of tea, then turns over the lid, which holds the wet leaves in a neat mound: the infusion. He sticks his nose into the warm, limp leaves to take in the full range of aromas, from sweet and malty to fruity, lime blossom to tarry. In the infusion, he can gauge if the firing has been right. Acrid notes, burnt tones, and stewiness indicate that the firing has been too hot or too long, with too much moisture zapped from the overtoasted leaf. The reversed pot lid is set on top of the infuser pot, displaying the damp leaves.

The dry leaf is also examined for the color—shades of grays, greens, and browns—and size of the rolled leaf. "The appearance tells you whether you've withered it right. It'll tell you if you've rolled right," explained Sanjay Sharma at Glenburn during a warm but drizzly late-second flush tasting. "You want that twist and style." He held a handful of dry leaf on a stiff sheet of white cardboard and sifted a pinch through his fingers. He snapped the cardboard taunt a couple of times, making the leaves dance while checking their sort. A loud, vintage air-raid siren sounded across the estate. The lunch break was over. A number of pluckers carrying faded umbrellas passed by the tasting-room window en route to a field just below the factory. "It will tell you if you sorted it right. Sorting is basically about size." Part for quality and taste, part for aesthetics. "You don't want your teas looking like long-grain basmati rice, you know," he said with a smile. "That would be boring."

It's also important to check what H. R. Chaudhary at Namring calls "the cleanness of leaf," checking for any stems or twigs, as well as the percentages of tips (buds), for fine-plucking.

Again starting with the teas on the left, Dhancholia moves to the liquor itself. He is looking at its color, briskness, quality, and strength. After noting the shiny clarity and depth of color in the liquor, he takes in the aroma. He leans in close, nearly doubling over his tall frame, with one arm held tightly behind his back in the position of a speed skater. In the other hand he holds a large spoon like a pencil and stirs and splashes the liquid to get the aromas flying around. His nose is visibly sniffing in the various scents among waves of tea spilling over the rim as he moves from cup to cup in rapid succession down the line. Nothing in his actions is delicate—or haphazard. It's messy, and the Rajasthan-born Dhancholia wears an apron made of a tight blue-and-white-check material like that of picnic tablecloths and a matching cap that comes down low on his fore-head and sits like a moppy beret.

Finally, back at the first cup, he tastes the tea. He loudly slurps a generous mouthful of liquid off the spoon. Holding it for a moment, he takes two or three quick and sharp aerating sucks that flood the liquor around the palate and send it up into the olfactory organ in the nose in the manner of an animated wine taster. The tip of the tongue gauges sweetness and saltiness, the middle tartness, the back bitterness, and the back edges sourness. But he is also *feeling* the tea: the inside of the gums, cheeks, and the back of the tongue catch the astringency or pungency by sensation rather than taste. Tannins are responsible for the penny-brownish color of liquor and the astringency that gives tea its body and bite—its briskness. In a final exhale, Dhancholia spits out the mouthful of tea in a powerful stream into a tall, steel spittoon locally called a *gaboon*. He hesitates for a beat, gathering last impressions from the residual flavors on his palate, and then moves to the next. It's all over in a few seconds. The mouth has registered the flavor, briskness (the opposite of flat or soft), pungency, and strength and caught any flaws.

And so on down the row of cups lined up along the counter, quickly, quietly, gruffly, keeping within the spell of the tasting in an almost hurried sense of trying to hold a complete set of impressions before any distraction can occur and break their imprint.

Outside the tasting room, Dhancholia is quiet and unassuming, soft-spoken. In a film, he might be cast as a provincial high school music teacher who coaxes greatness from his charges through subtlety, sensitiv-ity, and talent. His physical, almost aggressive style of tasting seems at first out of character, until one understands that the seriousness he puts to the daily task drives him to literally jam his nose into warm leaves and splashing tea. Tasting demands complete focus. He calls the concentra-tion required "a type of meditation."

"You need a fresh mind—and a clean tongue," said Girish Sarda at Nathmulls tea store in Darjeeling. Rajah Banerjee agrees. But you also must be highly practiced. Superior olfactory perception (and recognition) might be inherent in some, but it needs to be honed and cared for through years of repetition. "Because the tongue is a wonderfully sensitive bit of equipment that has many nerves that trigger in us a certain emotional message to the nerve center: sour, sweet, salty, sugary, bitter, whatever. It is a combination of all these sensations that one has," Rajah said in a 2005 documentary about Makaibari. "So triggering of this abstract emotion instantly needs the fusion of a fine tongue, a palate, a good nose, training for it, and of course the discipline of a good lifestyle."[1]

In summertime he said, "It's a natural talent that can't be sullied." By that he meant personal habits, much in the way an actor cares for the voice and an athlete the body. No chewing betel nut, no *gutka* (an addictive, powdery mix of tobacco, betel nut, and other flavorings sold in small, silver packets that litter the Darjeeling hills), nor even too much spicy food. Smokers, for Rajah, are hopeless tasters. "Mimics," he said on a cold autumn evening, scoffing at the number of those who are professionally tasting teas yet carry on with such habits. "We've become an industry of mimics."

"You can't make it one hundred percent perfect," Sanjoy Mukherjee, the production manager at Makaibari, explained during a first flush batch tasting. "But we can minimize the error percentage." While he reckons that amount is just a single percent, good tasters—he ranks Rajah among the best—can pick out all the faults from rolling, withering, fermenting, and firing.

The teas aren't tasted just a single time. It's essential to sample them at varying temperatures as they cool. Certain tea aromas are volatile and dissipate—"high-strung" Sanjay Sharma calls them. Others hang around, a good sign. "The aroma should intensify as it cools," Dhancholia said. "As it cools down, if you get the same flavor, then that is best." In Delhi, Sanjay Kapur, India's best-known taster and blender, also favors teas with "fixed flavors" that remain as the temperature decreases and the teas grow inward and intense. But his take is more practical, from a merchant's perspective. These are more desirable because it is realistically how they are drunk, he explained. "Sipped, while talking. Enjoyed."

Dhancholia keeps going back to certain cups in the tasting room, slurping and sniffing as he splashes the liquid with a spoon, occasionally curling a hand around the top of the cup so that nothing escapes as he leans down and draws in the aromas. He rechecks the dry leaves and the infusion of the teas he particularly likes—or dislikes. All the while, he is commenting on the teas and asking for certain details from the factory manager.

Banerjee offers his comments (or commands) in a high, weedy voice in a blend of Bengali and English as he goes back through the teas, slurping and sniffing. "Damn good! Damn good!" he repeatedly marveled about a handful of cups during a first flush tasting with sixteen batch samples lined up. When he considered one anything less, it was immediately obvious to those in the room by his exaggerated grimaces and dramatic spitting of the tea into the *gaboon* followed by a calflike moan. While Dhancholia and Sanjay might be a touch less theatrical, they are just as demanding.

Most tasters note the better batches by moving the tasting bowl one position forward or backward like a chess pawn, or even above on the small tile ledge of the window, mixing up the once-orderly line and leaving the tiles wet with splashed tea and stray infused leaves.

While tasting has a routine and a ritual, it is not fully quantifiable nor scientific. "There is a science to it, yes, but also an art," said Sanjay Kapur, a round soupspoon in hand. In his late fifties, Kapur is tall, refined, articulate, and well-read, with a penchant for tailored dress shirts and dapper boardroom blazers, and the patient way of listening of a diplomat. He also possesses one of the most discerning palates in the business.

Kapur gingerly picked up a cup and smelled the aroma before tasting a spoonful of it for the fourth or fifth time. Two wooden trays held porcelain tasting cups partially filled with first flush teas shining greenish gold. He had been tasting that morning, returning to the teas at leisure as they cooled.

His tea boutique, Aap Ki Pasand, and the offices behind (and above), edge a chaotic jumble of lanes in Old Delhi's Daryaganj neighborhood not far from the majestic Mughal-era Jama Masjid and Red Fort. Outside, gusts of hot April winds, laden with dust picked up off the parched plains, gave the sky an insulating haze. But once inside, the heat and grit of the old city immediately receded. The quiet inner room—part laboratory, part atelier—acts as Kapur's work space. Along a counter, old gadgets sit in mugs (magnifying glasses, various thermometers, a small barometer) among a small digital scale, antique Chinese teapots, and tall stack of guides to herbs and histories of tea in various languages.

Kapur's tastings are different from those in batches on an estate. As he samples at the same time teas from a handful of gardens, the differences from cup to cup are greater. The teas he selects and buys will end up not being sold under the garden name but his own label, San-cha Tea, India's most selective, gourmet brand of tea. The best Darjeeling becomes Presidents Tea. Sipped by leaders that include Mikhail Gorbachev and Bill Clinton, this was India's state gift at a G20 summit in 2010.

Kapur did not come from a family with a background in tea. When he finished his master's degree in management and marketing at the highly ranked Jamnalal Bajaj Institute of Management Studies in Mumbai—set up in the 1960s in collaboration with Stanford's Graduate School of Business—he went to Kolkata to work in the tea industry and never turned back. He experienced every aspect of the business, even working in Darjeeling, where he met and married the daughter of a tea planter. In 1981, Kapur moved to Delhi to open a dedicated tea boutique and the only one focusing on high-end teas. He not only selects, packages, and sells teas, but creates bespoke blends for clients ranging from hotels and restaurants to individuals around the globe.

"You can learn the science," he said after slurping tea spooned from another cup, "but the art must be cultivated." The latter, developed slowly over many years and many thousands of teas, is an appreciation and sensitivity to the nuances of fine teas.

Even then, tasting remains an exercise in articulating the intangible.

During the first flush, Rajah Banerjee, who tastes in a particularly exuberant burst of energy, swiftly, and with such confidence in his perceptions that he finds no need to linger over the cup, said that trying to describe the smells and tastes of teas was "talking about the abstract in purity."

But was it *good*? Before or beyond anything else, it is about taste. As the Chinese poet and tea master Lu Yü put it more than a thousand years ago, "Its goodness is a decision for the mouth to make."[2]

CHAPTER 9

Knocking Down

India has two models for selling tea, and most Darjeeling estates use both. One is through private sales, where the garden sells directly to a client—be it wholesaler or retailer—or uses an export merchant. Less than half of Darjeeling tea trades this way.

The remaining is sold at auction. A single brokerage firm—and a lone auctioneer—handles 95 percent of that. J. Thomas & Co. in Kolkata sells 55 to 60 percent of all Darjeeling tea, about 4.5 to 5 million kilograms a year.[1] A weekly auction takes place every Tuesday.

On a late-June day, just two weeks shy of the ten-year anniversary of Makaibari's world record being set in the same room, J. Thomas held Sale No. 26, offering early second flush teas from the 2013 harvest. Buyers began arriving at eight thirty or so, darting into the building from the morning monsoon squall that was splattering fat, pregnant drops.

The ten-story Nilhat House is a fine example of early–1960s functionalism, a niched and reticular brilliant white building, trimmed with bold, accentuated colorfulness in Himalayan sky blue. It sits a couple of blocks off the central square named BBD Bagh* along Mukherjee Road—originally Mission Row, purportedly the oldest street in the city—just a few buildings down from the Old Mission Church, a splendid 1770 building with a small, enclosed garden whose unharvested fruit trees conceal large, noisy birds.

---

*This is shorthand for Benoy-Badal-Dinesh Bagh but still often called by its original name, Dalhousie Square.

Mukherjee Road is narrow and tree-shaded, for much of the day its sidewalks crowded as a subway platform. Stretching along both sides of the street are hundreds of semipermanent food stalls that offer everything from scalding-hot chai in unfired-clay cups to fried *aloo bonda* (potato balls). As tea buyers made their way to the auction house that morning, stalls were already preparing for the lunch crowd by peeling potatoes, slicing eye-watering mounds of onions, and getting blackened kettles of stews and dals simmering. Across from Nilhat House, an elderly man squatted on the street and ground copious amounts of coriander seeds with a long, cylindrical pestle on a coarse slab of stone the shape of a tombstone. Another slapped chapatis between his palms. Wide, woven baskets displaying mangoes and nested clusters of still-green bananas sat between them.

Shaking out their umbrellas, the buyers followed the wide, curving stairwell, lined with a wall of small tiles in vibrant shades of California blue, to the auction room on the second floor. With six gently tiered rows, each with a dozen or so seats and an aisle running up the middle, it has the feel of a college lecture hall. A square of wood attached to the armrest unfolds into a small table.

Buyers greeted each other as the seats gradually filled. Some made last calls on their BlackBerrys or stepped outside into the foyer for a cigarette. They all carried the day's auction catalog, some fifty or so pages thick. Its closely printed sheets showed the lot number, garden, grade, date packaged and dispatched, number of kilos and of packages in each lot, and the valuation of the tea up for auction. Each lot had been available to taste beforehand, and buyers had put tick marks beside the ones they hoped to get—teas that fit their own purchasing levels and desired flavor profiles. A handful of women stood out among the mostly male crowd.

Just moments before nine A.M., three J. Thomas men entered the room. They shook a few hands as they came through the door and nodded to acquaintances, but didn't dawdle on their way to the front, where a long desk sat on a dais. A gentleman in his sixties took a seat at one end, a man in his twenties sat at the other, and in the middle, a step higher and with a slightly raised lectern before him, was a man in age between the other two wearing a striped dress shirt, silk tie, and angular glasses that gave his face a somewhat severe look. This was the auctioneer, Anindyo Choudhury, the most influential man in Darjeeling tea.

Going under his hammer that day were 794 lots from fifty-some gardens, a mix of low-, medium-, and high-end—or priced—teas. They had largely been produced a month or so beforehand as the harvest moved from the shoulder *banji* period into prime second flush.

Choudhury's copy of the catalog sat open before him. His right hand held a pencil to jot the final sales amount and his left a wooden gavel. No microphone, no laptop. At the back of the room, above the heads of the buyers, is a clock—the same plain, efficient digital type that hangs in schoolrooms, cinema lobbies, and rental-car agencies—which Choudhury watched closely. When the red numbers flashed 9:00, he began.

He gave the lot number, name of the garden, grade of tea, and a line about quality if superior. For most lots, he moved up in Rs 5 or 10 increments, but on some of the higher-fetching teas that fall for thousands, he would skip 100 at a time. For tea that had been valued in the catalog at Rs 1,000, say, he opened at Rs 700 to 750.

"Tata five hundred," he called out during the bidding on an early lot, acknowledging the Tata Global buyer's nod. Rs 505 got a nod from another buyer, and Tata agreed to 510. "Five-ten Tata," Choudhury said. "Five-fifteen? Any takers at five-fifteen? Any takers at five-fifteen?" He paused only a beat and then said, "Knocking to Tata at five-ten," smacking down the gavel. The two men flanking him both noted the buyer and agreed price. (A young woman from J. Thomas sitting among the buyers did likewise.) Choudhury penciled a quick note in his catalog and within a breath moved on to the next lot.

And on down the list, page after page, in a clipped, slightly impatient pace. Far from the chanting singsong of a southern-American auctioneer filling a room with a steady river of musical phrasing, or offering praise or eulogies to the tea on offer, his style is professional, perfunctory, even a bit dry. He only pauses to sharpen his pencil.

J. Thomas & Co. is the oldest and largest existing tea auctioneer and broker in the world. (The London tea auction ceased in 1998, after more than three hundred years.) The first public sale of tea in India took place in their Calcutta office on December 27, 1861, a consignment of 250 chests from the East Indian Tea Company and another hundred from the Bengal Tea Company. Originally named Thomas Marten & Company, the company began not as brokers of tea but of shellac, jute, and, foremost, indigo. "The color seeped from the packed chests [of indigo] and stained the length of Mission Row a deep abiding blue," wrote a historian of the company.[2] The current building's name—from *nil* (indigo) and *hat* (market)—reflects its legacy in dye, as does its colorful trim. For a century the company was controlled by the British. The first Indian chairman was appointed in 1962; the last member of the Thomas family, the fifth generation, left a year later; the company's final Brit departed in 1972.[3]

Today, J. Thomas handles about one-third of all tea auctioned in India—almost 500 million pounds (200 million kilograms) a year. It conducts auctions not just at its main Kolkata center but also in other tea producing areas: Guwahati (Assam), Siliguri (the Dooars and Terai), Cochin (Kerala), Coonoor (in the Nilgiris of Tamil Nadu), and Coimbatore (a couple hours farther south in the same state). They also keep correspondents at the other main tea auction houses in Asia and Africa—Colombo (for Sri Lanka teas), Chittagong (for Bangladesh), Jakarta (for Indonesia), Mombasa (for Kenya, Uganda, Tanzania, Rwanda, Malawi, and others), and Limbe (for Central Africa).

Over the last few years, tea auctions in India have become computerized, with buyers sitting silently in a room in front of identical laptops clicking their mouse to make bids or done anonymously online, where buyers do not even know who they are bidding against. That is, all except for the Darjeeling tea auction at J. Thomas's Kolkata branch. The tradition simply remains too entrenched to halt. Anindyo Choudhury is the only tea auctioneer left using the open outcry system.

Choudhury came to tea, like many in the industry, randomly, almost on a whim. "It was an unknown field, mostly word of mouth, family connections," he explained in his office. "When I finished university"— the University of Delhi, one of India's highest-ranked institutions— "someone said, 'You want to try tea?'" Choudhury smiled at the thought, at the simple suggestion that led to his life's work.

He spent a year with Tata Tea and then joined J. Thomas. After working in their Siliguri office, he moved to the headquarters in Kolkata. For the last few years, he has been in charge of Darjeeling tea for the company.

As auctioneer, though, he does more than simply call out lots and take bids. Choudhury spends just one day a week in the auction room. He passes more time in the tasting room, where he personally tastes each lot going up for sale and sets its value. That means that he tastes around 60 percent of all tea produced in the district. Every week, in a day and a half, he tastes a thousand different Darjeeling teas. The renowned wine critic Robert M. Parker tastes ten thousand bottles a year.[4] Choudhury does that many second flush teas alone.

Located on the fifth floor of Nilhat House, the long, narrow tasting room is at least twenty-five generous paces in length, with windows running along one wall and four parallel and unbroken rows of tasting benches cleaving it into strips. Choudhury pulls on a snug blue apron fronted with a deep V-neck that shows off tie and collar and works quickly down the long rows of tasting pots, cups, and teas. An assistant pushing a wheeled podium and a massive ledger follows behind, jotting down his remarks and initial values. Choudhury tastes not only each of those coming up for sale, but also retastes certain ones from the previous auction to see why they sold higher, or lower, than his valuation.

"I am tasting with the manufacturing process in mind. What was right about the tea, what was not," he said. J. Thomas furnishes gardens with reports on what they send to auction, and Choudhury travels frequently to Darjeeling to taste at the gardens themselves. He wants each tea estate to produce the best-quality tea it can, but also to help the gardens "get in line with the market." No one is more intimately attuned to what Darjeeling's gardens are producing and what buyers are demanding. He sits in a prime position to gauge the desires, changes, trends, and needs of the market and translate those to the planters.

Assessing Darjeeling tea is the most "intricate," according to Choudhury. The vast differences in quality from garden to garden, and even from week to week at the same garden, creates huge discrepancies in prices. "This makes it trickier," he said, than other styles of Indian teas that lack such a flavor and price spread.

That June morning, one lot that had been dispatched on May 30 sold for Rs 545 while an identical grade and type from the same garden produced the following week, when better weather had kicked in and the season had moved more solidly into second flush, sold for Rs 1,050. "One week can make all the difference in Darjeeling," the female J. Thomas assistant whispered after Choudhury slapped the gavel down on the sale.

Darjeeling tea is traded based on its quality rather than on a futures exchange like coffee, and on its daily—as opposed to seasonal or yearly—harvest. "It has a valuation structure based on quality," said Steven Smith, the legendary American tea pioneer who founded (and sold) both Stash Tea and Tazo and now has his own high-end, eponymous brand of tea, in his office-cum-workshop in Portland, Oregon. It's about the taste in the cup sampled from each invoice. Steven Smith Teamaker offers a small, well-curated selection of the world's finest teas, and Smith samples around two hundred Darjeeling options a year—preselected by his associates in

India from thousands of teas—in selecting tea to fill the roomy loose-leaf sachets of his boutique brand.

Choudhury gives each tea that sells in his auctions the price he thinks it is worth or that he wants to get for it. At the end, he is a salesman, Darjeeling's biggest. He wants the prices to be high. To be sure, the company earns a percentage on each sale. (J. Thomas is "a feature in the formula," he explained, "that the Tea Board of India is in charge of and negotiates.") But as a champion of Darjeeling tea, he wants the market to accurately reflect Darjeeling tea's value.

With unwavering punctuality, when the digital clock on the back wall reads one P.M., Choudhury breaks for lunch. Most of the buyers head down to the food stalls along Mukherjee Road and around the old law courts that offer everything from simple *dosas* (crispy filled South Indian savory crepes made from a fermented batter of rice flour and ground dal) to full *thalis* (a selection of small dishes with rice and bread and a dollop of pickle or chutney).

The J. Thomas staff, meanwhile, heads upstairs to the Tiffin Room. "Just like they used to," said one junior member. And he meant it. The lunch menu remains mostly English, with chicken cutlets, beefsteaks, and, that June day, shepherd's pie. Friday is Indian food. One of the two tables is for the dozen senior members, and the smaller one is for junior members. The room is not large and the staff must eat in turns. Stiffly poised black-and-white portraits of past J. Thomas leaders line the walls, confident men with tightly buttoned collars, narrow ties, and, on a few, regimental mustaches.

A seldom-used boardroom off the Tiffin Room guards another Raj-era tradition at J. Thomas. Into the shiny gloss of a Burmese teak dining table, each outgoing director since 1870 has carved his initials. Ashok Batra recently etched A.B. 1972–2013 cleanly into the polished wood with a penknife at the end of his four decades with the company. While his father retired as vice admiral of the Indian navy and his four uncles were also military men, Batra joined J. Thomas fresh out of college in Pune. "Tea is a gentleman's industry and I learnt so much from it that I've no hesitation to say what I'm today is due to tea," he said upon retirement in a newspaper interview.[5]

Hanging in these back rooms are a number of framed certificates commemorating records reached in its auction rooms. They illustrate the price difference between orthodox teas and CTC ones produced in the same area. One commemorates the Assam orthodox record being set at Rs 6,999 a kilo in August 2012 (then worth $127.25) by the Duflating Tea Estate. That same month, at the Halmari Tea Estate, the Assam CTC record was also reached: Rs 390 ($7.09), a paltry 5 percent of the orthodox tea's amount. Halmari alone produces more than 2 million pounds, about 1 million kilograms, of tea annually, 95 percent of it CTC.

The money, as the junior J. Thomas member pointed out when looking over the certificates, is in volume.

At two P.M. Choudhury and his team are back in the auction hall trying to sell the remaining few hundred lots by three thirty or four P.M. Afternoons are more challenging; energy among the buyers can lag, and Choudhury presses hard to keep the auction moving at a steady pace.

"I want to keep buyers around at the end," he said of his strategy in preparing the order of sales. It's neither alphabetical nor organized by value. "I start with traditionally good producing gardens, spread out the quality in pockets, mix it up." The key is the beginning, as the first five or so pages of the catalog—about a hundred or so lots—set the "market mood." Choudhury wields complete power in the order, another element of his far-reaching influence.

While most gardens sell via private channels as well as at auction, some sell only through private means. These include those of the Ambootia group and the Chamong group, which counts Chamong, Marybong, Lingia, Tumsong, and Bannockburn in their Darjeeling fold of highly respected estates. According to Sujoy Sengupta, a marketing manager and key taster at the group, part of the issue for opting out of the auction was being "under the umbrella" of generalizations: good, medium, or bad. Chamong didn't want their gardens to be characterized within these narrow categories. "Such simple terms don't reflect our crop."

Some who trade within the auction system quietly say that the gardens who only sell to private buyers don't have confidence in their tea's quality. Chamong, though, likely knew they could sell their product for higher prices outside the system. Especially when dealing with high-end retailers such as Harrods, Whittard of Chelsea, Twinings, and Fortnum & Mason, even Nathmulls in Darjeeling, direct deals can make a garden more money.

Tea merchant Vikram Mittal in New Delhi offered another reason for direct sales: Many private buyers simply don't have access to the

Kolkata auction system. He said, "They can pay a little bit more—and would rather get it directly from the garden." The immediacy and intimacy is appealing. "At auction there is a wall between garden and buyer—the broker."

Direct purchasing can also avoid one of the biggest disadvantages to the auction, the time lag, said Mittal, who buys using both methods. He puts that difference at about four weeks, the time it takes for samples to be drawn and sent to the broker, tasted, graded, valued, listed, shown, sampled, auctioned, and then dispatched to the buyer. (Choudhury estimates that about eight kilograms, or eighteen pounds, is lost in every lot from samples, a notable amount from the garden's point of view.)

The urgency in getting first flush teas into shops means many gardens and buyers prefer the direct method for spring teas. "Buying time is short," said Choudhury. "The crop is small. The season is short." Yet, he added, "there is a huge buying requirement." The excitement of its being the year's first teas adds a touch of frenzy. The second flush is longer and larger and has a bigger showing in auction.

While Ambootia's and Chamong's estates might have opted out of the auction, the majority of Darjeeling's gardens have not. Between 60 and 65 percent of them still send teas to J. Thomas, including top producers (and price getters) Jungpana, Castleton, and Thurbo.

The auction room has a frisson and buzz. It's riskier, to be sure. After selecting tea to bid on from the catalog, a buyer might get it for less that hoped for, or more. Or, maybe not at all. Gamesmanship, strategy, and tradition are all on display.

On the afternoon following the auction, in his office at the end of a fourth-floor corridor, the Kolkata-born Choudhury was much more relaxed than he had been behind the dais with gavel in hand. Cordial and clubby in a congenial way, he has a willing laugh. He appears trim and erect in an athletic rather than military manner—the comparison is not arbitrary; he studied at an Army Public School in Delhi before going to university—like someone who plays squash (aggressively and against a younger colleague) a couple times a week.

He was reviewing the catalog from the previous day's auction. Held together by a thin, brown thread, the stack of printed sheets was heavily marked up with pencil in a quick, loose hand. His office was sparsely decorated, the walls largely empty, as if he had initially hesitated on what to hang and then just got used to it. A window looks over the company parking lot. Leaves, blown down in a brief but fierce midday downpour, stuck to the roofs of cars like postage stamps.

Choudhury had already tasted the upcoming lots and given them provisional values. Now that he had the current pulse of the market, he could assign them their final numbers. Reporting on that just-completed sale, the *Economic Times*—India's most widely read business newspaper (and the second most widely read one in the world after the *Wall Street Journal*)—noted that the market, which had been a touch subdued, had begun firming up. "Darjeeling teas showing an improvement in quality was readily absorbed."[6] The superior crop was coming in. The teas were increasing in depth and appeal.

The stern demeanor of Choudhury's face had softened (in part from not wearing his glasses), and he seemed more patient than he had in the auction room. He needs to keep the buyers in order, he explained with a sly smile, smoothing down his black mustache. "If I lose concentration, I may knock something down early, so they try to distract me, say something, make jokes."

His style for cupping the gavel is more practical than original. "If you hit it too hard, the damn head is liable to go flying off," he said with a hearty laugh. Beside, cupping it also diffuses the noise, a not insignificant point when he bangs the gavel down more than seven hundred times on auction day.

Precisely at three thirty P.M.—punctuality clearly an inherent, or inherited, J. Thomas trait—an elderly bearer in a white cotton uniform glided along the corridor with a cart, serving tea to each office.

Darjeeling? "No," Choudhury said with a sheepish smile. Most Indians, he explained, don't like such light teas. "They want some body in their cup." There was only Assam orthodox, brisk and bold, offered with milk and sugar.

A half dozen reddish biscuits sat on the cup's saucer. Similar to Wheat Thins but flakier and saltier, they had a generous seasoning of masala spice. After dipping one in the tea and taking a bite, it was clear the office demanded some body in their snack, too.

With his power, exceptional palate, continual tasting, and acute sense of what the market is producing, it's hard not to see Anindyo Choudhury as

Darjeeling tea's Robert Parker. "Tasting," Choudhury said, "is like a skill, like having a memory on your tongue." Parker clearly possesses the ability to not simply distinguish among the nuances of taste and aroma in wines, and express those traits in a graspable manner, but also recall them, with precision, later.

While Parker is a prominent global figure, outside the confined world of Indian tea in India, Choudhury is unknown. He has no newsletter or bestselling guides like Parker. Shop owners do not wait to see his valuations to buy or to set prices, nor has he changed, to any discernible degree, the style of teas being made in Darjeeling to fit his taste preferences.

But within the industry, Choudhury is a sought-after ally. "Everyone wants him on their team," according to one prominent Indian tea merchant, who said Choudhury is the "most powerful" person in the business. His word alone can do wonders. "When he recommends a garden to a buyer . . . ," the merchant said, pausing, a little breathless at the thought. "How he can talk about a tea for five minutes—or nothing, or neglect you. By his auction ordering."

As brokers rely on the trust of both producer and buyer, integrity is considered the guiding principle in hiring at J. Thomas, reported a piece in the *Hindu* a few years ago celebrating the 150th anniversary of the first public tea auction in India, and recruitment is "based on sound background, schooling and sportsman-like qualities."[7] Sports clearly remain important. Company profiles of J. Thomas's current top management show men who play table tennis and badminton, cricket, and tennis, and Kavi Seth—the auctioneer of the Makaibari record and now one of its top directors—is a former number-one-ranked squash player in Bengal.[8]

But also integrity. In listening to dozens of people in the industry, Choudhury's image seems unblemished, his reputation excellent, even if people don't always agree with his pricing. That's imperative. For the system to continue to function, buyers need to have confidence in his impartiality and judgment. He is more than just a middleman between garden and buyer.

While one day he will no doubt leave the auction room to a younger colleague and move from senior management to join Seth as one of the half dozen or so company directors, for the moment he remains the front man of Darjeeling's industry, through whose fingers more than half its tea passes.

• • •

The reputations of auctioneers and tea brokers haven't always been as pristine. From the beginning, their scruples have not infrequently been called into question. The first written use of the word *tea-broker* in English can be found in a news item in Edmund Burke's *The Annual Register: or A View of the History, Politics, and Literature for the Year 1770*: "Coyde, a tea-broker, charged with forging a warrant for the delivery of three chests of tea at the India House, was brought to be examined before a Court of Directors at the India House."[9] Perhaps it was included in Burke's *Register* not so much for the crime—minor news compared to the paragraph above it that reports on forty thousand people crowding Rome's Piazza del Popolo to see the execution of two murderers—but because, while the court debated Coyde's case, the tea broker escaped from the three police constables guarding him. Few things help make a crime newsworthy more than an escaped villain. Unscrupulous, but also wily.

That the first use of "tea-broker" appeared in this context would surprise no one who deals in Darjeeling tea today.

Darjeeling's tea is unduplicable. But—as with any limited, luxury product—that doesn't mean others don't try. With its cachet, high prices, and declining output, mislabeling is rampant and blending common-place. Some has been done legally—Germany can use 51 percent Darjeeling tea in a blend and still call it Darjeeling—and some not. Such problems are not exactly new. Blenders have been passing off teas from Sri Lanka, and then Kenya, as Darjeeling since the 1960s, and now teas from Nepal are surreptitiously being brought across the Indian border and sold as Darjeeling on the domestic market.[10] As well, green leaf from Nepal is getting processed in Darjeeling factories and being mixed in, say numerous sources in Darjeeling. "Everyone knows where it is going," said a tea merchant in Darjeeling. "No one says a word."

Industry officials estimate that some 40 million kilograms of "Darjeeling tea" are sold on the market each year. That is over four times the amount that the area actually produces.

Monsoon Flush

(July through September)

*M*onsoon: from the Arabic mawsim, *"season," itself from* wasama, *"to mark." A punctuation in the subcontinent's year, its most important natural feature, its most anticipated change. The country receives 75 percent of its annual rainfall in just four months. In May, as India's heat burns across the plains, warming the land faster than the oceans that surround it, the southwest monsoon winds begin to gather, circling the Bay of Bengal. They pass over the southern tip of India sometime around the first of June, and then sweep heavy clouds northeast along the coastline, pushing straight over the Terai toward the Darjeeling hills to meet the impassable barrier of the Himalayas and drench the foothills with the remainder of their moisture.*

By mid-June, after weeks of building-and-bursting thunderheads and short, lashing storms that strip and scatter the heart-shaped leaves from pipal trees, the rains around Darjeeling become sustained and pound in steady patterns on the tin roofs. Lightning flickers. Electricity cuts out. Fog and mist, rising up from the humid valleys, trim visibility to mere feet. Overhanging eves on shops and verandas drip, and the edges of paper curl like shells in the dampness. The city empties of tourists, the pace slows. Couples in knee-high gum boots and oversize rain slickers huddle under shared umbrellas as they hurry down Laden-la Road to one of the family-run Tibetan places in the lower bazaar to have lunch, a bowl of thukpa *(noodles) or a plate of* momos *(steamed stuffed dumplings) dipped in tongue-withering chili sauce.*

In the long grasses and humid forests, leeches lurk. They work their way undetected between rolled pant cuffs and thick socks to latch onto the soft skin somewhere around the ankle. (They also drop from branches and grasp ahold on the back of the neck.) They bloat unnoticed with blood and then fall, while their anticoagulant keeps the small, round lesions bleeding for another hour or two, unnoticed, until later, sitting on a dry verandah sipping a cup of tea, a subconscious brush of the leg with the fingers comes away wet with blood.

The sky and mountains disappear behind a sheen of white for months on end, and the rain is both heavy and steady. While Darjeeling has received on average thirty inches of rainfall during the month of July, recently it has been closer to forty inches or more. Retaining walls collapse, the topsoil dissolves, and the dozen rivers that course down the valleys' slopes—the Teesta, which divides Darjeeling from Sikkim, the Great Rangeet and the Rungdun, the Balason, the Kaljani, and the Torsha—run swift and murky. Landslides are a danger. Dirt roads on the estates get washed out. Getting in to the Club or a branch of the State Bank of India from a garden, along the steep, twisting, and narrow paved roads, is difficult, even impossible.

But how the tea gardens glisten in a spectrum of greens! Lime. Jade. Teal. Mossy. Olive. Toady. Drops of rain dangle from the leaves like Christmas pendants. In the drizzle on Jungpana, an isolated garden reached only by hundreds of slippery steps, men trim the weeds between tea bushes wearing large strips of plastic in the style of hooded capes. Pluckers wrap similar sheets around their midsections and knot them high above their waists like industrial butchers. They wedge the handle of an umbrella between neck and shoulder and keep plucking with both hands.

After absorbing the moisture for a few weeks, the tea bushes begin to flush out great quantities of leaves—larger, coarser ones than those of the other harvests. But also with less flavor. "Because it jumped!" H. R. Chaudhary, Namring's long-serving manager, said by way of explanation. "The slower you grow, the more the flavor. Same for mango, banana, for anything." Down lower on Rohini, at the base of the hills, B. B. Singh said in a soft voice, "Slow growing, good flavors. Fast growing, no flavors."

How are you? "Flushed out!" Sanjay Sharma on Glenburn called out in reply on a rainy day. "The trees are flushing like crazy."

Factories struggle to keep up with the amount of green leaf coming in. Half the year's harvest in a single flush. But the dampness also makes withering and fermenting harder to manage and producing fine, delicate teas, appreciated for their nuance, difficult.

Rain teas: quantity over quality.

During this wet harvest, the nature of the tea liquor changes, becomes stronger, and turns the deep reddish brown of a Spanish cedar cigar box. Even ruddier.

And prices drop. *The leaves picked during the monsoon yield the majority of the blends and are sold non-estate-specific. It's blenders' season in the J. Thomas & Co. auction room.*

One ducks through the open door of Nathmulls, in the center of Darjeeling, from a sudden squall and finds—as always—Girish Sarda standing patiently behind the counter. Nathmulls sells 150 different Darjeeling teas. Not a single one is monsoon flush. In front of Girish sit three dozen large, old-fashioned candy jars. They have wooden lids, rounded as mushroom caps, with the grains running across the tops like the oversize whorl of a thumbprint, and hold prize black teas from the first and second flushes plus one or two from the previous autumn.

But now, on one end of the long glass counter in Nathmulls, some jars contain fine green teas. More estates are using this flush to make a style of tea not traditionally associated with the region. Being unfermented, they carry the natural vegetal notes of the season rising up from the saturated soil: brothy and grassy, at times even kelpy, with hints of artichokes and silky spinach.

"It's got that tinge, that certain taste of Darjeeling tea, a sweetness there," Sarda said one soggy morning, *"a certain taste that comes through that inherent bitterness intrinsic in green teas."* He stood with his arms crossed watching the steady parade of people with umbrellas passing outside the shop as a fresh curtain of water sluiced the city. Rivulets of water cascaded down Laden-la Road, so steep and slick that nugget-size stones have been embedded directly into the tar for traction.

CHAPTER 10

The Raj in the Hills Above

The British thirst for inexpensive tea significantly shaped the history and rule of India. "The Flag went forth so that Trade could follow," wrote Jan Morris, keen chronicler of British colonialism, "and very often, in point of fact, the order was reversed."[1] Trade and empire swung hand in hand, and indeed commerce brought the British to India—initially in the guise of the East India Company, *merchants*! Soon profits and tax revenues helped develop this most dazzling and extraordinary imperial possession. "As long as we rule India we are the greatest power in the world," Lord Curzon said as viceroy in 1901, referring to modern-day India but also Pakistan, Bangladesh, and Burma. "If we lose it, we shall drop straight-away to a third-rate power."[2]

India was not a settler colony like Australia or Canada. Most British returned back home at the end of their working life. But they were not transients. The relationship lasted three centuries, and some 2 million Brits died in the subcontinent, most prematurely, many by tropical diseases.[3]

The degree of interaction between the British and those they ruled is unexpected, wrote acclaimed Delhi-based author and historian William Dalrymple. "Contrary to stereotype, a surprising number of company men responded to India by slowly shedding their Britishness like an unwanted skin and adopting Indian dress and taking on the ways of the Mughal governing class they came to replace."[4] Some wore *lungis* (a sort of cotton loincloth) and ate spicy local dishes; others went further with friendships, business partnerships, love affairs, even marriage, and not infrequently children. At times they did this in dramatic fashion.

Calcutta-founder Job Charnock notoriously snatched a young Hindu from her husband's funeral pyre and lived with her and their extended family.

Numerous Company employees became exceptional scholars, studying Sanskrit and producing treatises on temple sculpture or translating classic religious texts. Charles Wilkins did the first English translation of the *Bhagavad Gita* in 1785; a decade later, William Jones—linguist, founder of the Asiatic Society in Calcutta, and judge on the Supreme Court of Bengal—prepared one of the important Vedic discourses known as *Manusmriti* (The Laws of Manu). Both were sponsored by the first governor-general for British India, William Hastings.[5] With a mastery of Urdu and Hindu, Hastings also backed translations of important Islamic texts,[6] founded an Islamic college in Calcutta,[7] and ordered the construction of a Buddhist temple along the Hooghly.[8]

The depth of involvement for many men was profound. Dalrymple found that more than a third of British men working for the East India Company in India in the 1780s left in their wills their possessions to Indian wives or children from Indian women.[9] Children with a father rich enough were often sent back to school in England. "According to one estimate of 1789, one boy in every 10 at English schools was 'coloured'— but not too dark," Ian Jack observed,[10] responding to reports that DNA tests showed Prince William has Indian blood, traced back to Eliza Kewark, the housekeeper of Theodore Forbes (1788–1820), a Scottish merchant working in the port of Surat, and passed down on Princess Diana's side.

But such intermingling didn't last. Along with the starched mores of Victorian society imported into India's ruling class, two events hastened its end and set up the environment for Rudyard Kipling's famous edict that "East is East, and West is West, and never the twain shall meet."[11]

One was the opening of the Suez Canal in 1869. The journey from Britain to India around the Cape had been reduced from six months to three or four with the advent of the steamship in the mid-nineteenth century and was further trimmed down to as many weeks by cutting through the canal. Wives and children could join the men, friends come for the cool season, and visits be made back to Britain. Home became harder to forgo and impossible to forget.

European womenfolk, though, needed to be secluded, or at least protected. That included wives, sisters, and aunts, as well as the young, unmarried ladies who traveled out to India to spend the festive winter season with married relatives. Their annual influx was dubbed the Fishing Fleet. With a (European) male-to-female ratio of roughly four to one, India became fertile husband-hunting ground among colonial administrators, army officers, businessmen, and even planters. Fit from plenty of sport, dashing when in uniform, and craving attention from the opposite sex, the men feted the eligible ladies with balls and afternoon teas, shooting parties (a tiger hunt with a bejeweled maharaja for the truly connected), races at the Gymkhana, and picnics in tea gardens or under Himalayan deodars. They escorted them on morning rides and walks in the hills to see orchids and rhododendrons, played afternoon games of tennis on the clay courts, and danced at the Club to gramophone records in the evening, all chaperoned of course. Romances were, by necessity, quick, as the hot weather spelled an end to the social season. Young ladies who failed to snag a spouse by the heat's arrival traveled back to Britain as "Returned Empties."[12]

Those who *did* catch a husband became full memsahibs and often ended up in remote posts, not only far from the London (or Oxford or Edinburgh) society in which they had spent their lives, but also from the parties and exotic excursions where they had first been wooed in India. Along with not succumbing to cholera, typhoid, smallpox, dysentery, and malaria, avoiding prickly heat and snakes, and trying to adapt to life in a highly unfamiliar country, they frequently had to endure large chunks of time alone while their husbands traveled through the districts they administered or went off on military maneuvers. Fellow foreigners were generally few, or too far away, to visit. Contact with Indians remained largely restricted to their servants and often limited to a level of the local language known as kitchen Hindustani. Children brought a measure of comfort, though both boys and girls were nearly always sent home—a place they had never set foot—to boarding school, often as young as eight years old, to forge independence and proper British character.[13]

Another major event that hampered the intermingling of the British with the locals was the uprising of 1857, also known to the British as the Mutiny and to Indians as the First War of Independence. Tensions between the rulers and the ruled had been mounting for some time on the street and, more dangerously, among the Indian soldiers—sepoys—in the East India Company's barracks. The tipping point came when their

Enfield rifles began using a new cartridge rumored to be greased either in tallow (beef fat, which was offensive to Hindus) or pork fat (offensive to Muslims). The cartridges had to be bitten open before they could be used, an act that made a Hindu lose caste and defiled a Muslim.

The rebellion started in Meerut when Bengal army soldiers shot their British officers, moved to Delhi, drew in the aging Mughal emperor Bahadur Shah Zafar as their figurehead, and eventually spread along the Gangetic plain. The rebellion was put down ferociously but not swiftly. It took the British more than a year to fully quell it. The costs were dreadful, and reprisals on both sides viciously brutal. Zafar's heirs—his two sons and grandson—were killed in cold blood, and the last Mughal emperor was exiled to Rangoon, where he died as a prisoner and was buried in an unmarked grave. In the aftermath, mutual distrust increased along with separation, racial isolation, and British feelings of superiority.

The rebellion, Dalrymple wrote, "marked the end of both the East India Company and the Mughal dynasty, the two principal forces that had shaped Indian history over the previous three hundred years, and replaced both with undisguised imperial rule by the British government."[14]

It was a decisive moment in the British rule of India. In 1874, the East India Company, "formidable rival of states and empires, with power to acquire territory, coin money, command fortresses and troops, form alliances, make war or peace, and exercise both civil and criminal jurisdiction,"[15] was effectively dissolved, and the British Crown assumed all of the Company's responsibilities and administration of the country. The metamorphosis from commercial traders—*boxwallahs!*—to imperialists was official. The governor-general was now viceroy, and within a couple of decades, Queen Victoria would become Empress of India. "We don't rule this country anymore," Ronald Merrick says in Paul Scott's *The Raj Quartet*. "We preside over it in accordance with a book of rules written by people back home."[16] He wasn't exaggerating. In 1901 less than a thousand British officials of the Indian Civil Service (ICS) administered, with unshakable self-confidence, the affairs of more than 300 million people. They were backed by 60,000 British troops and 120,000 Indian troops,[17] not to mention the tens—or hundreds—of thousands of Indians who supported the ICS and ran the day-to-day operations of the country and did the main work of the administration.

After the uprising, the British in India, went the convention, had to remain above India (and Indians) and not become a part of it (or equals among them). The narrator in Kipling's story "Beyond the Pale" baldly states the prevailing opinion: "A man should, whatever happens, keep to his own caste, race and breed."[18] In the years that followed the rebellion, Dalrymple noted, "There was almost complete apartheid, an almost religious belief in racial differences, and little friendship or marriage across strictly policed racial and religious boundaries."[19]

As the eminent Indian intellectual Gurcharan Das commented, the British, for the most part, "did not interfere with our ancient traditions and our religion." They were generally religiously tolerant of their Hindu and Muslim subjects, and India preserved its spiritual heritage, customs, and monuments. Past invaders—Aryans, Turks, Afghans, and Mughals—"merged and became Indian." The Brits were different. "They did not merge with us and remained aloof to the end."[20]

Hill stations were a physical rendering of such aloofness.

The British "could start from scratch" on distant hilltops to be "celestially withdrawn from the Indian millions on the plains below," live "a few months in the year entirely for themselves,"[21] and "pretend that India had receded from their lives."[22]

The stations, built for Europeans, developed as oases of European civilization in the form of idyllic English or Scottish villages: churches with Gothic edifices, stained glass, and bell towers, bandstands for concerts with strident military tunes, the mall—limited to pedestrians and horses—for strolling, and, most notably in Shimla, a lively amateur theatrical season. Half-timbered, Tudor-style bungalows with low roofs and porches perched precariously on hillsides and offered stunning views. Owners christened them with names such as Willowdale, Springbrook, and Briar and surrounded them with roses and ornamental plants often raised from British seed. These flowering beds formed "a cordon sanitaire to keep India at bay."[23] For "Britishers," hill stations were a fundamental part of life during the colonial era.

But hill stations were not intended to be tourist resorts as they are today. Rather, they were built as sanitariums for East India Company employees to rest and recuperate. With excruciating summer temperatures on India's plains and tropical maladies cutting short the life span of British soldiers, whose numbers increased greatly after the uprising of 1857, Britain began building convalescent settlements in the mountains in the second half of the nineteenth century. Within a couple of decades, some eighty hill stations, from the grand (Shimla, Ooty, Darjeeling) to the less noted (Yercaud in Tamil Nadu, Almora and Ranikhet in Uttar Pradesh), were spread across the subcontinent.[24]

Ranging from four thousand to eight thousand feet in elevation, their initial attraction was a less oppressive climate that offered a chance to regain health and recoup one's old vigor. Heat was a frequent source of problems, although not infrequently exacerbated by inadequate clothing. Soldiers were still dressing in woolens and colorful Napoleonic-era uniforms with heavy ornamental insignia more suitable for a Central European battlefield than the scorching plains of the Indian subcontinent. The diet contained often excessively and unsuitably heavy food and too many bottles of fortified Madeira from Portugal. "We blame India for all our ailments, forgetting to accommodate our habits to its climate," *The Complete Indian Housekeeper and Cook*, the domestic bible for the British in India that ran through at least ten editions between 1888 and 1921, sternly admonished,[25] mindful that it took far too long for flannels to be replaced by cotton undergarments and girdles left in the closet.

At first modest, hill stations grew into a pure and distilled expression of the Britishness of the Empire[26] and potent colonial emblems. From 1864 until 1947, the summer capital of British India was an improbably small and inaccessible mountain resort. "From Shimla were directed the affairs of 308 million people—two and a half times the population, by Gibbon's estimate, of the Roman Empire at its climax," Morris noted.[27] Or, at the time, about one-fifth of mankind.

Shimla might have been comfortable, even somewhat familiar, but it took weeks to reach from the capital. Until 1911, when the newly crowned King-Emperor George V transferred it to Delhi, the capital of British India was Calcutta, some twelve hundred miles from Shimla. But when the heat arrived, as Kipling wrote:

> . . . the Rulers in that City by the Sea
> Turned to flee—
> Fled, with each returning Spring-tide, from its ills
> To the Hills.[28]

The level of British organization and the depth of desire, even desperation, to flee the heat culminated with the yearly move of the entire central government apparatus piece by piece from the capital into the hills when the hot weather arrived, and then back down again when it receded.[29]

The caravan of bullock carts, camels, and elephants, syces (grooms) and scribes, guards, memsahibs and children, cooks and ayahs making their way slowly to the hills was befitting of kings and conquerors on the move. "Hannibal's army crossing the Alps," Geoffrey Moorhouse noted, "had nothing on the British Raj ascending to its summer retreat."[30]

Shimla had the viceroy and commander in chief in summer residence, as well as the Delhi and Punjab secretariats. But Darjeeling was the Queen of the Himalaya. Many tailgates on beefy Tata trucks and snub-nosed lorries plying the road from Siliguri today refer to it as "Queen of Hills." Even the exacting authors of *The Complete Indian Housekeeper and Cook* called the scenery the "finest of all the hill stations." Though not before noting that it was also the dampest one in India and "leeches and ticks are a perfect pest."[31] In 1911, the year the Indian capital shifted, Darjeeling town had possibly the highest concentration of Europeans in the country with a ratio of less than ten Indians to one European, where it was overall many thousands to one.[32] During the summer months, the European population doubled.

The town spread almost vertically along a semicircular ridge, with buildings plastered to the shelves of the hillside. At the top sat the European quarter (residential bungalows and cottages, the lending library, pharmacy, Club, and church, with the steeple of St. Andrew's as the apex), then came the cheap hotels, bazaars, huts, and native tenements below in descending consequence but increasing density down to where the rickshaws waited and carriages loaded.

Along with being Bengal's chief sanatorium for the convalescing, Darjeeling acted as the provincial summer capital for the regional government whose seat was a distant Calcutta, some four hundred miles south. Men working in the civil or military administration and businessmen sent their wives and children into the hills to spend the hot months in the mountain air and, if lucky, joined them for a fortnight. Early Darjeeling also attracted some wealthy Indians and a few local princes. The maharaja of Cooch Behar built a sumptuous summer home there as did the maharaja of Burdwan.

The visit in the spring of 1880 by Lord and Lady Lytton, the viceroy of India and his wife, marked the hill station's arrival. The heavily bearded statesman and poet and his wife, who had been a lady-in-waiting to Queen Victoria, arrived with a thirty-one-gun salute and departed five days later under another regal salvo into the March sky. Darjeeling had "come of age."[33]

Not every early visitor was impressed, though. "Darjeeling itself is not so striking in its beauty as Lucerne or Chamounix or St Moritz," wrote John Oliver Hobbes in 1903. "It may be questioned whether it is beautiful at all. The town has no plan, and it straggles apparently over several hillsides."[34] What caught the attention, pen, and hyperbole of Hobbes was the bazaar, with its picturesque elements that Darjeeling's Swiss and French rivals could never match:

> One could buy skins of beasts, turquoise earrings, silver girdles, prints of the gods, bangles, dreadful drugs from the native apothecary, prayer wheels, rice, maize, yellow ochre and powdered carmine for one's face, bangles and dress materials. The girls often have their cheeks stained horribly with the blood of goats or chickens, and they wear their wealth in necklaces made of rupees for which they are sometimes murdered.[35]

The city remains, as when Hobbes experienced it, essentially a set of tiered landings and switchbacks with steps and steep ramps running between, jammed with buildings, shops, and cafés, and all roads leading up to the long, broad plaza at the saddle below Observatory Hill. The Chowrasta is the city's flattest point and meeting spot, where four important pedestrian streets come together, and everyone in town seems to pass through at least once during the day.

"In any town in India the European Club is the spiritual citadel, the real seat of the British power," Orwell wrote in *Burmese Days*,[36] his scathing portrait of British attitudes during their rule of British India (including Burma) and Ceylon (Sri Lanka). The Club—like the Company—was given a capital *C*, and often a capital *T*, too: The Club.

Their beginnings go back to the early coffeehouses in London, men-only places where every class and trade had a favorite in which to gather. Eventually they set up their own private establishments. Such exclusivity transplanted effortlessly around the Empire. In India, Calcutta's Bengal Club, established in 1827, was the first, followed by the Byculla Club in Bombay and the Madras Club five years later. After the uprising in 1857, they appeared in nearly every station across India.

The Club was "a symbol and center of British imperialism," wrote Leonard Woolf—writer, editor, and husband of Virginia—recalling his seven years as a colonial administrator in Ceylon. "It had normally a curious air of slight depression, but at the same time exclusiveness, superiority, isolation. Only the 'best people' and of course only white men were members."[37]

Club membership was based, foremost, on race. A system that would essentially allow any class of white but no class of Indian, no matter aristocracy or Oxbridge education, was ironic and particularly galling. Yet, in a country where Hindu castes were rigid and many Brahmans would not eat food touched by lower castes, such segregation was not unique.[38] (The decision, at the end of Britain's rule, to begin allowing in *some* Indians divided members—and Empire.)

Membership was, secondly, based on occupation. *Boxwallahs*, a rather contemptuous name for all those engaged in trade, fell well down the rank across India except perhaps in port cities such as Calcutta and Bombay, where commerce dominated affairs.[39] Those in the army were above nonofficials, but residing at the top were ICS men—generally recruited just out of Oxford or Cambridge. Know as "Heaven-born," these were "the colonial equivalent of the Hindu Brahmin caste."[40]

"Ironically," lamented Eugenia Herbert, "in the new order of things, the once-glorious merchants (*boxwallahs*) and planters ranked virtually on par with untouchables."[41]

Not so in Darjeeling. While ICS, British army officers, and railway officers drank at the Planters' Club, the planters themselves and *burra sahibs*—head managers at the tea gardens—were its aristocrats. It was the hub of social life for British working on Darjeeling tea estates.

Established in 1868, the Darjeeling Planters' Club was built on a parcel of land donated by the maharaja of Cooch Behar, who was the only one allowed to park his rickshaw on the main porch of the Club. It was a place to meet, swap stories, commiserate, and talk shop.

"The life of a planter was very lonely," observed the Club's current assistant secretary, Shabnam Bhutia, on its open verandah with brilliant white walls and tea-leaf-green doors during a spring day. Dozens of potted purple and white flowers had symmetrically been arranged on a stepped, three-tiered platform beneath sets of mounted horns. Wide wicker chairs were turned toward the midday sun like sunflowers. The planters had little chance for social activity. Gardens were remote, and even ones side by side took time to reach.* With a staff of servants, cooks, houseboys, bearers, and gardeners, life on a tea estate could be comfortable for the planter, but lonesome. Society and even other Westerners were generally too distant for regular contact. Applicants in Europe wanting to work on a tea estate were required to be bachelors, wait some years before marrying, and then secure permission to do so from the *burra sahib*[42]—which is to say, approval not just of the marriage but also of the woman, often found among the small Anglo community in Darjeeling.

Being a planter or a European working on any of the tea gardens obliged becoming a Club member, and being a member was a key part of the social life. Liquor played an important role at the Club, but was governed by an unwritten rule: beer from eleven A.M., gin in the afternoon, and whisky not before sunset.[43] Billiards and bridge were offered, and, in the evenings, dancing to songs already out of fashion in Britain, but that hardly mattered. On Club night it was packed: Attendance was obligatory. The Club had a couple dozen rooms available for the planters to stay over, or for their guests. After Mark Twain gave a lecture in Darjeeling, he retired to one of its rooms.

Most didn't sleep over, though. The junior members of a tea estate— the assistants and engineers—needed to make the garden's dawn roll call no matter how late they stayed at the Club. So the men made their way home, somehow, late at night. They would ride back along the network of precarious paths, crossing on horseback streams and rivers whose swollen torrents were dangerous in the rainy season.[44]

Until just a few decades ago, horses remained a principal means of transport on a tea garden, and planters received a horse allowance. "Every manager rode his estate, and horses were considered more expensive than wives," according to Gillian Wright. "Even in 1971, a planter was allowed Rs 300 a month for his horse and Rs 150 a month dearness allowance upon marriage."[45]

While managers now make that late-night drive in a jeep, the roads are frequently washed out by monsoon rains, overrun by streams, and, in most cases, remain just as wild. "Driving home at around midnight from the Club," Vijay Dhancholia, a member since 1992, recalled, "I saw a

---

*They still do today. Traveling from the manager's bungalow on the Bannockburn Tea Estate to the one on the neighboring Ging Tea Estate takes close to an hour by jeep. This is rather standard.

leopard on the road with a deer, and it crouched there until we went right next it."

Such an evening out today is an anomaly. While most garden managers are members, like Dhancholia, they now rarely go. Planters' families live with them on the estates, and with Internet, mobile phones, and satellite TV, most planters don't need the Club for entertainment or even to socialize.

Today officially called the Darjeeling Club, it has 470 members. In the late 1990s, it opened admission to professions other than planters. Joining is very expensive, although it is currently not taking new members. Yet few come these days. "Just two or three," said a receptionist on an April evening that had cooled enough to require coal fires to be lit in the guest rooms and a heater turned on at the feet of the receptionist. And before? "Three hundred," he said flatly.

At the base of Nehru Road, across from the Planters' Club, is Keventer's, a popular, decades-old, inexpensive café with a roof terrace shaped like a ship's bow. On Sundays it fills with junior boys from Darjeeling's elite schools ordering cheese-toast sandwiches and bottled Maaza mango sodas.

During the nineteenth century, Darjeeling became famous for its English-style boarding schools modeled on Eton, Rugby, and Harrow. St. Paul's School was the first. It started in 1823 in Calcutta and opened a branch in Darjeeling in 1864 as the highest school in the world. Located on the outskirts of town, the beefy buildings with peaked, red roofs and a massive quad comprise one of the area's top institutions, along with St. Joseph's at North Point, Mount Hermon, and Loreto Convent (where Mother Teresa spent ten years doing her novitiate). They draw students from beyond the hills and also India itself, with scores from Bhutan, Nepal, Bangladesh, and Thailand (including royalty). The town's numerous students stroll around in V-neck sweater-vests, slate-gray trousers or long skirts, striped ties, and crested blazers.

Even when there is no chance of rain, and Darjeeling is suffering from drought, the boys of St. Paul's still carry their ubiquitous black umbrellas. Asked why they had them on a sunny day when it hadn't rained in weeks, one tall boy with a fuzz of hair just appearing on his lip said, "Tradition, sir!"

"What if you get caught without an umbrella?"

"We wouldn't be able to come into town, sir."

"How often can you come into town?"

"Once a month, sir."

"Really?"

"Tradition, sir."

CHAPTER 11

Nostalgia

If there is a hint of what V. S. Naipaul called mimicry on the Indian side in the school crests and clubs with hunting trophies, dress codes, and the same elitist rules that once excluded them, there is nostalgia on the Anglo side. It's located in the heritage hill station hotels with snuggeries displaying steam-train memorabilia, the solid, gray-stone buildings with wisteria, and the evocative smell of coal smoke in the evening air. In Darjeeling, no one traffics better in nostalgia than the city's most exclusive hotel, the Windamere.

Established in the 1880s as a cozy boardinghouse for bachelor English and Scottish tea planters, it was converted into a hotel by the father of the current owner, who bought the property in 1939. Strung across the narrow back of a hummock, with stunning views dropping straight down on both sides and a royal guest list, the old-fashioned, self-contained Victorian cottages, annexes, and planters' suites are the only buildings on Observatory Hill. Rooms have spacious closets (one had to dress for dinner) and a second, smaller room (to change perhaps, or for an attending footman). Full meal plans are obligatory, menu cards typed out daily on an old machine, and waiters breeze among tables wearing white gloves even to serve breakfast. The porridge is memorable, roast beef and Yorkshire pudding are served on Sundays, and desserts lean toward British public-school staples—which is to say Raj standards—such as bread-and-butter pudding with plump golden raisins, sponge cakes, and jam roly-poly, all smothered in hot custard. When evenings are cool, which is most of the year, coal fires are lit in the rooms while guests are down at dinner, offering heat along with soothing sounds of embers shifting in the grate as they burn down during the night. A hot-water bottle wrapped in flannel is surreptitiously tucked into the sheets, too.

"This place isn't just a throwback to the early 20th century," wrote the Canadian journalist Muhammad Lila. "It *is* the early 20th century."[1]

The tug of nostalgia pulls the firmest at afternoon tea, which, every day at precisely four P.M., is offered fireside in Daisy's Music Room.

The Windamere's tradition began seventy-five years ago by copying the British fashion and has carried on with little change since. A server wearing a frilly lace pinafore and white gloves pours out tea from a silver pot and offers platters of macaroons, Bundt cake with candied cherries, and scones to slice open and generously spread butter and clotted cream across their soft crumb face. Arranged in orderly layers on silver platters are petit triangular sandwiches that have been filled with cucumber, boiled egg, or cheese and had their crusts shaved off with a long, serrated knife.

The music room is not overly large, and with the curtains drawn and a fire blazing, it becomes intimate and cozy. Stacked on the piano among candelabra are heavy, black-boarded photo albums of past Windamere celebrations. Lovingly separated by sheets of onionskin are treasured images of New Year's Eve bonfires, dances, and dinners with Christmas crackers and shiny party hats. On the wall, frames encase regimental ware, portraits of long-dead royalty, and notes from famous guests. A card from Jan Morris contains this handwritten ode:

> As the glow of Kanchenjunga
> Faded with the passing of each year—
>
> When the whistle of the Toy Train
> Dies at last upon my ear—
>
> In my heart I still shall cherish
> Dear old Windamere.

The British tradition of afternoon tea originated with Anna Maria, the seventh Duchess of Bedford (a lady-in-waiting to Queen Victoria), in the early nineteenth century as she began having a little pick-me-up between the then-standard two meals a day, breakfast and dinner. At first private affairs, afternoon teas moved to the drawing rooms of the fashionable set—ladies only; the men had their clubs and pubs—and soon after to teahouses and hotel dining rooms. In some ways, this was a beginning of women's emancipation. Starting in 1865, the year the luxurious Langham Hotel on London's Regent Street opened and began offering afternoon tea in their dazzling Palm Court, ladies had a place to go out together in public without risking society's moralizing gossip.

As with many British fashions, afternoon tea became popular on the subcontinent, too. In Victorian India, tea was drunk as in Britain, with milk and sugar, though that sweetener might have been jaggery,[2] a dark brown sugar made by evaporating the sap of palm trees. Some Brits enjoyed tea Mughal style, with spices, and *The Raj at the Table* offers a rather baroque recipe that includes palm starch (sago), almonds, cardamom, rosewater or dried rosebuds, milk, sugar, and "just sufficient tea leaf."[3]

In gardens of hill stations during the summer social season, and in the sunny winter down on the plains, tea was served along with sweets— tiffin cake, dholi buns, Bombay golden cake, and gymkhana cake, which included plums and currants. Baking in British India was not without its challenges, even for experienced cooks. High-quality flour was hard to come by and butter difficult to keep fresh. Yeast was perhaps the trickiest ingredient to obtain, so cooks often prepared homemade versions from cookbooks "using ingredients as diverse as potatoes, hops, bananas, barley, toddy (palm sap) and a fruit flower known as *mowha*."[4] Even if a cook could whisk up all of the ingredients, ovens were primitive and formed a final obstacle to pulling off a decent cake.

Beforehand, the lady would most likely have checked her well-thumbed copy of *The Complete Indian Housekeeper and Cook*. The fourth edition, published in 1898 at the height of the Raj, contained forty-three chapters that instructed on every element of housekeeping and colonial life on the subcontinent, from getting a piano to the Himalayas for the summer to throwing a perfect garden party. "Cakes and bonbons suitable for tennis parties are legion, and, as a rule the one thing to be observed in selecting them is to avoid stickiness or surprises," advised coauthors Flora Annie Steel and Grace Gardiner. "It is not pleasant to find the first bite of a firm looking cake result in a dribble of liqueur or cream down your best dress."[5]

For afternoon tea, the two ladies recommended serving warm slices of Ferozepore cake, named for the ancient town in the Punjab that under the British housed one of the largest military garrisons on the subcontinent.

To the standard quartet of flour, sugar, butter, and eggs, the recipe adds almonds and pistachios steeped in cream and, to tart it up, lime, which they exotically called "green citron."

To be sure, if the hostess had consulted Mmes. Steel and Gardiner for her menu, she would have been firmly discouraged from serving anything beyond cakes and scones to accompany the tea. "In England, the fashion of having various kinds of sandwiches at afternoon tea has of late gained ground but as it means a necessary disregard of dinner, it is not to be encouraged by any one who sets up for being a gourmet."[6]

The Mesdames did, however, yield—even if slightly—to fashion and offered a handful "of the latest" sandwiches, albeit "given in the proper place," at the end of the book. (The penultimate chapter, added only "by request," contains eight "native dishes" that the authors warned "are inordinately greasy and sweet.")[7] The limited selection included an eternal standby, egg sandwiches. But little else. "Almost anything can be made into sandwiches, so it is unnecessary to give more recipes," the book drily noted.[8]

Lovely sandwiches can be found at afternoon tea in the Elgin Hotel. Built as the summer palace of the maharaja of Cooch Behar, the Elgin has a snug interior bedecked with etchings and lithographs, period teak furniture from Burma, oak floor paneling, plush red sofas with ample throw pillows, and fireplaces that crackle in the winter. In the well-lit drawing room that runs across the ground-floor front of the stout, white building, the Elgin's waiters—clad not in frilly lace but turbaned, regimental uniforms—serve afternoon tea on the heavy, polished wood side tables inlaid with mother-of-pearl. Among the monogrammed cups and saucers and silverware covered in a gossamer of spidery patina, waiters set down a stacked tea tray (known in Edwardian days as a curate), with three hoops to hold plates of delicacies and a loop handle on top to carry it.

While the Windamere might prepare moister scones and clotted cream that can suspend a spoon upright, the Elgin serves just-fried *pakoras* (fritters) made of onions, vegetables, or boiled eggs to accompany their selection of sweets and savories, and, along with a long list of fine, single-estate Darjeeling teas—including Margaret's Hope, Balasun, and Puttabong (Tukvar)—a sublime masala chai that's aromatic and perfectly spiced.

"Under certain circumstances there are few hours in life more agreeable than the hour dedicated to the ceremony known as afternoon tea," begins Henry James's masterpiece *The Portrait of a Lady*.[9] Sitting by the fire in Daisy's Music Room on a drizzly day, or by the large windows of the front lounge at the Elgin with tea and *pakoras* when the mists clear for a moment to shed a quick glimpse of the ethereal Kanchenjunga hovering just above Darjeeling, it is hard to disagree.

For British in India, though, liquor, as much as tea, defined the Raj experience, especially in the popular imagination. "Of course drink is what keeps the machine going. We should all go mad and kill one another in a week if it weren't for that," proclaimed Flory the timber merchant in Orwell's *Burmese Days*. "Booze as the cement of empire."[10] A battery of servants took care of most tasks, and the British often had little to do in the evening but whine about the heat and drink. Measuring out pegs of whisky and generously diluting them down with soda or water became a ritual. So did enjoying a gin cocktail to be served out on the verandah for a sundowner. Or earlier on weekends. "The hour or two before Sunday *tiffin* [lunch]," wrote Jennifer Brennan in her Anglo-Indian cookbook-cum-memoir, "was the time for several pristine gimlets or pink gins."[11]

The gimlet was synonymous with British India. Four parts dry gin to one part Rose's lime juice shaken with ice and strained into a cocktail glass. Limy sweet and refreshing in the heat, they go down easy. The Windamere still shakes the stiffest in town in a pickling ratio of six to one. At the Elgin, the barman adds a squeeze of fresh lime. Little else has changed.

But tea planters considered pink gin their drink. Just two ingredients that play off one another: gin, preferably Plymouth gin, which is a touch sweet, and Angostura bitters. The latter was developed in 1824 as a medicinal elixir to cure soldiers' stomach ailments by a German doctor, Johann Gottlieb Benjamin Siegert, a Prussian army veteran of the Napoleonic Wars who fled to South America, where he was appointed surgeon general of Simón Bolívar's liberation forces. Originally called Amargo Aromatico (Spanish for "aromatic bitter"), the wily blend of spices, herbs, roots, and berries eventually took the name of the Venezuelan town where Siegert lived. It helped assuage seasickness in sailors and rouse the appetite of those living in unfamiliar, tummy-troubling lands. The gin was meant to disguise the unpalatable, acrid taste of the saucy, brown concoction, but in reality the bitters help cover the searing taste of cheap, local gin.

In 1939, the year the Windamere Hotel opened, the American Charles Henry Baker Jr. offered the perfect recipe for pink gin in his indispensable *The Gentleman's Companion*:

> Take a thin, stemmed cocktail glass. Shake in 4 or 5 dashes of Angostura, tip the glass like the tower of Pisa and twirl it between thumb and fingers. Whatever Angostura sticks to the glass through capillary attraction is precisely the right amount, although a lot of old India hands whose stomachs are lax find that a lot more Angostura than that is in order to stimulate appetite. Gently pour off the extra bitters that do not cling. Fill glass with gin. That's all. Superfluous bitters go back in the bottle, on the floor, or out the port hole or window—depending upon who, where and what we are.[12]

On a cold autumn evening, the quiet, somewhat aloof Lepcha barman at the Windamere prepared it a touch differently. First he chilled the glass by wildly swirling a couple of ice cubes around a wide champagne glass like high-speed roulette balls. After flinging these into the sink, he shook in three or four drops of Angostura, then twirled a new pair of ice cubes around the glass for a few moments before pouring the gin over the top. He set the drink down, silently and without ceremony, on the Chinese-red bar counter.

The color of a pink gin is less Hello Kitty pink than "the orangey-pink of the inside of a conch shell," as Ian Fleming described it in the final 007 novel.[13] From Fleming's pen—and dangling from Bond's fingers—the drink exudes sexiness and daring.

Not so from Graham Greene. A number of Greene's forlorn and doomed characters, stranded in dingy, half-forgotten, and always-neglected British colonial outposts, go "through the doomed motions of mixing another gin and bitters."[14] Scobie, in *The Heart of the Matter*, "grinned miserably at his glass, twisting it round and round to let the angostura cling along the curve."[15] He and his wife drink them out of boredom and despair: "Life always repeated the same pattern; there was always, sooner or later, bad news that had to be broken, comforting lies to be uttered, pink gins to be consumed to keep misery away."[16]

In British-ruled Malaya the drink was called *gin pahit* ("bitter gin" in Malay), a favorite tipple in the Far Eastern tales of W. Somerset Maugham, Britain's other great observer of far-flung colonial fatigue. As the narrator remarks about an Irishman in the story "P. & O.," "He had lived too long in the East to drink anything else."[17]

The same could have been said for many of the men standing at the bar of the Planters' Club. This is perhaps a more fitting coda for colonial-era tea planters on isolated Darjeeling estates than afternoon teas and warm scones with clotted cream.

CHAPTER 12

Planters and Pluckers

Tea is one of the most labor-intensive of all crops to cultivate, and Darjeeling's pioneering planters had to settle vast numbers of laborers to work on their isolated estates. They quickly became sprawling, self-contained communities housing thousands of people. They still are. The average garden has just 224 hectares (553 acres) of tea with production of around 100,000 kilograms (220,000 pounds). It is surprising how many people the limited amount of tea must support. Workers number in the hundreds, but many times more live on the estate. Marybong has a dozen small villages scattered across its 395 hectares (976 acres) that are home to about 6,000 people. Just 741 of them work on the estate. About half are schoolkids. Some of the others might work off-garden jobs, from laborers in nearby villages to serving in the military, but most are supported by the family member who has a position on the garden. Ging has just 692 laborers and 67 staff but supports 7,000 people in two dozen small villages. Ambootia has eleven villages housing 4,500 people. Tukvar supports more than 5,000 people with just 636 of those permanent workers on the estate. Namring is even larger—450 out of its 1,068 total hectares under tea, with 1,398 permanent workers, and yet it's home to 10,000 people. Considering its fame, Makaibari, covering 573 hectares (1,415 acres) with 250 hectares (617 acres) of tea and about 1,500 people living on the estate and some 650 employees, is relatively modest.

Tea garden land is not owned by the estates but rented on a freehold lease from the government of West Bengal for renewable thirty- to ninety-nine-year periods. A lease can be transferred or sold, but a new owner inherits the workers living on the garden and must employ them. The clear and rigid hierarchy has the planter at the top. "It was a system created by Britishers," Dhancholia said. Medieval and serflike, it remains firmly in place.

Darjeeling's early tea planters, wrote E. C. Dozey in *A Concise History of the Darjeeling District Since 1835*, "will be remembered among those who led the forlorn hope, who planted the banners of civilisation and industry on these mountains; and in sowing the seeds of the tea plant have laid the foundations of India's increased prosperity."[1]

Published in 1922, that is perhaps rather generous in spirit. A lively and opinionated contemporary Darjeeling historian offers a different appraisal of the same men:

> In the early days, only those Englishmen who failed to make it as soldiers, sailors, clerks, and by default, with nothing else to lose and nowhere else to go, took up life as a "tea planter." They knew nothing whatsoever about tea and it is doubtful if they had even set eyes on a tea bush. Scoundrels, rascals, and scallywags enlisted to become lord and master of a little fiefdom called a *tea garden* in the exotic misty hills of Darjeeling.[2]

Such a scathing assessment was echoed by Major (retired) Sandeep Mukherjee, the secretary and principal adviser for the Darjeeling Tea Association. "They were the riffraff, the criminals; the persons [the British] thought would pollute the society were sent here," he said on a cool spring morning at the association's office beside the Planters' Club. Tall and upright, with a strong jaw and neatly parted hair, he still holds the military bearing of his days as an aide-de-camp to the Chief of Army Staff in Kashmir. "Nobody at home, they became somebody here," he said at his large desk, turning over a cigarette packet. He wore three rings on his right hand, including, on his pinkie, a luminous pearl from South India as big as a marble. "Nobodies who had nothing to lose." Driven, at times brutal, and continually busy, they began from scratch, planting the steep, heavily forested hillsides cut by ravines. But, he acknowledged, "It would have been impossible to create this industry without such personalities, and that idea of superiority."

Undeniably the planters were a mixed bunch. Many came from the working or middle classes—shopkeepers, chemists, retired army officers, sailors. A handful of minor gentry also headed to India's tea gardens from Britain to make something of themselves. Or, at least not disgrace the family back home. The protagonist in Rudyard Kipling's story "Yoked with an Unbeliever" who is "sent out to 'tea'" is typical of this kind:

> What "tea" meant he had not the vaguest idea, but fancied that he would have to ride on a prancing horse over hills covered with tea-vines, and draw a sumptuous salary for doing so; and he was very grateful to his uncle for getting him the berth. He was really going to reform all his slack, shiftless ways, save a large proportion of his magnificent salary yearly, and, in a very short time, return to marry Agnes Laiter. Phil Garron had been lying loose on his friends' hands for three years, and, as he had nothing to do, he naturally fell in love. He was very nice; but he was not strong in his views and opinions and principles, and though he never came to actual grief, his friends were thankful when he said good-bye, and went out to this mysterious "tea" business near Darjiling. They said, "God bless you, dear boy! Let us never see your face again,"— or at least that was what Phil was given to understand.[3]

Like Phil, planters rarely lacked faith in being able to do the job— then or in the years that followed. "I had been brought up in an era of empire, and inculcated with the idea that for the British to go out and run colonies and tropical enterprises was perfectly normal," wrote tea-planter-turned-author Roy Moxham about going out to Malawi in 1961 as an eighteen-year-old. "I had read the short stories of Somerset Maugham, and from his acute observations had a surprisingly good idea of how planters behaved. I had read a good deal about young men who worked in the tropics. The job was challenging but not daunting. I knew nothing about tea, but I could learn."[4] Moxham couldn't even drive—in his telling, seemingly the only real requirement for the position. But he winged that, too, and taught himself on the rain-slicked dirt roads of the estate before anyone could find out otherwise.[5]

Determined and confident (more than heroes or scallywags) are perhaps more accurate generalizations of Darjeeling's pioneers. But also inexperience, even ignorance. Their most common trait was having no idea how or where to plant tea bushes, nor process the leaves. "With no previous experience," Lama wrote, "they had to rely on information obtained hearsay and it was a pure learn-as-you-earn industry or go-broke-as-you-work business."[6] The workers in the factories and fields also had to learn to prune, pluck, and process tea as they went along.

The planter's duties were "multifarious," as the 1907 edition of the *Bengal District Gazetteer* for Darjeeling noted, and included

> the supervision of the cultivation, the control of the manufac-
> ture, the management of the large labour force employed, the
> construction of roads in the estate, and often the erection of
> the buildings. He must therefore combine, as far as possible,
> the knowledge and skill of an agriculturist, engineer and archi-
> tect, and even, to some extent, of a doctor; and above all, he
> must have firm control over his labourers, the art of manage-
> ment, and generally the power of conduct.[7]

While few planters act as doctors or road surveyors today, many of the other tasks still exist in the job description, plus a few more. "Police and judge," said one. "Banker and counselor."

Not all the planters during the British era in Darjeeling were English or Scottish, and some of the eclectic array of foreigners came to the hills for reasons other than tea. The Reverend William Start, an Anglican-clergyman-turned-Baptist-evangelist, brought a band of Protestant missionaries from the Moravian Church in Germany to India in the late 1830s.[8] The small group of young men and women from outside Berlin traveled to Liverpool and then on to India, an arduous journey that took five months around the Horn by ship to Calcutta. From there, they had a further month's journey to reach Start's mission on the plains. The rever-end believed in communal work, and the Germans had little time to spread the gospel in their day-to-day efforts simply to survive. After two years, Start ordered them to his Tukvar Mission just north of Darjeeling. They started over and struggled even harder in the mountains. Within a few years, the venture failed, and Start—angry, no doubt, that there had not been a single conversion—withdrew his financial backing. The Germans had to abandon Tukvar, the homes they had built, and the fields they had planted that were, finally, beginning a return on their considerable efforts.

Without means to return to Europe, they settled in the newly established town of Darjeeling and tried to support themselves by selling produce, doing carpentry, or whatever they could. Darjeeling's nascent tea industry soon offered opportunities, and their names are strewn throughout its pioneering decades (and found on gravestones in Darjeeling's rather unkempt Old Cemetery). The most frequent that crop up are from the Wernicke-Stölke dynasty, with various marriages between them and involvement on numerous estates.

The most successful was the second-generation Andrew Wernicke. Just a handful of months old when his family arrived at the Tukvar Mission, he grew up in the hills. Yet by the time he was coming of age, Wernicke had no plans to work in tea. He was a scholar of Greek and Latin with intentions of entering the church. At the end of 1863, while he was working on a B.A. at Bishop's College in Calcutta, his father died suddenly, and Andrew was compelled to break off studies and return to Darjeeling to support his widowed mother (a Stölke). His younger brother, Fred, was an assistant on the Soom Tea Estate, and Andrew reluctantly followed, gaining an assistant's position on Captain Masson's Tukvar Tea Estate.

Almost immediately, he nearly truncated his new career with a gun accident. "Using an old-fashioned muzzle-loader gun, he returned to his bungalow from green-pigeon shooting. The gun had been wetted by rain. Resting the gun on the edge of the bed, he was wiping it down when it slipped to the floor, exploding with the concussion, and discharged the shot, which shattered the left hand and wrist."[9] His arm had to be amputated below the elbow. Wernicke wore a knitted sock over the stump and carried on. While needing help to get dressed and cut his meat at the table, he rode ponies, played billiards, and even shot birds on occasion. Within a few years, he left Tukvar to manage Makaibari, where he soon married a girl a decade his junior, the sixteen-year-old Elizabeth Niebal.

In the 1870s land was becoming available for planting. With his brother, Andrew opened out Lingia and then Tumsong estates, "a bold and arduous venture for father and Fred," Andrew's son Frank said years later, "and it was only by exercising the most rigid economy and sacrificing even the simplest of luxuries that they were able to achieve their objective." A new tea garden doesn't immediately start repaying its investment. "It takes 5 or 6 years before the tea bush comes into bearing and manufacture can begin. These must have been lean years indeed, waiting for the first returns from the sale of their tea."[10]

Andrew Wernicke was over six feet tall, lanky, and heavily bearded. "He walked with a slight stoop and one shoulder slightly depressed, owing to the loss of his left arm," his son recalled late in his own life. "In expression his face was rather pale, somewhat care-worn and meditative. He seldom smiled and I don't think I ever heard him laugh. His dress was always simple, and to my childish critical eyes, shabby."[11] Decades of living an arduous, austere life damaged his health. By 1883, Wernicke, severely suffering from rheumatism, was forced to retire. But he wasn't done with tea, acquiring Glenburn Tea Estate in 1895 and then Bannockburn across the Rangili Valley from it.

Wernicke died in 1904. By then, the Wernickes and Stölkes had owned or managed more than a dozen gardens: Lingia, Marybong, Tumsong, Steinthal, Soom, Glenburn, Bannockburn, Makaibari, Risheehot, Pandam, Aloobari, Goomba, and Tukvar. This impressive list includes some of the most illustrious gardens in Darjeeling.

Among the colorful foreign figures in the nineteenth-century annals of Darjeeling tea is Louis Mandelli. His father, Jerome, from an aristocratic Maltese family, was raised in Milan and fled as a young man to South America to join freedom fighter and Italian patriot Guiseppe Garibaldi, who led the Italian Legion in Uruguay's Civil War (1838–51). He returned with Garibaldi to capture Sicily and southern Italy from the Bourbons, events that led to the unification of the country. Falling out with his family, Jerome changed his surname from that of his father (Count Castel Nuovo) to that of his mother (Mandelli), which he passed down to his son, Louis.[12]

Or maybe it was the son himself who fought for Garibaldi in the late 1840s as a very young man. Accounts of Louis Mandelli's early life are riddled with gaps, and the sketchy dates that are known do fit and can apply to him rather than his father.

But in 1864 Louis Mandelli *did* somehow finagle a position managing the Lebong & Minchu Tea Estate. He appears abruptly on Darjeeling municipal records, and on those of the Catholic Church, as he married in January 1865, not long after arriving. That he had no experience with tea seemed to matter little. Soon under his command were two more estates,

Mineral Springs and Chongtong. He now controlled 550 hectares (1,350 acres), a not insignificant amount considering the effort involved in moving between properties. "Being so busy looking after the three gardens under my charge," Mandelli wrote in a letter, "and each of them is at a great distance from one to another, so I have to remain at each for days & days."[13]

Before long, Mandelli became a partner in two other gardens. One was the picturesque Kyel Tea Estate. When a division of Lingia next door was given to Mary, the daughter of Lingia's owner, as a wedding present in the 1870s and added to Kyel, the new estate was rechristened Marybong ("Mary's place" in Lepcha). Even today, the winding fourteen-mile journey from Darjeeling to Marybong takes about ninety minutes by jeep in the dry season. Mandelli did it on horseback.

"I can assure you, the life of a Tea Planter is far from being a pleasant one, especially this year," Louis Mandelli wrote to a friend down on the plains in 1876, "drought at first, incessant rain afterwards, & to crown all, cholera among the coolies, beside the commission from home to inspect the gardens, all these combined are enough to drive any one mad."[14]

The rugged, feral life on an isolated garden, the hundreds of laborers under a planter's responsibility, and the fickleness—and all too frequent cruelty—of nature when farming tea in the hills took their toll. So did the unhealthy climate and tropical diseases. "Quinine every morning, castor oil twice a week, and calomel"—also known as mercurous chloride, a poisonous white power used as a purgative, antiseptic, and fungicide—"at the change of the moon,"[15] went the planters' preventive, self-medicating prescription.

Mandelli found solace in ornithology, shooting and skinning some specimens, but mostly preserving ones that local collectors had shot or trapped for him on lengthy trips to Sikkim, Tibet, and Bhutan.

But deep losses on the estates and mounting debts to the bank began to wear him down, and he even found his beloved hobby exhausting. "The rains are frightful, the dampness horrible & the fog so dense that you cannot see few yards before you," he wrote of collecting around Darjeeling, adding that any excursion into neighboring Sikkim is "simply madness, as the leeches will eat you alive."[16]

But surely the biggest blow came from an English rival, Allan Octavian (A. O.) Hume. "Yes, Hume is a brute, in fact, I call him a swindler, as far as birds are concerned," Mandelli wrote to a friend in January 1876:

> What else would be thought of a man who promised to help me / <u>and very grand and magnificent promises they were</u> / to make my collection of Indian birds as perfect as he possibly could, in order only to get out the best & the rarest things to be found up here, & then leaving me on the lurch now, as he has found out that I am no more his slave subservient to his sneaking and bland manner & hypocritical ways?

Such robust underlining is not typical in Mandelli's letters, except when writing of Hume. "I should say that swindler is too mild a term for such a man after having got out from me about 5000 birds & given only in return about 800, the commonest birds in India, 400 of which went down the khud [ravine or precipice], as they were not worth the carriage."[17]

But how to complain about Hume, except in private letters like this? ("The only consolation I have in this matter is that I am not the only one who has been victimized!!!")[18] Hume had become director-general of agriculture in India in 1870 and was the country's preeminent and most powerful ornithologist. Although considered the father of Indian ornithology, Hume is far better known as the founder of the Indian National Congress Party—the party of the Gandhi and Nehru clans, and still a dominant political force in the country. Hume made an open call to students in 1883, and during the party's historical first meeting in 1885, the Brit was nominated to be the party's general secretary, a position he held for nearly a quarter century.

Reading Mandelli's letters it is impossible to picture him dancing in black tie at the Planters' Club or playing a game of cards after a couple of rounds of pink gins. His bank, creditors, and poor health are frequently mentioned. "For the last two or three months I have been unwell & troubled with slow fever, cough, deafness etc. etc.," Mandelli wrote in March 1877. "In fact I think old age is creeping fast on me."[19] He was just forty-four years old.

By the end of 1879 Mandelli was no longer in charge of any of the four gardens that he had recently been running or owning, an incredible turn of events. His problems—debts? poor harvests? depression?—must have severely worsened. In February the following year he committed suicide.

Mandelli left behind a wife and five children in Darjeeling. Municipal records show them steadily liquidating his property for cash over the next two years. They sold what remained of Mandelli's prized bird collection to none other than A. O. Hume.[20]

The cause of Mandelli's death was listed as "unknown" in the Bishop's Death Register, but this was perhaps done by a sympathetic official knowing that burial in the church cemetery would be impossible if the truth was recorded. Before long, though, news of his suicide was considered common enough knowledge that when the British Museum, with thirteen of his birds in their collection, published an appreciation of Mandelli in 1906, the text clearly stated that Mandelli had taken his own life, though how remains a mystery. Mandelli used arsenic in preparing bird skins, and perhaps some grains helped him to end his life and hide the way he did it.[21] This could be another reason his death was "unknown": arsenic poisoning has many of the same symptoms as other ailments and, until the eighteenth and nineteenth centuries, was difficult to detect, especially in a station as distant as Darjeeling.

Mandelli's grave is impossible to locate today. The tomb is not in the main Old Cemetery, but the Catholic-dominated Singtom Cemetery, at North Point below St. Joseph's School. Built in 1858, it is known as the New Cemetery. In both graveyards, the tombstones of settlers, soldiers, wives, and children are tipped over, cracked, broken, and obscured by moss, vines, and weeds. The inscriptions on the older ones have been worn away over the years, and vandals plucked out the brass letters on other ones during the violent, agitation-filled mid–1980s, rendering names and dates into a series of faint dots like a marquee with broken lightbulbs.

Mandelli's legacy lives on not in tea but the animal kingdom. At least a half dozen birds carry his name, including Mandelli's bush-warbler, Mandelli's willow-warbler, Mandelli's snow-finch, and Mandelli's tit-babbler. The rare red-breasted (or Bhutan) hill partridge (*Arboricola mandellii*) is another. A dozen samples of these had been gathered by "Mr Mandelli's hunters" but "nothing absolutely is known of its habits, food or note," informed the three-volume *The Game Birds of India, Burmah, and Ceylon*,[22] coauthored by Hume, generous, at least, in his attribution. Details of Mandelli's spotted babbler (*Pellorneum ruficeps mandellii*), a rufous-colored bird with a puffy, pale breast streaked with browns and an upright tail, are more forthcoming. "They are very restless, energetic birds, constantly on the move and keeping up a never-ending chatter amongst themselves," reads the 1922 edition of another guide to British India's fauna. They are easy to watch if "perfectly still, but a movement of hand or foot sends them scuttling off into denser cover," the volume warn. "They have many sweet notes as well as harsh ones, but their prevailing note is that of the genus, a constantly repeated 'pretty-dear, pretty-dear.'"[23]

During Darjeeling's early decades, "all the managers and assistants on the estates [were] Europeans," the *Darjeeling Gazetteer* noted in 1907.

> It is a remarkable fact that, though educated natives are much cheaper than Europeans, it has not been found economical to employ them generally, although here and there a few natives have done remarkably well, and have proved themselves worthy of full trust in positions of responsibility. The result is that although the industry in the hills is now fifty years old, it is still almost entirely in the hands of Europeans.[24]

The exception was Makaibari. By the time this edition of the *Gazetteer* was published, the estate was already in its second generation of Indian ownership.

The man, though, who originally began planting out the garden in the mid-nineteenth century was a British officer, Captain Samler. After five years in the East India Company army, he had deserted along with ten Gorkha sepoys. They raided an armory at the base and headed 150 miles north to the heavily wooded slopes below Kurseong. It was the start of the monsoon, and the men planted maize—which would later lend the land they settled its name, Makaibari, "cornfield." By time the ears were tall and ripening, the military police had located the renegades. The men were prepared, though, and repelled a series of raids. Eventually the authorities left the fugitives alone. From the tea nursery that Dr. Campbell had started in Kurseong—the town hovered on the ridgeline above them—Samler swiped saplings and planted them on Makaibari.[25]

Meanwhile, down on the plains, a precocious fourteen-year-old boy named Girish Chandra (G. C.) Banerjee, from a rich land-owning Bengali family, ran away from home on his horse. With perfect English and impeccable handwriting, he found work on a British base.[26] He was clever, says Rajah Banerjee, his great-grandson, and by sixteen G. C. had cornered the pony express service between Kurseong and Darjeeling and then began buying prime land. At twenty he was already the wealthiest man in region. He had also become a close friend of Samler's.[27]

The British Crown granted Samler amnesty for his help during the 1857 rebellion, which some infer to mean that he helped track down and kill anyone suspected of taking part in the uprising.[28] (Rajah denies this.) The government recognized his estate. In 1859, he was appointed agent for the Darjeeling Tea Company and made legal owner of Makaibari. Samler died the same year, but a month before passing away, he sold the estate to his friend G. C. Banerjee, the first of four generations of Banerjees to control it.

While planters and their assistants on Darjeeling's estates were largely European, the laborers were all Nepalese. Cultivating tea in the hills requires a vast labor force, and manpower shortages have been a problem from the beginning. Even during Darjeeling's pioneering decades, growth outpaced the available labor supply.

When the British began establishing gardens in the mid-nineteenth century, the population of the Darjeeling region was scant. Unable to get enough local Lepchas, they brought in Gorkhas from Nepal. Outside the region Gorkhas are best known for their legendary military prowess and ubiquitous large, curved kukri swords. The British fought them in the Anglo-Gorkha War (1814–16) and then incorporated them into their army.*

Save for one caveat, the 1907 *Darjeeling Gazetteer* carried the typical enthusiastic attitude of early commentators on their work ethic: "The Nepalis, who form the great majority, although extremely improvident, are a cheerful, hardworking, and enterprising race, courageous to a degree, and pleasant to work with, so long as they are treated with fairness and consideration."[29] But the gardens required not just labor but *inexpensive* labor, which was, as the *Gazetteer* noted in that global and timeless dictum of economically profitable agriculture, "a matter of vital importance to the [tea] industry, as cheap labour is essential to its prosperity."[30]

Ultimately the gardens set up a system that would entice the workers to come and, importantly, remain. Along with daily wages, they were

---

* The British spell their name with a *u*—*Gurkahs*—though around Darjeeling it always has an *o*. They generally prefer to be called Indian Gorkha.

offered housing and basic necessities. Because the gardens were so isolated, they also received food rations. Workers and their families settled on the estates in small villages based largely on caste or clan. Spread over a garden's hillsides and surrounded by fields of tea, these consist of tight clusters of small, wood-framed homes with two or three rooms and a covered but usually open-air kitchen. Flowering plants, herbs, and the occasional ripening chili pod grow in chipped clay pots, chickens poke around, and pale pye-dogs lounge in the morning sun. Garden villages contain schools, temples, a day care, and a medical clinic, plus small shops selling staples from potatoes and batteries to soda and umbrellas.

Pay amounts are fixed across all of Darjeeling's estates in an agreement negotiated every three years between the Darjeeling Tea Association (DTA) and the Darjeeling Indian Tea Association (DITA), representing the gardens,* various unions representing the workers, and the West Bengal government. For April 1, 2011 to March 31, 2014, the daily pay rate was set at Rs 90 (about $1.60), with full pay for twelve weeks of maternity leave and two-thirds pay for sick days. Workers in the factories get another five or so rupees a day as they are considered "technical." This applies to spraying teams in the field as well. The extra money is known as "pay-of-post." Wages do not go down if a garden loses money.

But wages are only part of labor expenses. On top of salaries, a garden covers medicine and education costs. It contributes to a provident fund for retirement of fifteen days per each year of work, so that after forty years a worker receives the equivalent of six hundred days' pay. Babies get formula, infants get child care (allowing mothers to work), and children get schooling. Upon death, the garden provides wood for a pyre or a casket, depending on belief or preference. Per week, each permanent worker is allotted just over two pounds of rice plus eighteen ounces for each minor dependent, and five pounds of atta flour plus twenty-four ounces for each minor dependent for making flatbreads. And, of course, tea. Clean drinking water is provided, as well as blankets, rubber boots, firewood, and lime to whitewash their houses. Some estates encourage farming by giving tools and seeds for growing cardamom, ginger, turmeric, and oranges.

---

*The two are similar umbrella organizations. The DTA is older, larger—it represents about three-fourths of Darjeeling's gardens—and more active in labor issues.

Positions are hereditary. When a plucker retires, she can pass her right to a position on the estate to one of her children. Or sell it.

"Only in tea plantations are you taken care of from birth to death," Sandeep Mukherjee of the DTA said. In 2013, these additional items were valued by the Indian Tea Association at Rs 93.97 per worker per day, just above the daily wage.

Talking to a handful of men who grew up on Makaibari, the perquisite they remember most fondly as children was getting balls and boots to play on the estate's rough soccer pitch—a barren, flat expanse of dirt that drops immediately off to a nearly vertical ravine—among themselves but also in highly competitive intergarden games. While sport across India is dominated by cricket, Darjeeling (and Sikkim) is soccer country, and young boys frequently wear knockoff maroon-and-blue-striped Barça jerseys with, ideally, MESSI and the number 10 stenciled in gold across the back.

CHAPTER 13

Midnight's Planters

I ndia gained independence on August 15, 1947. A new era for the country ensued—and for Darjeeling tea. Many European owners sold their estates to wealthy Indians, perhaps believing they would never enjoy the same authority they had before.[1] In some cases, suppliers became owners. Local contractors, for instance, supplied wood for chests used to pack tea and, over the years, accrued credit. They tallied the IOUs and then paid the difference between what they were owed and the value of the estate.[2]

The changeover often meant that the new owners had fewer ties to the land. "Darjeeling's old managers had been rooted in the soil; they were linked to the pioneer planters and closely connected to each other through business or by marriage. Plantation labour accepted them as heaven-sent patriarchs. Tea was more than an industry, it was a way of life. The new proprietors were often wealthy businessmen who cut costs, demanded quick profits and operated long-distance."[3] They were looking closer at bottom lines than traditions.

During the nineteenth century, estates had been planted out in a forty-forty-twenty scheme: 40 percent for the tea crop, 40 percent left wild as a natural buffer and soil anchor, and the remainder for housing and workers' facilities. But many of the new crop of owners had terraces removed, shade trees cut to plant more tea shrubs, and allowed encroachment on the natural portions, all of which destabilized the land and caused topsoil losses. Following the industrial development so strongly advocated by the country's first prime minister, Jawaharlal Nehru, the new owners embraced the latest generation of chemical applications. Fascinated by science and believing that it "must be made the handmaiden of economic progress," Nehru was keen to make India a modern, industrialized nation as quickly as possible,[4] with farming a priority. "Everything else can wait," he said not long after independence, "but not agriculture."

"Until 1955–56 there were no chemicals in tea. It was organic," said Marybong's Vijay Dhancholia. That was when India began striving for food independence, Dhancholia explained, instead of buying "third-rate stuff from Australia and the USA" to feed the country's surging population. *Jai Jawan, Jai Kisan* (Hail the Soldier, Hail the Farmer) was a catchphrase coined in 1965 by the country's second prime minister, Lal Bahadur Shastri, to cheer on India's soldiers battling Pakistan along the Kashmir border, as well as farmers in their agricultural revolution. Fueling that modernizing sprint and spirit were chemical fertilizers, pesticides, herbicides, and fungicides. The 1966–67 harvesting year marked the onset of the *green revolution* in India, a term that didn't refer to the contemporary sense of natural or organic farming but rather making the best use of higher-yielding varieties and chemical inputs to increase production. This began a cycle of using progressively larger amounts of such inputs just to keep yields from falling.

As elsewhere in India, yields initially climbed on Darjeeling tea estates. Darjeeling estates produced 7.8 million kilograms (17.2 million pounds) of tea in 1951 and topped 10 million kilograms (22 million pounds) by 1960. To sustain levels above 10 million kilograms a year, more chemicals were thrown at the plants. These killed off useful microorganisms and also sapped the land of natural nourishment. The ground between the tea plants was kept clean so that the chemicals would be absorbed by the bushes, not weeds, which further contributed to soil erosion.

Farming had moved, within a few decades, from one extreme to another.

Although ousted as colonial rulers, the British still controlled the tea sector until 1974.[5] On the first day of that year the Foreign Exchange Regulation Act (FERA) of 1973 was instituted.* It tightened currency controls on foreign companies in India and instigated the Indianization, or rupeeization, of companies in the country by limiting foreign-owned stakes, making it harder to take profits out of India, and restricting

---

* This was replaced in 1999 with the Foreign Exchange Management Act, FEMA.

expansion and diversification.[6] Some companies complied with the new laws, but others simply left as a result. (Mostly famously, Coca-Cola pulled out rather than partner with an Indian company and turn over its secret recipe as the government demanded; they didn't return until 1993.)

While sectors, including those engaged in trading, could retain a maximum 40 percent foreign-equity holding, tea companies were given a special dispensation that allowed 74 percent ownership.[7] Even that was unpalatable. British firms in the tea industry that had stayed after independence had steadily been losing interest and had already begun exploring alternatives to growing tea in India. The new regulations provoked further divesting and accelerated development of estates in Kenya.[8] The East African country was blessed with altitude and rainfall—and room to expand. "The British had a major advantage in Africa," wrote E. Jaiwant Paul, onetime director of tea giant Brooke Bond India, "because they could take full benefit of their decades of experience in other countries and incorporate the more recent technical advances both in cultivation and in manufacture on the African estates."[9] Or, as Sandeep Mukherjee put it, "Any handicaps they had here they did away with in Kenya."

The shift was swift. The year of independence India exported 127.2 million kilograms (280 million pounds) of tea to the UK, half of its total production and the lion's share of its total exports. A decade later it hit 135.4 million kilograms, but then began to slide.[10] By 1977 UK imports had dropped to 74.3 million kilograms, and in 1987 they were a paltry 22.4 million kilograms, down nearly 85 percent from their 1947 level.[11] Currently Indian tea exports to the UK sit around 16 million kilograms. The UK now gets about 60 percent of its tea from Africa.[12] Today Kenya is the continent's tea giant and the world's fourth-largest producer. Grown largely in the highlands and nearly all CTC, the tea is bold and vigorous, fresh, and brews a reddish-coppery liquor. It is used in blending, often in breakfast teas.

When India lost the UK market, the USSR and Eastern Europe stepped in to replace it. In 1947, the Soviet Union imported just 4 million kilograms (8.8 million pounds) of tea from India; by 1991, imports had risen to 104.5 million kilograms (230 million pounds), 51.5 percent of India's total tea exports.[13]

Soviet buyers preferred dark brews rather than the fine and floral qualities of tea from the Darjeeling hills. "They wanted the cheapest," recalled the third-generation tea merchant Vijay Sarda in his Darjeeling shop Nathmulls. He sat on a stool at the door greeting acquaintances passing along the narrow sidewalk, while his son, Girish, stood behind the counter. "They'd say, 'We want tea in this price category and good for human consumption.' Those were the guidelines." He laughed and shook his head at the memory. "'And good for human consumption'!"

The breakup of the Soviet Union in 1991 threw the Indian tea industry into crisis. The trade agreements between the two countries that the industry had to come to rely on suddenly vanished. "We put all our eggs in one basket and pushed away the competition," the joint-secretary of the Indian Tea Association said in a 1994 *BusinessWeek* piece on Darjeeling's post-Soviet troubles.[14] With less money to spend, Russians began buying cheaper teas from places such as Sri Lanka instead of India, much less the pricey Darjeeling varieties.

Demand for Darjeeling tea plummeted and prices followed suit. That meant even less money to keep up the estates or reinvest in improving them. Many fell into ruinous conditions, were abandoned, or sold off. The total number of gardens, which had stood at 102 in 1990, fell to 83 by 1995.[15]

So Darjeeling turned its attention to Western Europe and Japan. To satisfy the Soviets' preference for big brews, heavy on liquor but less so on flavors or aromas, many Darjeeling estates had planted at least some Assam leaf, often on their lower, warmer sections. Estates began pulling these up and replanting with the smaller-leaf, slower-growing, and lower-yielding China *jat* on which Darjeeling's fame largely rests. Along with these, they began planting some of the excellent high-end cultivars grown from cuttings of strains well suited for Darjeeling's conditions that were being developed. And the gardens also began to urgently adopt farming practices that reduced their chemical and pesticide residues to permissible levels. With the Soviets, this had not been a concern, but Europeans were becoming much more conscious of the issue.[16]

Today, most Darjeeling tea is exported. The majority goes to Europe, and now sales being hit by the Eurozone crisis. "You can't avoid drinking water, but you *can* avoid drinking Darjeeling tea," said Mukherjee.

After independence, the Indian government began rupee-to-ruble trading with the USSR for machinery and fuel to grease its industrial revolution.[17] Tea was an important part of the goods that India bartered in exchange.[18] The concept was not new. The Chinese traded tea with the Tibetans for warhorses as far back as the seventh century, with the Russians for furs from Siberia in the seventeenth and eighteenth centuries, and then with the British—indirectly—for opium in the nineteenth.

In the spring of 2013, India once again floated the idea of bartering tea for oil, this time with Iran. "Iran used to be the highest paymaster," said Namring's H. R. Chaudhary, who has been managing in Darjeeling since 1971. "They went for quality, while the Russians, quantity." Europe and Japan today are, in Chaudhary's phrase, Darjeeling's top paymasters, and Iran may join them, at least in kind, in oil.

It seems more likely, though, that Russia, with its emerging moneyed class, could pay the highest amounts. An October 2013 charity auction in Moscow that offered 1.2-kilogram (2.6-pound) lots of first flush teas from twenty different Darjeeling gardens showed widespread interest. Chamong received $1,076 for one of their lots, but the winning bid went to a Castleton tea for $1,384.[19]

Today *tea planter* is a synonym for *garden manager* or *superintendent*. Though considered the most humble title of the trio, it retains romantic associations.

No one symbolizes that romance in Darjeeling more than Swaraj Kumar "Rajah" Banerjee on Makaibari. *Rajah* means "king" or "prince"; the nickname was earned at Goethals Memorial School, a Catholic boarding school between Kurseong and Darjeeling run by the Irish Christian Brothers, when he led a group of junior boys against senior bullies. The name stuck. Around Darjeeling, he is, by some distance, the most famous man in the business, and it feels appropriate. He has his world record, of course. He's published a glossy book, a documentary has been made about him, and the media make a direct line for Makaibari when looking for a sound bite or television segment on Darjeeling tea. Guests arrive daily, from famous agronomists and foreign tea makers to students.*

---

*Rajah Banerjee is a galvanizing figure and the lone person in the area about whom everyone offers an opinion. From fellow managers it is rarely positive. One source of recent criticism is that Makaibari is now packaging lower-priced green tea and a black tea called Apoorva and selling them widely on the national market from leaves sourced outside his garden. "It has degraded his brand," one merchant said. But it has made it the best-known Darjeeling tea in India, with forest-green or bright yellow packets emblazoned with Makaibari's ubiquitous logo widely recognized across the country. "Envy," his defenders call such sniping. Even his detractors say, "You have to appreciate his ability," and acknowledge what he has done in terms of the reputation of Darjeeling and its teas and his ability to soak up most of the media attention.

As he strolls confidently through Makaibari or sits behind his wide desks handling a stream of petitions, the title seems particularly fitting. He cares for the business as well as the aesthetics: he is house manager and head chef. He looks after its vision as well as day-to-day minutiae.

Nearly all of Darjeeling's tea estates are owned by Indian companies that have their headquarters in Kolkata. Some are small, family-run organizations with just a couple of properties in their portfolios. The owners of Glenburn have a single garden in Darjeeling and another in Assam, as is the case with Goomtee and also Jungpana. Selimbong has one in Darjeeling and another in Dooars. The Saria family, which controls Rohini and Gopaldhara, has another pair of tea estates in the Dooars. These tend to be run by multigenerations and passed down through the family.

Darjeeling, though, has, over the last few decades, become dominated by a handful of larger, in some cases global, groups that have been snapping up gardens appearing on the market. The Bagaria Group, with interests in steel, real estate, and wind farms along with tea, has three gardens, including two of the largest in Darjeeling (Phuguri and Gayabaree & Millikthong). The Goodricke Group—part of Camellia Plc UK, one of the last surviving London-controlled tea companies in India—owns eight gardens in Darjeeling, including the preeminent properties of Castleton, Margaret's Hope, Barnesbeg, and Thurbo. (They also have eleven gardens in Assam and another dozen in Dooars.) Jay Shree, part of the industrial conglomerate B. K. Birla Group, which refers to itself as the "First Family of India Inc.," has twenty-two gardens in India, six of them in Darjeeling, which produce about 11 percent of the area's total output. Ambootia's eleven gardens contribute more than 12 percent of that. Currently the Chamong group is the largest in the area, with thirteen gardens—eleven acquired between 2001 and 2004—that produce around 20 percent of Darjeeling's total tea.

All of these estates are run by managers who live on-site. They might have to decide exactly when the tea should be picked and exactly how it gets processed, but they answer to stakeholders often more concerned with numbers and shorter-term gains.

Yet, while some managers are almost clerks taking orders from the head office in distant Kolkata, this seems to be the exception. Darjeeling's tea planters are different from those elsewhere. To be successful in these hills, they must have deep passion. Even those running an estate for the largest groups care as much for the garden as if it were their own. While most managers start in the Dooars or Assam—where there are more gardens, more tea, and more job—once they end up at Darjeeling, they stay.

"Other areas don't have the history that Darjeeling has and don't have people who have lived there for more than twenty years," Vikram Mittal, the owner of Mittal Stores in New Delhi's Sunder Nagar market, said. As a top taster, blender, and merchant specializing in premium Indian teas, he is Sanjay Kapur's (and Aap Ki Pasand's) only real competitor in Delhi. Mittal's father opened the shop in 1954. Originally it sold a hundred items including tea. (Why tea? "The horoscope of my father said he should sell something black.") Gradually the other products fell away, and in 1978 it became a dedicated tea shop. Mittal Stores' selection is not extensive but is well chosen. Nonetheless, it doesn't fit inside the tiny shop. When it opens in the morning, a pair of assistants cart out large metal tins with tea, cardboard boxes, and sacks of bags and labels, and stack them in front of the shop in order to make room for customers. In the evening, they move it all back inside.

"People who fall in love with this place don't want to go anywhere else," Mittal observed. "They start interacting with the plants and factory and begin doing amazing things. Many of the people who have been producing good tea in Darjeeling do not have a lot of education but have a fertile mind. Over the years they have learned how, and when, to produce the best tea." There is no specific teacher-led training, but rather a clear sense of apprenticeship and learning on the ground.

Longevity is a Darjeeling trait. Rajah Banerjee was born on Makaibari and has been working on the estate since 1970. Namring's Chaudhary has been here in the hills for forty-four years and Singbulli's Satish Mantri for twenty-nine. Both men are among a number of Rajasthani planters. Chaudhary's brother is the manager of Lingia. Dhancholia at Marybong is also from Rajasthan, as is Rajesh Pareek on Tukvar. These men arrived in the green of the hills and never left, gaining an intimate knowledge of their garden in order to obtain the finest results from its unique set of materials and microclimate.

B. N. Mudgal personifies this ideal in his twenty-three years on Jungpana and in the isolated nature of the garden to the east of Kurseong. After a bouncing ride down a windy, rough dirt track through Goomtee Tea Estate, the road ends abruptly at a river. A wooden footbridge, slick on misty monsoon mornings, arcs over the tumbling runoff, and a trail heads up 638 uneven, slippery steps embedded in the hillside to the Jungpana factory and offices. The altitude change and climb leave an unaccustomed visitor's legs rubbery and heart palpitating, sweaty from the hike and the humidity but chilled by the high-elevation breezes.

Everything needs to be carried in by foot, including machinery parts and fuel for the factory as well as well as rice, atta flour, and other food staples. All of the tea is carried out. Every other day, men load wooden chests of tea on their backs, with a wide, steadying trump-line stretched across the forehead, and head down the hill.

For the first decade after independence, the Nepalese royal Rana family owned Jungpana before selling it to its current owners, the Kejriwals, in 1956. The estate's name comes from a legend of a Gorkha called Jung Bahadur, who was mauled by a leopard while hunting with a British sahib. The hunter carried Jung, calling out for *pana* (water), to a stream, where he died. Ever since, the area has been known as the place where Jung took his last drink. "We don't know the facts, but that's what the elderly people on the garden tell us," said Mudgal.

The south-facing garden is small, having just 73.6 hectares (182 acres) under tea, and spans from 2,900 to 3,300 feet, with a significantly higher-up out section called Mahalderam that ranges from 5,642 to 6,001 feet. The plucked leaves from those fields are loaded into gunny-sacks and slid down a steel cable to the factory to be processed—nearly three miles and a three-thousand-foot drop in just six minutes.

Jungpana produces only about 36,000 kilograms (80,000 pounds) of tea a year, a limited but consistently excellent output that is much sought after by clients that include Harrods and Fortnum & Mason in the UK, Mariage Frères and Fauchon in France, and the royal family in Japan. Many experts are calling it Darjeeling's top producer. Once the 2013 season wrapped up, the front page of the *Calcutta Telegraph* proclaimed A NEW CHAMP TAKES DARJEELING CUP.[20] Jungpana had knocked Castleton off its perch as the area's finest tea, the article argued. In the 2014 World Tea Championships held in the USA, Jungpana won the award for top Darjeeling tea.

Wholesale buyers seemed to agree with such judgment. In 2013, from April through the second week of November, the average price Jungpana's tea fetched at auction was Rs 856.33 per kilogram, far more than the next one, Castleton, which went for a third less at Rs 569.15.[21]

Darjeeling's best tea? "Each tea needs to be approached with an appreciation of its peculiarities and individual characteristics. You really can't compare between a Rembrandt and a Picasso. If my pockets are deep enough, I would buy them all!" Krishan Katyal, the chairman and managing director of J. Thomas & Co. in Kolkata, is quoted as saying in the *Telegraph* article.

Sanjay Sharma embodies the unsettled young man who ends up in the hills on a tea estate as randomly as his British predecessors, finds a passion when he begins interacting with the leaves, and creates something special.

Still in his early forties, he's young and confident, exceedingly sharp, with both handyman cleverness and book smarts, and, although somewhat wild as a young man, is no rogue. Or at least not completely. His father was one of India's most decorated fighter pilots, an expert on MiGs—he helped bring over the first planes from Russia—who fought in the 1971 war with Pakistan and, for three years, was head flight instructor at the Air Force Academy. He met Sanjay's mother, a nurse, while recuperating in a hospital after a faulty ejection from a jet. Sanjay was educated at St. Mary's High School, an Irish Christian Brothers boarding school in Mount Abu, Rajasthan, and then La Martinière College in Lucknow, finishing at a precocious fifteen. After two years studying at a medical college in Patna, Bihar, he realized the field didn't fully interest him and, at eighteen, transferred to the elite St. Stephens College in Delhi to study literature. Casting about for something to do after graduation, Sanjay landed an interview with a large international tea company that controlled numerous estates.

Of tea he knew almost nothing. The company was looking for OLQ, Sanjay explained using Indian air force jargon, "officer-like qualities." As in the recruitment ideals at J. Thomas & Co., they were seeking sportsmen. Bright and energetic, he had the ability to lead and the drive to win. They hired him and sent him to work on their Soom Tea Estate.

Sanjay immediately took to the isolated life in the hills, a turn that surprised his friends and fellow Stephanians, who were getting rich in the media and financial worlds, writing books, or entering politics, while he worked as a modest assistant on a tea garden. "As a new assistant manager, you basically know nothing," he said, walking up through the nursery. Fields of tea rose all around. The morning light caught dozens of greenish spiderwebs strung between tall shade trees that held palm-size golden orb-weavers with striped, yellow-jointed legs. "Technically you're an executive, but even the lowest-paid worker on the estate knows more about tea than you do." He watched and listened carefully—he quickly picked up the local language—and was lucky to have had a good head worker who taught him much. Stopping at a covered mound of composted earth, he took a handful and breathed in the humus and loam. "As a planter," he said, "you have to love the smell of soil."

In 2001, at twenty-eight years old—the youngest in modern Darjeeling history— Sanjay was named manager of Glenburn when the garden was taken over by new owners. "I jumped the queue," he quipped, adding with a laugh that this didn't endear him to many at the Planters' Club. Sanjay has a deep and infectious enthusiasm for what he does, and a sense of pride that permeates his undertakings. No matter if he has been up into the late hours of the night, he rises early to check on the factory. He is energetic but has a calm presence and uses a quick and gentle wit to diffuse moments rather than his voice. Things get quietly done. He carries complete authority on the garden, but out of respect rather than fear, and appears extremely well liked by the Gorkhas, with whom he banters in their own language.

"Tea planting, as a profession, is unrivaled in the varied interests it involves," wrote tea historian William Ukers in the 1930s, "but its greatest attraction lies in the fact that it appeals to the creative instinct in man."[22] That appeal remains. Tea planting, Sanjay said, "is unrivaled in scope for creativity. It's endless."

For him, there is creativity in dealing with a thousand full-time workers and all the elements that come with running a 758-hectare (1,873-acre) estate with eight villages housing 708 families and some 5,000 people. There is creativity in the field, getting the bushes to produce the best leaves they can, and in the factory, eking out the finest possible teas from them.

When Sanjay began at Glenburn, the garden was not known for its consistently high-quality teas. Under him, Glenburn began steadily turning out excellent harvests, with a few of his vintages being simply superb. Tubelike canisters, decorated with antique botanical drawings of tea plants and flowers, of Glenburn's various flushes sell in some of the most exclusive shops in India and abroad.

While one of the estate's newly developed specialty teas recently won an important industry award, Sanjay is particularly proud of the excellent monsoon teas, made when the leaf quality is the worst and the conditions are the most difficult, much in the way a chef admires a sublime dish created using only the cheapest, boniest fish in the sea: taking inferior raw materials, working within—even being inspired by—their constraints, and, as he says, "throwing them out in a certain fantastic light."

One duty that Sanjay, perhaps uniquely, relishes is that of snake catcher. Glenburn has cobras, kraits, and vipers—the Big Three of deadly snake families in India—as well as other, less venomous species. "Snakes control the rodents on the farm," he said, scrolling through some recent photos on his smartphone of him holding snakes. "There used to be a reward paid for every snake that was killed. Now I pay a reward for every snake that is *alive*." He shrugged. "So they call me."

His snake catching began at five and has not been without its mishaps. A highly venomous Indian cobra—*Naja naja*, with its flared hood and double-monocle markings—bit him on the left hand. "I was thirteen and holding a cobra and riding a 250 cc motorcycle," Sanjay said, screwing his finger into his temple. He spent two and half months in the hospital as the doctors tried to stop the local necrosis—where the flesh dies and rots away—on his hand and danger of gangrene. At one point, doctors even wanted to amputate his arm at the elbow, he explained, sipping a well-watered Scotch whisky on the *burra* bungalow's deep, wide verandah. They managed to save it through a series of surgeries, including a skin graft from his thigh to a sizable part of the top of his hand. The scar runs from above the wrist to near the knuckles.

On Glenburn he continued to use his bare hands to catch snakes, placing them in an old plastic bag and driving to a secluded spot on the estate to release them away from the villages. Sometimes plans go awry. In late spring, a ten-foot-long python he had captured slithered out of the bag in the backseat. The snake wound under the driver's seat and nestled around the pedals as he jolted down a steep gravel garden road. He laughed at the absurdity of it and found a photo of himself catching hold of the snake near the steering wheel. He wrested the python back into the sack and continued down to the river. He slipped off his shoes and crossed the low, premonsoon river to let it go. In one hand he held the snake's head—the size of a small dog—and with the other its body, as the serpent wound a stretch of itself around his upper arm, slipping the tip of the tail under a loop as if tying a nautical knot. As Sanjay stood on the shore, the snake cinched its grip. In a photograph of him at that moment, his head has quickly turned, his expression changed, his flashy smile gone.

He laughed at the image and looked down at his empty tumbler. "It's time for dinner, yeah?"

CHAPTER 14

Crises

Vast as a continent, India has an appetite that's great, and potential that's even greater. We are in her century. The country is growing in power and stature on the world stage. Flexing newly toned muscles causes global repercussions as it vies to become one of the century's three great powers. She's an innovative, dynamic place where the modern and the traditional exist side by side—IT workers and naked, ash-smeared sadhus, tridents held high, striding with righteousness down a city street; bullock carts and Google glasses; pilgrimages up the Ganges and a mission to Mars.

The country's population is more than 1.2 billion and set to eclipse China's by 2030[1]—the same year it is slated to become the world's third-largest economy. The swelling middle class now numbers around 300 million, up from just 25 million in the early 1990s. Such economic clout is not without precedence. "During the first millennium A.D. merchants referred to India as the 'Bird of Gold' due to the glittering dynamism of its market," the global consulting firm McKinsey & Company stated in a 2007 paper on the rise of India's consumer class. From A.D. 1 until A.D. 1000 India had the world's largest economy, accounting for a third of the global gross domestic product (GDP)—three times greater than Western Europe's and significantly higher than the entire Roman Empire's 21 percent.[2] By 1500, India had fallen to second, at 24.4 percent (compared to China's 24.8 percent). During Mughal rule, it maintained its vigor and ranking, but then slipped under the British. By 1820, it had fallen to 16 percent (to China's 33 percent), and at independence in 1947 to a meager 4 percent. The slide continued, its global GDP shrinking to 3.1 percent in 1973.[3]

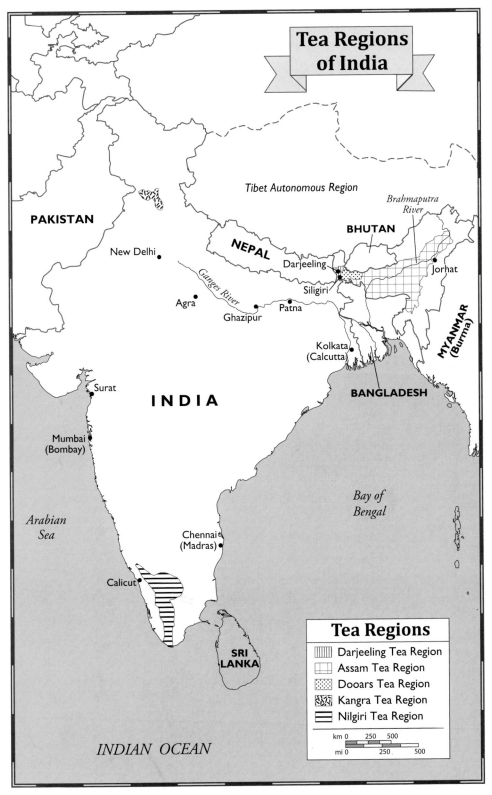

Tea Regions of India

PAKISTAN

Tibet Autonomous Region

Brahmaputra River

NEPAL

BHUTAN

New Delhi

Darjeeling

Jorhat

Siligiri

Ganges River

Agra

Patna

Ghazipur

MYANMAR (Burma)

Kolkata (Calcutta)

Surat

I N D I A

BANGLADESH

Mumbai (Bombay)

Bay of Bengal

Arabian Sea

Chennai (Madras)

Calicut

SRI LANKA

Tea Regions

▦	Darjeeling Tea Region
▦	Assam Tea Region
▦	Dooars Tea Region
▦	Kangra Tea Region
▦	Nilgiri Tea Region

km 0   250   500

mi 0   250   500

INDIAN OCEAN

India produces about one billion kilograms of tea a year. Each of the country's growing regions gives a different character to the final cup. (Gary Antonetti)

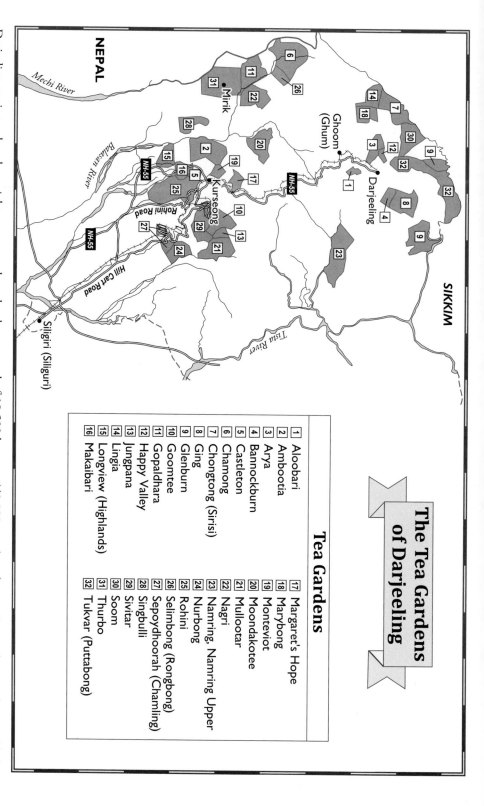

The Tea Gardens of Darjeeling

Tea Gardens

1 Aloobari		17 Margaret's Hope	
2 Ambootia		18 Marybong	
3 Arya		19 Monteviot	
4 Bannockburn		20 Moondakotee	
5 Castleton		21 Moolootar	
6 Chamong		22 Nagri	
7 Chongtong (Sirisi)		23 Namring, Namring Upper	
8 Ging		24 Nurbong	
9 Glenburn		25 Rohini	
10 Goomtee		26 Selimbong (Rongbong)	
11 Gopaldhara		27 Sepoydhoorah (Chamling)	
12 Happy Valley		28 Singbulli	
13 Jungpana		29 Sivitar	
14 Lingia		30 Soom	
15 Longview (Highlands)		31 Thurbo	
16 Makaibari		32 Tukvar (Putabong)	

Darjeeling tea is produced on eighty-seven gardens that have a total of 19,500 hectares (48,000 acres) under tea. Recent harvests have yielded only around eight million kilos of finished tea. (Gary Antonetti)

The leaves, flowers, and seeds of *Camellia sinensis*—tea.

Darjeeling was originally established as a hill station retreat for East India Company employees to rest and recuperate in the cool mountain air. Mt. Kanchenjunga overlooks the city.

As governor-general of India, the controversial Lord William Bentinck formed the Tea Committee in 1834 and was instrumental in helping to establish India's tea industry.

In the 1840s, the great botanist and explorer Joseph Dalton Hooker spent three years in the Darjeeling hills, Sikkim, and Nepal identifying and collecting plants.

Early Darjeeling tea pluckers with a European overseer. (James Sinclair)

Established in 1868, Darjeeling's Planters' Club (on the right) was, until recently, the center of social life for tea planters. (Ratna Pradhan/DAS Studio)

Dr. Nathaniel Wallich was superintendent of the East India Company's botanic garden in Calcutta for three decades and was at its helm when wild tea was found growing in Assam. Considered the Empire's nursery, the garden was fundamental in developing a tea industry on the subcontinent. (Wellcome Library)

The Scottish plant hunter Robert Fortune added, by his own estimation, nearly twenty thousand Chinese tea plants to the young Indian industry, giving it the quality it desired. (© President and Fellows of Harvard College, Arnold Arboretum Archives)

Robert Fortune gradually perfected the technique for sending tea plants and seeds from China to India in glass Wardian cases.

The charismatic Rajah Banerjee tastes some of Makaibari Tea Estate's iconic teas. His family owned Darjeeling's most famous garden for more than 150 years. (Getty Images)

Winding up through tea estates, the road to Darjeeling from the plains is slow, steep, and scenic.

Ambootia Tea Estate, one of Darjeeling's biodynamic gardens

Makaibari Tea Estate, just below Kurseong. On clear days, the view stretches down to the plains.

Sanjay Sharma inspects a field of young tea interwoven with blossoming marigolds on Glenburn Tea Estate.

Autumn on the Ging Tea Estate with the snow-capped Himalayas in the background

The view from Glenburn Tea Estate of Mt. Kanchenjunga. At 28,169 feet, it's the world's third-tallest peak behind Everest and K2.

High-end specialty teas like Glenburn Tea Estate's Silver Needle have recently become an important part of many gardens' portfolios. These are packed in traditional wooden chests to prevent breakage.

A classic Darjeeling pluck consists of just the tender first two leaves and a still-curled bud. It takes about twenty-two thousand of these to make a single kilogram of tea.

Tea pluckers working a section of Castleton Tea Estate during the first flush.

Plucking in Darjeeling is highly selective, can only be done by hand, and is made more challenging by the steep terrain. The average plucker produces under four hundred pounds of finished tea a year, less than a quarter of one in Assam.

After being weighed, freshly plucked tea leaves are withered overnight in long, narrow wooden troughs where they lose about two-thirds of their moisture. H. R. Chaudhary checks the leaves on Namring Tea Estate to see if they are ready to be rolled.

Rolling the withered leaves initiates the fermentation (or oxidation) process by rupturing the cells and releasing the natural juices of the leaves. When exposed to the air, they begin to oxidize, which acts as a catalyst for the characteristics associated with Darjeeling tea.

Once the leaves have been rolled, they are spread out on fermentation beds where they develop their pungency, strength, and aroma. Determining when the leaves have reached their peak and when the fermentation process needs to be immediately halted by firing them in a dryer is the most critical part of tea making.

The liquor—the infused liquid—of Darjeeling tea changes in color throughout the year. First flush teas are pale gold, often with a hint of green.

A range of second flush and monsoon teas on Goomtee Tea Estate. The liquor has deepened in color to amber, copper, and tawny. Teas from the final flush in autumn tend to be ruddy copper, bright auburn, or even burgundy.

A hand-stenciled sack of tea on Goomtee Tea Estate

Vijay Dhancholia conducts a daily tasting on Marybong Tea Estate with the assistant manager, Normal Chhetri.

Girish Sarda at Darjeeling's storied tea store Nathmulls. Opened in 1931, Nathmulls sells around 150 different Darjeeling teas.

Christened "Tea Deva" by Rajah Banerjee when first found on Makaibari Tea Estate, the insect mimics a tea leaf.

The verandah of the Planters' Club. Today it is officially known as the Darjeeling Club.

But it turned, eventually. The sluggish economy built momentum and sprinted ahead to double digits, hitting 10.5 percent economic growth in 2010. Though it has since cooled, the World Bank hailed this turnabout as "one of the most significant achievements of our times."[4]

Yet among breakneck growth and staggering accomplishments that include the doubling of life expectancy, leaps in literacy, becoming polio-free, and an agricultural revolution in which India has achieved self-sufficiency in almost all products (and surpluses in staples such as rice and wheat), stiff growing pains remain for the world's largest democracy. Poverty continues to be a major challenge for India. While the percentage of those in poverty has decreased over the last years, because of population growth the gross number of poor has actually increased. More than 400 million live below the extreme poverty line of $1.25 a day, a third of the world's total living in such poverty.[5] Per capita expenditure on food has risen while, paradoxically, caloric intake has decreased: More than 30 percent of India's population are getting below the benchmark twenty-four hundred calories a day.[6] An overwhelming 40 percent of the world's malnourished children are in India, an estimated 217 million.[7] Amid the many other serious health matters, the country has a quarter of the global burden of tuberculosis, with an estimated 2.2 million new cases every year[8]—someone in India dies every ninety seconds from TB.[9] Delhi is now the world's most polluted city.[10]

Creating jobs is a challenge for the government. Nearly half of India's population is under twenty-five years old—a bottom-heavy demographic that could become a time bomb if the GDP hits the breaks and growth decelerates too much. Providing energy is another challenge. India has around 17 percent of the world's population and is the fourth-largest consumer of energy after the USA, China, and Russia,[11] but according to OPEC, it has only about one third of a single percent of the globe's proven oil reserves.

Inflation has hit double digits, and the currency has lost a third of its value in the last two years. For the first decade of the twenty-first century the exchange rate varied between Rs 40 and Rs 50 to $1. In August 2011, it was trading just above Rs 44 when it began to slide. And then tumble. It lost more than 13 percent of its value in three months over the summer of 2013, bottoming out at Rs 68.85 at the end of August, when it sank 3.7 percent on its biggest single-day percentage drop in more than two decades. As 2014 began, it had edged back closer to Rs 62, but it would take significantly more push to return to its Rs 55 level, where it had been before its historic summer 2013 nosedive.

While these are all serious issues that directly or indirectly affect Darjeeling, a number of specific local problems are particularly pressing and immediately more devastating to its tea industry.

Darjeeling tea is under serious threat. India's marquee product is fighting for its future on three separate and crippling fronts that have already pushed production numbers down to their lowest level in many decades and thrust the industry into dire straits: changes in the climate, labor issues, and a political fight for independence from West Bengal.

Hurry Mohun Sannial, overseer of Bengal's Public Works Department, wrote the first history of Darjeeling authored by a person of Indian origin and to be published in Bengali. He fretted that the weather was changing. The cutting of timber and large-scale clearing of the forests was causing it to rain less. Streams carried less water, temperatures were rising, and Darjeeling was receiving less snowfall than before. Deforestation was causing problems with water retention, and he worried about the effect on the vegetation and sustainability of the land. The influx of people was also contributing to the rising temperatures. "Only God knows how densely this place, now a sort of sanatorium, will be populated in times to come."[12] He wrote his book in 1880. The viceroy had just visited Darjeeling, the town was on the cusp of being fashionable, and its tea industry would soon accelerate its growth with the arrival of the Darjeeling Himalayan Railway.

What would Sannial think today? The 2011 census put the population of Darjeeling's district at more than 1.8 million, up 15 percent since 2001 and nearly 25 percent since 1991. (The Darjeeling municipality is 120,000.) This unprecedented growth has brought urbanization, industrialization, and road building. Increased traffic has resulted in a keen uptick of pollution and further destabilization of already unsteady slopes with the continual vibrations from heavy trucks and buses. Long backups make getting to Darjeeling from the plains arduous, and traffic jams in the city itself form in the early hours of the day and last into the evening. The hills are being overharvested for food and overgrazed by animals, stripped illegally of their timber to use for firewood and home building, and gradually being deforested. With climatic changes, the weather has become erratic. Glaciers are receding. Daily temperatures have risen, nights don't cool as they once did, and a sudden hailstorm can batter a hillside of tea bushes with ice.

Particularly problematic is the erratic and unpredictable monsoon. "The spread is uneven," said water-management consultant R. N. Chatterjee. "In total, not a significant drop if you see the general statistics," but the monsoon now generally begins later. As rain affects a garden's production during the prime manufacturing periods, some gardens have started irrigating their dehydrated bushes as a precaution. Irrigation isn't to increase yield, Chatterjee added, "but as a tool against, or insurance against, crop loss. It's only for obtaining what they would normally have attained." This is especially important with the opening harvest. Hitting first flush is key. "It's like running the hundred-meter dash," said Sanjay Sharma. "If you stumble out of the blocks, you are still running, but you can never catch up."

"We always start the new year with a drought," the DTA's Sandeep Mukherjee said. "When we want rain, there is none, and when we don't, there is too much" goes the typical complaint by tea planters. At Glenburn, rain measurements show the garden received nine inches *less* during the 2013 monsoon than in the previous one. But then the rain came when it wasn't supposed to. "In October we had sixteen centimeters [6.5 inches] of rain, compared to less than two centimeters [0.75 inches] in 2012," Sharma said at the end of the season.

The key for tea is that the rainfall be evenly distributed. The Darjeeling area lacks ponds or reservoirs to trap the abundance when it does fall. The water just runs off the land rather than being absorbed into it. Natural underground wells and perennial springs are not being refilled. The streams have been reduced to trickles, and taps frequently go dry.

The felling of timber is exacerbating the situation. The trees not only absorb the monsoon rain and gradually release moisture into the earth and mountain springs, but also anchor the land with their roots and protect topsoil. With their disappearance when it rains, the soil on the steep slopes erodes, and landslides are a severe problem. Deep, V-shaped gullies scar the hillsides. Seen for miles around, they are eyed with concern as they slowly expand and threaten to slide even farther. The tradition of harvesting ginger, potatoes, onions, and other root crops in September and October, just after the monsoon, makes the land even more vulnerable to erosion by breaking up the soil.

Even the soil that isn't being washed away is worn-out, depleted. Decades of use of pesticides and fertilizers have rendered the soil barren and reduced its quality.

The tea bushes are dying and being replaced at a rate of only 2 percent a year. Time is a primary factor, as it take years for a bush to come to full bearing. Five years plus one additional year for every thousand feet, runs the planter's rule of thumb, but various factors, including the weather, affect this. A section on Gopaldhara planted at seven thousand feet took fourteen to fifteen years to produce a good, full harvest. Added to this is the fear of tearing up the fragile hillsides and of compromising quality by replacing the often-century-old bushes. "The old ones have the quality that Darjeeling is known for," said Vijay Dhancholia at Marybong. "You don't want to mess with Darjeeling quality."

Quality remains the optimal word. With limited output and high production costs, Darjeeling can never compete in price or volume. "You have to make quality teas," said Rishi Saria at Gopaldhara. "Unless you are making excellent-quality teas, why should anyone talk to us?"

The Darjeeling tea industry employs around fifty-five thousand permanent workers and another eighteen thousand temporary ones during the mid-March-to-mid-November plucking season.

But unauthorized worker absenteeism has become acute. In summer, Suman Das, assistant manager at Thurbo, said it was 30 percent on the estate. "Fifteen years ago when I started it was five percent maximum. *Max*imum." Even just five years ago, it was only 5–10 percent for most gardens. No longer. When the 2013 plucking season began in March, the DTA put the average at 25 to 30 percent. Yet it ran higher than that on most estates as the season progressed. "The leaf is there," said the factory manager at Goomtee in July, "but the workers are not." Goomtee was seeing 30 to 35 percent absenteeism. Some days it hit 40 percent. Several gardens struggled to contain levels that reached close to 50 percent.

Money is the knee-jerk answer given for the sudden change. From 2001 to 2008, the daily wage for a plucker rose just a total of Rs 12.10. In 2008—after a fifteen-day strike by workers—it was increased from Rs 53.90 to Rs 67, with a cumulative Rs 13.10 increase spread over three years. In 2011, the unions wanted the daily wage to rise to between Rs 120 and 154. Predictably, owners balked. As the first flush got under way, unions embargoed the dispatch of all tea. Gardens were heavily guarded and not a single leaf was allowed to leave. In early April, the owners, desperate not to miss out on their important spring harvest, agreed to Rs 90 plus perks valued around the same amount. That was a 34 percent increase—the largest annual wage increase in Darjeeling's history. As 70 percent of the cost of producing tea is labor, that immediately pushed up a garden's total production cost by nearly a quarter.

Among some management, the thought was "Well, we'll pay, but at least they'll show up to work," one planter recalled. "They didn't."

For many workers, the pay is simply not enough for essentials, much less to get ahead. "Life is too expensive," a worker on Makaibari complained. "You can buy nothing with ninety rupees." In nearby Kurseong, a liter of petrol costs Rs 85 (roughly $6.20 per gallon), and a chicken in the market costs Rs 180. Individual cigarettes sell for Rs 6 in the small shops around Makaibari (a day's work for fifteen smokes!), a single building brick for a house costs Rs 7, and a two-liter bottle of Coke costs Rs 52. Prices are higher on gardens farther from towns and their markets. That same Coke costs Rs 68 on Glenburn, and a bar of Lux soap goes for Rs 22, with the more luxurious Dove for exactly double that.

So pluckers look for work elsewhere.

Yet, because of the live-in system and the convoluted laws about firing workers, gardens continue to pay periodically absent workers and cannot easily replace them.

But even if they could, the vacuum is nearly impossible to fill. Estates along main roads can try to import day laborers. Castleton, which edges Kurseong, for instance, is in a privileged location, and with absenteeism running around 35 percent, according to one of the garden's accountants in autumn, it was bringing in a few hundred workers every morning in the back of pickups. These could be seen grinding up the steep, narrow roads to Kurseong in the early morning. But busing in a daily workforce is difficult and expensive and is merely a stopgap. During the 2013 harvests, few gardens were even attempting it. Some tried to make up their labor deficit by offering their own workers higher bonuses or extra plucking hours for those who wanted more work, and by pulling women out of retirement. Others simply chose which sections of the estates to best focus their workers' energies on.

Mechanizing is not an option. The steepness of the slopes and the selective plucking required make this impossible, while the continually shifting leaf and climate variables make automation in processing tea equally unfeasible.

Ironically Jungpana, long hindered by its isolation and the additional effort in bringing up goods and getting out tea, is seeing the lowest absenteeism in the district. "It's not an issue," said Jungpana's assistant manager, S. K. Choudhary, while walking through the misty monsoon fields of the garden. "Just ten or eleven percent." For one, it's too far to go for workers to find other day jobs.*

Labor shortages do not just reduce the quantity of tea a garden can produce, but can also harm its quality. Tea bushes need to be plucked every week, and gardens require a crew that can manage a seven-day plucking round.† The quality of the tea suffers if the leaves cannot be plucked at that interval.

Finding workers is exacerbated by the promise of higher salaries elsewhere. Dreams of a more middle-class lifestyle are drawing the labor pool away from Darjeeling's gardens, as is the Indian government's rural-development scheme that offers guaranteed work on low-skilled projects such as road building.

But doubling, even tripling, pay does not appear to offer much of a solution.

"There are three reasons why the labor problem is not only about wages," explained Sandeep Mukherjee in his office during the first flush. First is education. The parents of today's workers were illiterate. "Now the kids go to school and don't want to follow what their parents did." While many do not finish their studies and few go on to university, they are far from uneducated. The schooling, even half-finished, is a stepping-stone off the garden. At Glenburn, Namring, and many other estates, education is a priority for management, and they do what they can to supplement the government's resources. Namring has sixteen schools on the estate. The garden now offers a choice between Nepali-medium or English-medium schools. Paradoxically, managers acknowledge they are actively, passionately, and purposefully educating away their future workforce.

Television also plays a major role in the labor problem. Previous generations of pluckers were not exposed to the world beyond the tea estates. They stayed "cooped up" on the garden, spent their whole lives

---

*Even Jungpana is not immune to labor issues. During the 2014 monsoon flush, the owners took the unprecedented step of temporarily suspending all work operations along with pay and rations. They cited intimidation and threats from union officials interfering with managerial decisions. Tactics included *gharaoing*, a protest method of surrounding someone with a large group of people—often for many hours—until demands are met. It took two weeks and three rounds of meetings to negotiate the garden's reopening.

† As there is no plucking on Sundays, a seven-day round is actually six plucking days.

there, and usually knew little outside the hills. Now they have TV and can glimpse the rest of the world. "They can't help but see what others have and what they have and compare the two." Mukherjee stopped there, not needing to add the connecting thought: now they want more.

Exposure to education and the world at large has produced aspirations. "They know that if they stay, they will go no further than their parents," Mukherjee said, watching his cigarette smoke float out an opened window. "They want to go further than their parents." And the parents want their kids to go further.

One father in his thirties at Castleton Tea Estate stands in for many. His mother had been a plucker on the garden, his grandmother, and most likely his great-grandmother. His wife plucked for two years before she quit. It wasn't worth it, they decided, and they sold her hereditary position on the estate for Rs 10,000 ($180). Their house was built and renovated by the family, and the garden cannot kick them out, he said, so they continue to live on Castleton but receive nothing from the estate. He works as a driver for a hotel in Kurseong and makes only marginally more than he would on the tea estate—Rs 3,500 (about $65) a month—"but I can learn more, like practice my English," he said. Here he has hope of advancing. He and his wife have two young daughters and are paying for a private school in Kurseong.

Would he want his daughters to work on the garden? "No way." He shook his head sharply. If the gardens paid not Rs 90 but, say, double that? "My wife would return," he thought. His kids? He shook his head again. Rs 400? Rs 600? He kept shaking his head. "If our daughter is working on a tea estate, we are not proud," he said self-assuredly. "If she is working a government job, we are proud."

What is happening in Darjeeling is part of a larger, nationwide trend—a global one, actually—of people fleeing rural agricultural work. Indians have become more mobile, able to go out and seek a better—or at least different—life away from the fields. Their parents and grandparents and great-grandparents did not have that option. The tea estates in Darjeeling are not immune, and the younger generation is fleeing the Himalayan foothills of their birth.

"No matter how much we pay," Mukherjee said, "the mind-set has already settled in the younger generation. Anything but pluck tea."

"There is no solution," said Rajesh Pareek on Tukvar.

Sanjay Sharma agreed, "There is no solution because it will continue to rise."

• • •

Another issue for Darjeeling is the separatist movement by ethnic Gorkhas, who make up three-fourths of the region's population and essentially all of the tea industry's workforce. Darjeeling is the northernmost part of West Bengal, a state about the size of Maine or Portugal with a population of more than 90 million people (to Maine's 1.3 million and Portugal's 10.5 million). Darjeeling remains under the administrative power of Kolkata, at the opposite end of the state some four hundred miles away, although not without significant local opposition. *Bandhs*, or shutdowns—those who dare open their shop risk having it burnt down—strikes, "agitations," violence, and curfews have been roiling the area and disrupting life in the hills (and even tea production) as Gorkhas press their demands for their own independent state within India.

The Darjeeling hills have, over centuries, been under the control of Sikkim, Nepal, and Bhutan, and then the British after they scooped it up in the 1830s, but not Bengal, argue statehood proponents, nor has it ever been politically, socially, linguistically, or culturally part of it. Outside the hills, Indian Gorkhas feel—and are treated like—foreigners, they say. "Historically and geographically, Darjeeling, the *land of the Indian Gorkhas*, has always been part of the Indian Nation—*but the people of Darjeeling* never were, and have no desire to ever be, part of the *State* of Bengal. It's as simple as that," wrote Basant Lama in the preface of his *The Story of Darjeeling*,[13] relying heavily on italics throughout for emphasis. "All the Indian Gorkha is asking for is that Darjeeling, the land of his forefathers . . . *be once again detached* from Bengal and restored to its original status as a separate homeland for the Indian Gorkhas within the constitutional framework of India."[14]

Sikkim, to the north of Darjeeling, with a population of only half a million and a land area of just 2,740 square miles (the size of Delaware), has its own state. But not Darjeeling.

According to the current chief minister of West Bengal, Mamata Banerjee, who has reiterated her stand in area rallies, West Bengal and Darjeeling are inseparable. Opponents of Gorkhaland's aspirations often argue against further fragmenting the country, or even the state. Bengal has been painfully divided before. In 1905 the viceroy of India, Lord Curzon, effected the partition of Bengal, only to have it reunited in 1911, until it was, again, divided in 1947 between West Bengal and East Bengal (which eventually became Bangladesh). Some opponents to independent statehood argue that the Gorkhas are new immigrants, settling only a century and a half ago, recent by Indian standards, and not entitled to carve out their own state.

Gorkhaland statehood demands aren't new. Calls for autonomy from West Bengal first sounded in 1907. In 1980, the Gorkha National Liberation Front (GNLF) was formed and launched a series of often violent protests. In 1987 a forty-day *bandh* culminated in the establishment of the Darjeeling Gorkha Hill Council (DGHC). Some years of stability followed. But a harder-line faction within the party thought the GNFL had traded the council for statehood ambitions. With conflicts and infighting marring the organization, a splinter group formed, Gorkha Janmukti Morcha (GJM), which took over power of the Darjeeling hills in 2008 and ratcheted up the bid for Gorkhaland with fitful and disruptive agitations.

At the end of January 2011, the GJM began a lengthy *bandh*—with a single exemption: tea plantations. That changed by early February when police killed three GJM activists. As 2011's first flush readied to be plucked, the hills were silent, businesses shuttered, roads empty. At the time, the managing director of one of Darjeeling's largest groups of tea estates said, "If the political problems remain, the Darjeeling tea industry will be ruined." Another group head agreed: "If political problems and shutdowns continue, it will spell the doom for the Darjeeling tea industry."[15]

Politically, though, the move proved effective. In July 2011, the GJM, the West Bengal state government, and the federal Indian government signed an agreement to set up an autonomous administrative body for the Darjeeling hills with substantially more powers over socioeconomic, agricultural, infrastructural, educational, cultural, and linguistic issues. Elections took place at the end of July 2012, with the GJM sweeping all 45 seats unopposed.

From the outset, whether this would lead to a significant level of autonomy, even independence, or whether it was merely a placating move on the part of the government remained to be seen. The leader of the GJM, Bimal Gurung, continued to insist that the agreement was "only the preparation for the separate state of Gorkhaland."[16] While Chief Minister Banerjee categorically refused to consider this option, Gurung saw it happening within a year. When Gurung was sworn in as the president of the newly created Gorkha Territorial Administration (GTA) in August, he reiterated his push for independence. "I will not let it delay further," he stressed. "In six months."[17]

The relationship between Gurung's GJM and Banerjee and her Trinamool Congress Party settled into an uneasy truce, even with the GJM rhetoric of "violence and bloodbath" if its demand for separated statehood was not met. While uncertainty dominated, 2013's first and second flushes passed without major political incidents on the tea estates.

But then at the end of July 2013, as monsoon teas were being plucked and processed, India's ruling Congress Party offered statehood to Telangana, in Andhra Pradesh. "They granted Telangana statehood, so why not Gorkhaland?" went the familiar cry. Gurung resigned as head of the GTA and called an indefinite *bandh*. A GJM supporter immolated himself. Tourists and students were asked to leave. Shops closed, roads emptied, and hotels shut. Schools canceled classes. Boarding students were sent home. Nothing could move. Vehicles on the road were burned. "There will be hardships but our movement will continue," Gurung said.[18]

Again, tea estates were given an exemption. Yet this time they could not bring anything into the estates—food, fuel—nor take any tea out. Bushes need to be plucked; harvesting continued. Sacks of finished tea stacked up as stocks of coal, fuel, atta flour, and rice dwindled. Whenever a day's relaxation in the *bandh* allowed people to restock basic necessities, convoys of trucks loaded with tea made their way down out of the hills as quickly as possible.

Finally, on September 10, 2013, after nearly six weeks, the *bandh* was suspended. Traffic returned to the roads. At the end of October, Chief Minister Banerjee arrived in the Darjeeling hills for a five-day visit. Gurung reversed his stance, met with her, and promised to call no more *bandhs*.

In the run-up to the 2014 Indian general election, Gurung took a new approach. The GJM switched its support to the Narendra Modi–led Bharatiya Janata Party's parliamentary candidate for Darjeeling. After the BJP's landside victory, Gurung was rewarded with an invitation to Modi's swearing-in ceremony in Delhi at the end of May. When the West Bengal chief minister returned to the hills for a visit in July to help rekindle her relationship, Gurung gave her the cold shoulder.[19] Their relationship had soured. The struggle for statehood continues, but now with a new ally.

During the 2013 monsoon season *bandh*, as tea piled up in Darjeeling factories and orders went unfilled, some buyers began sourcing their long-leaf orthodox teas for blending from other places. "This year with all of the problems [certain blenders] bought from Nepal," said one planter.

While Sikkim's lone tea estate, Temi, produces teas most similar in character to Darjeeling's, the neighbor to the west—Nepal—is the biggest potential competition, even threat, as the recent crisis laid bare.

Winding through India's Mirik Valley on the western flanks of the Darjeeling hills, past Chamong, Spring Valley, and Gopaldhara tea estates, and before cutting through Okayti and Thurbo, the road runs along the eastern India-Nepal border. On a foggy, drizzly July day, with mist hanging between the tall pine trees and upturned, white flowers shaped like old gramophone speakers along the weedy edge of the tarmac, messages from Vodafone India arrived on the mobile phone ("Hello, have a pleasant stay in Nepal") followed by ones from NCELL, the local Nepalese carrier. Tea estates spread along both sides of the road.

Although the first saplings planted in Nepal were said to be a gift to the prime minister, Jung Bahadur Rana, from the Chinese emperor in 1842, the industry developed with stock, not to mention expertise, from Darjeeling. In 1982, King Birendra declared five eastern regions a "tea zone." Ilam Tea Estate—the first commercial estate, planted out in 1863—remains the best. Overall, Nepal's 142 estates produced about 18 million kilograms (40 million pounds) of tea in 2012, roughly twice as much as Darjeeling. But only 2.4 million kilograms of that—some 13 percent—is orthodox. The rest is CTC. While nearly all of the CTC is consumed in Nepal, 96 percent of the orthodox is exported.[20]

The quality of Nepalese tea has been improving in recent years and carries similar taste and aroma profiles. Buyers and tasters have taken notice. "It's always in the back of the minds of producers," said Anindyo Choudhury of Darjeeling's growers after the 2013 season had ended, "that they will get into their market." Since then there has been a sudden awakening to the likelihood of this soon happening, and the issue has moved to the front of their minds. They are suddenly seeing it as one of their biggest challenges.

German and other European blenders have already begun marketing a "Himalayan tea" made with Nepalese leaves[21] that cost a third of what Darjeeling does. Perhaps of greater concern for Darjeeling gardens are domestic packeteers buying for the national market. They are looking for value for money. If the quality is there and the price is right, many are not that concerned about on which side of the border the tea was produced.

In the future, Nepal could be even more of a threat. In ten years, Nepal's National Tea and Coffee Development Board expects to expand plantings significantly and produce 45 million kilograms (100 million

pounds) of tea with 30 million kilograms of that Darjeeling-style orthodox, some fifteen times as much as is now produced.

Climate changes, labor problems, and severe political instability have all
contributed to significant reductions in Darjeeling's output. Darjeeling
once produced 16 to 17 million kilograms (35 to 37 million pounds) of
tea, and as recently as 1991 reached 14.5 million kilograms. The 2010
crop, hit by drought and then excessive rain, cutting the first flush by 25
percent, didn't even reach 8 million kilograms, the lowest since the 1950s.
The 2011 harvest edged back up slightly with better conditions, but then
2012 got off to a terrible start, with droughtlike conditions and yields
down a massive 40 percent. The 2013 harvest also began poorly. Tea
bushes need three or four inches of rain between October and March.
But no rain fell from the previous October until a sprinkling wetted the
tea bushes in February, causing the first flush to be delayed. During April,
the peak of the sought-after first flush, the harvest was down 24 percent
from the previous year. The 2014 harvest began even worse. The lack of
rain in the spring, with a more than two-month-long dry spell that lasted
into May, pushed the first flush down 30 to 40 percent below 2013's
harvest. Some gardens lost even more, depending on the microclimate of
the valley of the garden. "Gopaldhara [in the Mirik Valley] was down 33
percent, but Rohini [running up from the plains to Kurseong] was down
50 percent," said Rishi Saria, "and that from last year, which wasn't too
good."

    First and second flush fetch good prices at auction. Together, they
account for a third of the year's crop but about half its revenue. The
monsoon season contributes around 60 percent of the year's total production, but much of this is sold below production costs. Autumn flush
makes up the remainder.

    That leaves little room for the kind of climatic unpredictability that
stalks estates. In 2012, a hailstorm hit Marybong the first week of April
and devastated its valuable first flush harvest. The same happened to
Castleton in 2013, with a bruising of hailstones that knocked the quality
of its highly coveted second flush.[22]

    The heavy monsoons that drenched most of Darjeeling's valleys
during 2013 coupled with the summer political instability pushed down
prices for the rainy-season teas by as much as 50 percent at J. Thomas &
Co.'s auctions in Kolkata.[23] Then the cold came early and the 2013 season

wrapped up suddenly, quicker than expected. Most gardens missed their year-end targets.

Giving production declines an even deeper impact on profits is the recent leap in nonlabor input expenses. Sandeep Mukherjee puts them at 30 percent in a single year. Part comes from the significant increase in energy costs—electricity rates, coal prices, generator fuel—that jumped 15 percent between 2012 and 2013. Transportation costs shot up accordingly. Nearly everything in Darjeeling either comes from or goes down to the plains below. And now irrigation, which had not been prevalent in Darjeeling, is raising costs further.

Profit margins are thin. Today, a garden in Darjeeling is lucky if it is profitable. Final accounting numbers are known only by the highest levels of the head office and are rarely shared, but in the opinion of one owner with a number of gardens, the majority of Darjeeling estates are breaking even or losing money. Many are already in deep trouble. Soon-to-rise labor expenses will likely push more into the red in the upcoming seasons. Whereas a Rs 100,000 (about $1,800) per-hectare profit might be a round goal, he would be surprised if any garden is currently reaching that and figures a handful of well-managed groups might be making Rs 25,000 to Rs 50,000 ($450 to $900) per hectare. That isn't much. The average garden is cultivating just 224 hectares of tea. Larger companies with holdings beyond their Darjeeling gardens are better able to absorb losses, but a few more years of such dire numbers will spell doom for many of the family-held estates.

While production costs rise and output declines, lower-quality counterfeit "Darjeeling tea" from Nepal and elsewhere undermines its reputation and cuts both value and sales even further. Ecological predictions for the future of the Darjeeling hills could hardly be more dire. As one local government survey summed up, with the mounting problems and strain on its natural resources, "The future of the Darjeeling hills does not look very bright."[24] The report was referring to the land itself and landslides, but when looking at these major challenges, it may as well have been speaking about the entire tea industry.

Sitting in his office beside the Planters' Club, Mukherjee went even further in a flight of pessimism—or realism: "In twenty-five to thirty years, Darjeeling tea may vanish."

Autumn Flush

(October into November)

*T*he monsoon clouds have retreated, the skies cleared, and again the glacier-capped peaks of the Himalayas dominate the horizon. The slopes glow in serene lavenders, pinks, and pale golds in the last, softening light as the sun disappears early and darkness descends over Darjeeling by five P.M.

The final flush is short, just a few weeks or so on each side of the Diwali holiday celebrated at the end of October or early November. Baby-blue flycatchers with banditlike eye masks, woodcocks, and leaf-green magpies dart among the garden's shade trees. Marigolds bordering the fields flower ruddy yellow, their bases ringed with deep-orange petals. On the bushes, white tea flowers blossom: floral, fragrant, and tropical, they have the sweetness of jasmine, but not as cloying.

The autumnal leaves produce a liquor colored a ruddy copper, bright auburn, even burgundy. What a surprise to see claret tones glowing in the white tasting cup! So far from the greenish golds of spring. Sipped, the tea's flavor is round and more robust than that of the previous flushes, with mellowed hints of musky spice and smoke. There is a sparkle, a slight kick even.

"It's the most complex flush. It's the most sophisticated flush. It's the most refined flush," said Sanjay Sharma over breakfast under a pomelo tree just below the old planter's bungalow on Glenburn. "By this I mean it's got everything in it. It's a very fine tea." On this late morning in November, the chain of peaks shimmered to the north. "Fine," he repeated, drawing out the word, "smooth, mellow." As he spoke, his eyes remained on Kanchenjunga rising boldly up in the pristine sky with all the distraction of a flickering TV screen in a sports bar. *"It has that body, amber color, very defined flavors, from malts to chocolates to fruity notes, dried apricots. It just sits on the palate, just sits and sits and sits. Just lingers there."*

It has presence but not impatience.

And poetry:

> *Leaves: This beautiful autumn harvest surprises with twisted leaves in multiple colours (silver, green, brown, red).*
>
> *Nose: The nose is treated to notes of chocolate as well as woody fragrances, stewed fruit and plum jam.*
>
> *Liquor: From the onset, the brilliant amber liquor enchants us with a buttery, vanilla-laced background on which fruity notes (fresh Agen prunes, accentuated by cooked apple and quince jam), honey and a floral hint (rose, geranium) coalesce. The finale ascends with a halo of woody and liquorice notes lingering over this grand bouquet.*[1]

So goes the tantalizing description of a Castleton autumn vintage in a Mariage Frères catalog.

"Autumnal teas can be marvelously complex," said Sanjay Kapur at Aap Ki Pasand in Old Delhi. "Very easy to drink and intense in flavor."

For many insiders these are the year's finest teas, a last and final offering from the bushes. But they don't get much attention on the international market. "Europeans are done buying for Christmas, or distracted by Christmas, when these teas are ready," Kapur said. That means that they tend to be "underrated," which is to say less expensive than their first and second flush counterparts. He smiled at this delicious coincidence.

By the second and third week of November, the harvesting year winds down. Nights get colder, and then the days, too. Snakes disappear into burrows and rockery crevices. Birds migrate out of Central Asia over the Himalayas, while others simply come down from higher hills to the lower, warmer plains to winter. Ruddy shelducks, ibisbills with long, downward-curving, red beaks, and bar-headed geese pass through. Numerous black cormorants. Students from the elite English-medium schools sit for exams as the March-to-November school year comes to a close. They wear crested blazers and school ties, and even though the rains have stopped and there will be little, if any, precipitation until springtime, the boys from St. Paul's stroll through town with umbrellas.

Production slows. A batch tasting may consist of just a single tea or two.

The last of the leaves are brought in and processed. Workers pack the final chests of tea for the warehouses in Kolkata. A scattering of leaves have been left on the trees by workers, anxious to begin pruning.

The days grow shorter, the mornings crisper. Brisk winds blow off the icy peaks. A snap is in the air, the smell of coal smoke. Thermometers flirt with freezing. Hoarfrost spreads across the higher reaches of the estates. Snow dusts the tops of the hills, and then, gradually, the skirt of white begins to drop lower. At night, the brilliant, clear skies slur with rigid stars. The tea bushes go into hibernation for the winter.

CHAPTER 15

Positive Winds

Despite the severe challenges of climate, labor, and political stability, the winds blowing out of the Darjeeling hills still carry optimism and are redolent with promise. Even with the string of recent terrible harvests and current lack of profits, when asked about Darjeeling tea's future, nearly everyone involved with the industry answers "optimistic," "highly optimistic," or "extremely optimistic."

"Demand for Darjeeling tea has gone up leaps and bounds," said Sanjay Kapur in his Delhi atelier Aap Ki Pasand. "After some stagnant years, prices have gone up significantly." J. Thomas & Co.'s Darjeeling auctioneer, Anindyo Choudhury, agreed. "It has done a U-turn and is on the way up. It is around the curve. Two thousand one, 2002, and 2003 were low points. Two thousand ten is when the market really changed." He tipped back in the desk chair in his office. "There have been three or four very good years," he said. "The market is there."

Internationally, Darjeeling's most important markets—Germany and Japan—are strengthening; markets are growing in France and elsewhere in Europe; and North America has emerged as important. The Russians, with rising affluence, are eyeing higher-quality teas. Asia is also looking bright. Iranian and Middle Eastern buyers are moving from CTC to Indian orthodox teas, said Choudhury. Iran is now the world's fifth-largest tea importer and rising fast, with a twofold increase over the past two decades. For the moment the orthodox it buys is mostly from Assam, but Darjeeling appeals to clients looking for the highest quality. China, traditionally a green (and oolong) tea-drinking nation, is developing a taste for Indian black teas and has taken clear notice of Darjeeling's more refined (and expensive) offerings. "In the last two years, there has been an interest among the Chinese young crowd for black tea. Darjeeling tea is used for corporate gifting and on special occasions," according to Sujoy Sengupta of Chamong Tee.[1] In 2012, the group shipped around 250,000 kilograms (550,000 pounds) of tea from their gardens to China and expect to see an increase. In autumn 2013, the *Economic Times* reported that South Korea, predominately a green-tea market, ordered a staggering 1.5 million kilograms (3 million pounds) of Darjeeling tea, about one-sixth of its entire production.[2]

As a fine-tea merchant and taster, a prime source of Vikram Mittal's enthusiasm is in the flavor of teas raised on new stock propagated from cuttings of strains well suited for local conditions instead of with seeds from old China bushes. In the traditional method, seeds are sown in on-site seedbeds and then transplanted in small polyethylene sleeves of soil, about eight to ten inches long and as thick as baguettes, once they germinate, some four to six weeks later. Under a bamboo thatch of shade, they mature for nine or so months in a garden's open-air nursery until ready for planting. Old China leaf comes from a mix of parentage and sources, with leaf sizes all slightly different. When processing them, Sanjay Sharma said, "You sort of shoot for the middle. It's harder for tea making."

Now the new plantings on most gardens are with saplings from cultivars rather than assorted seeds. In Darjeeling these are referred to as clonal varieties, as they produce a replica of the parent plant. While India's Tocklai Tea Research Institute released its first clone in 1949 and has a few hundred on stock, three cultivars are by far the most popular in Darjeeling: AV–2, B–157, P–312.* Bushes behave more similarly and leaves are as uniform as possible, which means withering and fermentation can be more exact. "Clonal is easier to manufacture," Sharma said.

"Some you can't believe the flavor," Mittal said. "So intense." He can prepare a cup with lower-grade fannings and it comes closer to tea steeped from better leaves. "It's on a high pedestal."

Yet much of the current optimism among garden owners and managers—what keeps many of them in the business for the moment—stems not from such sales figures or even flavors but rather a recent legal ruling.

---

*These stand for Ambari Vegetative 2, Bannockburn 157, and Phoobsering 312, after the estates where the stock originated, but are always referred to in shorthand.

In 2004, to stanch rampant counterfeiting, mislabeling, and misuse of the name, and to discourage fraudulent claims, imitation, and adulteration, Darjeeling tea become the first product to which India, as a member of the World Trade Organization, awarded "geographical indication" (GI) status. This was a significant step toward seeking international protection for the product, which came in October 2011. Darjeeling tea was then awarded Protected Geographical Indication (PGI) from the European Commission, one of the first non-European products to receive such designation. Darjeeling tea is now a geographically protected product like Scotch whisky, Parmigiano-Reggiano cheese, and saffron from La Mancha, Spain.

While trademarks are used for private entities, geographic protection is communal and extends to the collective community producing a specific product in a specific area. According to the Tea Board of India, "Darjeeling Tea" means—only and specifically—tea that has been cultivated, grown, produced, manufactured, and processed in an orthodox manner on Darjeeling's eighty-seven tea gardens.

Forty million kilos of "Darjeeling tea" sell each year, insiders frequently reiterate, yet the area is actually producing just a fifth of that. "Once fully into force, you will have more demand than supply," said Vijay Dhancholia on Marybong. "Then you will get more price." Managers are saying the same thing all over Darjeeling, almost like a mantra.

"As of now, blenders in EU countries generally mix forty-nine percent of any tea with fifty-one percent of Darjeeling tea and still sell it as Darjeeling tea," Tea Board of India chairman M. G. V. K. Bhanu said after the ruling. "But it has now been decided that only those packets that contain one hundred percent Darjeeling tea can be sold as Darjeeling tea."[3] Such packets will carry the Darjeeling logo as well as the PGI logo.

As nearly 60 percent of exports head to the EU, and the majority of those to Germany, that's huge news. Germany is Darjeeling's largest importer and most important client. They buy in bulk and reexport much of it. "Germans are traders, not consumers," the manager at one top estate said. "They are big clients but not forever. It won't last long with the PGI changes," he predicted, indicating that many of the importers will lose interest when they can no longer blend and profits become harder to make. "Why should they continue to promote Darjeeling tea if they don't have a stake in it?" another manager said, arguing that Darjeeling tea was simply being bought and sold as a bulk commodity. "They will concentrate their efforts elsewhere—on Nepal."

The PGI notification took effect in November 2011 and started a five-year grace—or transition—period. The year 2016 is the most anticipated in industry memory.

Darjeeling teas will benefit, but which ones will benefit most isn't yet clear. J. Thomas's Choudhury thinks exports and high-end teas; Sengupta at the Chamong group's headquarters in Kolkata disagrees. "It will help everyone," he said, "and will help the middle and bottom teas even more." As the price of Darjeeling tea rises, the first to benefit will be those at the bottom as the price gets pulled up, he said. "The Rs two thousand [per kilo wholesale; $36] tea will now be Rs six thousand, the Rs three hundred [$5.50] tea will be Rs six hundred." Buyers used to paying a certain amount will want to pay about the same, he thought, and will go after a lower-level Darjeeling tea that has come up in price as opposed to spending more.

"It's about supply and demand," said Ambootia manager Jay Neogi. Small, white tea bowls, stacked upside down four levels high, ran along the white tile counter in the estate's large tasting room. "Darjeeling tea is a limited product. Other countries can increase production and just plant more tea bushes. In Darjeeling you can't." The hills are protected from further tea expansion, the clearing of the forests now illegal, and the area's topography and difficulties in irrigating makes planting out new gardens impossible. Resources—from manpower to water—are already being stretched. "So as demand gets higher than supply, prices will rise."

This hinges on the distinctiveness of Darjeeling tea and the impossibility of producing a similar one elsewhere. As a poster hanging on Ambootia's tasting room wall exclaims, "Darjeeling Tea. Born only in Darjeeling. Desired worldwide."

Among the lonely voices of those who don't think PGI designation alone will make a significant difference in how much their tea fetches on the market is Rishi Saria of Gopaldhara and Rohini estates. "Prices of Darjeeling tea will never go up unless Indians starting drinking Darjeeling tea."

Indians generally prefer stronger, brisker teas, with plenty of milk and sugar, over Darjeeling's delicate and fragrant flavors. Lack of a national Indian market with more readily accessible clients has long been what Sandeep Mukherjee at the DTA calls "an inherent handicap."

Nearly all of the tea needs to be exported to faraway clients. Some shift has recently occurred. The rising middle class means more Indians can afford the higher prices Darjeeling tea commands, but whether they will opt for it over colas and coffee is another matter.

In a small, randomly chosen grocery store on a side street in central Kolkata, among shelves of Amul Gold milk, mung dal, and hefty sacks of basmati rice, sat boxes of Darjeeling tea by Typhoo and Lipton as well as Tata Gold Fine Darjeeling Tea. "To enjoy the fine flavour—Brew," the front of the Tata packet instructs. "Do not boil," a distinct change in the way most Indians make their tea at home.

Also on the shelves were, more significantly for the industry, packets of popular Tata Tea Gold. These contain a blend of Assam CTC for strength and body and 15 percent Darjeeling long-leaf tea, which, says recent publicity, will "open up and release a superior aroma." That gives a staple drink something of a premium touch. Across the bottom of the familiar green-and-yellow package runs its catchphrase: "Rich aroma, refreshing taste."

Tata stormed the global market in the early 1990s and in 2000 consolidated its rise by taking over Tetley Tea; Tata is now the world's second-largest tea company, after Unilever (which has Brooke Bond, Lipton, and PG Tips in its portfolio). In India, Tata has a strong presence on supermarket shelves and in kitchen cabinets with a range of offerings from its various brands: Tata Tea, Tetley, Good Earth, Kanan Devan, Chakra Gold, and Gemini. At the Tuesday auction for Darjeeling tea at J. Thomas & Co. in Kolkata, Tata is now the biggest domestic player and the largest buyer in terms of volume. That has happened, said Choudhury, only within the last handful of years. "Knocking to Tata" is now heard over and over in his auction room, especially on midrange lots. According to Choudhury, Tata Global is buying about 12–15 percent of what is offered at auction.

"This has changed the complexion of the game," says Sanjay Kapur.

The emergence of Tata Global Beverages as the chief Darjeeling buyer for teas to be sold on the domestic market has been the major factor in the rise of auction prices of leaf-grade Darjeeling from Rs 204.67 per kilo in 2006 to Rs 490.93 in 2012, said Choudhury.

This has given an opening for individual estates to penetrate the Indian market. Darjeeling's gardens don't have money to individually promote their brand abroad because their production and resources are too small, and they generally need to rely on importers for that—namely the German importers, who many fear will lose interest in the teas once the PGI kicks into force.

But with the country's quickly expanding middle class and a larger product awareness among local consumers, Rishi Saria sees the Indian market as the place to focus his efforts. To spread the Gopaldhara brand and get closer to local clients, his family's company has begun selling tea online direct and opening up a handful of small retail outlets. Other individual gardens have been making similar small moves toward accessibility to directly target Indian customers.

Another significant change in the Indian market has been the recent craze for Darjeeling's *green* teas.

"We used to sell one kind of green tea," said Girish Sarda at Nathmulls in Darjeeling. "We couldn't get a whole invoice [about 150 kilograms] so we used to beg for one case [about 25 kilograms] and then take all year to sell it. Now we are selling ten to fifteen types. And buying complete invoices." Most of their walk-in customers come in looking for green tea, Sarda said. "They might buy black tea, but first they ask for green."

Numerous green-and-yellow billboard ads appear along Hill Cart Road promoting Nathmulls' "heritage shop," which Nathmull Sarda opened in 1931. It remains the most distinguished tea retailer in the city. Girish is the fourth generation of Sardas to run it. "It's in the blood," he said. He stood behind the counter, arms slightly spread and palms on the glass case. A trio of young men in jeans patiently measured out tea into small gold-foil packets, tied them in a cross of white string, and packed them snugly into boxes to airfreight out to online customers. Honking cars passed along the steep Laden-la Road just a foot or so from Nathmulls' always-open door.

"Health," said Sarda. "That's what green teas are all about." Drinking tea for medicinal benefits goes back to its earliest days in ancient China and Japan, and even in Europe. While an ever-increasing number of scientific studies are proving the health benefits of tea, some of the claims being put forward today in India sound almost as miraculous as Thomas Garway's seventeenth-century promises.

Nathmulls has printed a small brochure entitled "Green Tea: Your Prescription to Good Health," which gets included with each package and offered on the counter in the shop. Folded in half and smaller than the palm of a hand, it has the Darjeeling logo at the top, a two-leaves-

and-a-bud pluck at the bottom, and a pair of red crosses bookending "Good Health" in the title. It includes a short legend of the tea's healthy properties and also directions for preparation, but the bulk consists of eleven block paragraphs, a lengthy sentence or two each, on health:

GREEN TEA, being un-fermented, is a very rich source of ANTI-OXIDANTS.

TANINS (Polyphenols) namely EPICATECHINS and EPI GALLO CATECHIN GALLATE (EGCG) are among the strongest ANTI-OXIDANTS, active against many forms of Cancer and they also block the spread of the HIV Virus that causes AIDS.

When applied to the skin, they offer protection from free radicals present in sunlight and ultra-violet radiation, that damages the DNA cells, causing Cancer. These TANINS reverse pre-cancerous skin changes. QUERCETIN, another chemical found in tea, particularly inhibits the grown of Leukemia cells, thus preventing Blood Cancer.

It continues with terms in capital letters that the buying public may not know but sound sufficiently medically important.

Drinking tea can help control the Influenza Virus, restrain the growth of the Herpes Simplex Virus and can be helpful in checking Chronic Viral Hepatitis. The FLAVONOIDS also help relieve the oxidative stress to the eye lens, thereby lowering the risk of contracting Cataract.

And on, through a litany of diseases, with the promise of lowering the risk of dementia and Alzheimer's to controlling tooth decay and "slowing the onset of Atherosclerosis and Heart Disease."

As green tea's popularity has come full circle regarding the public's perception of its health properties, so have these selling points returned to the domain of local marketers, in their pamphlets and promises of cure-alls.

This surge in popularity has shifted the types of teas many estates produce. Green teas fit neatly into Darjeeling's harvesting cycle. During the monsoon, the leaves are at their largest and least flavorful of the year;

withering in the humidity is extremely difficult, and fermentation is tricky. Many monsoon teas sell below production cost because of the lack of interest from big-spending buyers. They fetch between a quarter and one half of the price of tea from the first two flushes and are used almost exclusively in blends.

Green teas offer an ideal option for Darjeeling gardens that sell their monsoon-flush black teas so cheaply. Being neither withered nor fermented, green teas are easier to make during the rainy season. The leaves are simply steamed to arrest any fermentation, rolled, and then fired.

Some tea experts, though, consider them simply monsoon filler and are far from enamored with the outcome. "You can't control quality during the monsoon," said Girish Sarda. As with Darjeeling's black teas, the best greens, he insisted, are from the other flushes. Indeed, demand has been strong enough for a couple of Darjeeling's top estates to begin producing limited amounts of green teas during their premium first two flushes—and getting premium prices for them.

Sitting along the glass counter at Nathmulls are ten jars of selected green teas, with a handful of others on a shelf behind. One contains Rohini's delightful first flush Green Enigma (Rs 5,800 or $105, a kilo), a leggy, large-leaf tea. Another holds second flush Emerald Green from Arya (Rs 6,400 or $115), which gives a light-colored liquor, mellow and aromatic, with traces of grasses and fruits.

For Sarda, Rohini's hand-rolled first flush Green Pearls was 2013's finest. "It's the smoothest green tea, very light and stylishly done." He smiled and plucked a couple of rolled pearls the size of earrings from a jar. Once steeped, the liquor shines a pale gold, a shade closer to champagne than hay. In the mouth, it's plummy in a fulsome and rounded way, with hints of vegetables and greens but no suggestion of bitterness or even the pungent notes so prevalent in other green teas.

Nathmulls sells it for Rs 8,000 ($145) per kilo. That makes it more expensive than all but a half dozen of Nathmulls' most exclusive and celebrated black teas. Such excellence comes at a price, even so close to its source.

The Rohini Tea Estate is one of the first gardens passed on the Rohini Road heading from Siliguri into the hills. Once it was the largest estate in Darjeeling. With the lowest section just above Siliguri, at the narrow, strategic neck of land that connects Assam and the northeast states with the rest of India, it has a quartet of borders within a brief bird's (or aircraft's) flight—Bangladesh (roughly three miles), Nepal (thirteen miles), Bhutan (thirty-four miles), and China (fifty miles). In 1962, the year of the Sino-India conflict when China abruptly launched a two-pronged attack along the high Himalayan border it shares with India and occupied part of Assam for a month, India's military took over Rohini's land, closed the garden, and converted it into an army base. Nearly 80 percent of the tea bushes were torn out. According to Rishi Saria, whose family now owns Rohini, the owner fought the central government for years to get it back. Finally, in 1995, 400 hectares (1,000 acres) of it were returned, although just 33 hectares (81 acres) were still under tea. By then, the owner, Saria explained, had exhausted his resources in the fight and sold it off. Part of the estate was reopened with some new plantings. In 2000, Rohini changed hands again, with the Saria family purchasing the garden. Replanting continued. Today 145 hectares (360 acres) of tea bushes are planted on the estate, which now measures 320 hectares (790 acres).

The lower reaches of the garden, through which a herd of elephants from the nearby forest reserve frequently pass (and, once, knocked down a wall of the factory), begin just before the foothills abruptly jut upward. From here, tea bushes sweep right up the slopes to the ridgeline below Kurseong, where it borders a handful of illustrious properties including Makaibari and Castleton.

One hot and hazy Sunday July morning, at the end of the long drive-way to the manager's bungalow set among banana trees and lavishly flowering plants, B. B. Singh emerged from the private temple built behind the century-old planter's bungalow. The Lucknow-born Singh has worked forty-two years in tea. Patient as a kind uncle, and generous, he began at Rohini when it reopened two decades ago and has overseen the replanting of the fields and restarting of the factory. "From zero to one lakh [100,000] kgs," he said proudly, pronouncing it *kay-gees*.

A few miles down the Rohini Road at the factory, an ugly if spacious building built in the 1940s when Rohini was significantly larger and producing many times the amount of tea it does today, Singh sent for someone to give a demonstration in how to roll the green tea pearls that Girish Sarda favors.

Production of these is limited—just 50 kilograms, or 110 pounds, in 2013. As the leaf is too small and delicate for adult fingers to properly handle, early in the morning before going to school, a dozen or so girls about twelve or thirteen years old from the estate come to the factory and roll pearls for an hour or two with their softer, smaller, and more pliant fingers.

Some minutes later, a girl with a moon-shaped face, large, dark eyes, and white scarf looped loosely around her neck slipped quietly into the tasting room. Her dress was sunflower yellow and flourished in white swirls, snug on her upper arms and frilled along the bottom hem. A delicate silver ring adorned the middle finger on one hand, and a pink, beaded bracelet encircled a wrist. She set down on the counter a handful of just-plucked leaves as tender as baby spinach. Two pink flower clips held her shoulder-length bob away from her face as she bent over slightly to roll the leaves between a thumb and forefinger and middle finger. When a leaf didn't immediately twist, she placed it in the palm of her left hand and spun the fingers of her right hand in a circular motion. The leaves are usually steamed first, and a half dozen get rolled into a single pearl, but the motion is similar.

The girl slipped out of the room as silently as she had come. A dozen small, leafy balls sat on the counter in a perfect row like an unstrung necklace.

Rohini is trying to do about 10 percent of its production as green teas. Some gardens are sticking to black—Marybong, for instance—but at least one of the Chamong group's Darjeeling gardens has converted more than half its production toward green.

"We have the finest raw materials in the world," said Sanjay Sharma of Glenburn, who questions whether green teas are the best use for Darjeeling's premium leaves. Certainly, green teas have less flavor range. From Japan to China to India, they often contain similar characteristics. They are not nearly as complex or sophisticated as black tea and have fewer variants in aroma and liquor. "Black tea offers a lot more variety than green tea, which can be mundane," Sanjay Kapur said.

The American tea maker Steven Smith noted that Darjeeling black teas offer a "sophisticated, flavorful cup" whose flavors have a broad and unparalleled spectrum from fruits, nuts, and florals to wines and muscatel. "But very, very few can pick out the unique qualities" of Darjeeling in its green teas. While Darjeeling's black teas command the highest prices on the international market, their green teas do not. "You will not get top dollar for the best ones like a Chinese tea," said Vikram Mittal in his New Delhi shop.

"The best black teas in the world are from Darjeeling. No one is near here," Girish Sarda insisted. "But while there are top-drawer green teas in

Darjeeling, they can't compete with the best Chinese greens." In part, the tradition is not as deeply established, and gardens, simply, aren't making that many green teas year after year. But they have nonetheless become an important part of the offerings alongside "specialty teas," which include white teas, high-end green teas, and oolongs.

At Glenburn, Sharma expanded the garden's portfolio. One of the most popular is the Autumn Oolong, a large-leafed traditional autumn tea with a twist. A tea maker, he explained, has to decide which characteristics to emphasize in the tea. "What we're highlighting is only the aroma," he said of the oolong. "Minus the body, minus anything else." It gets a light wither and then a light roll. "We just gently bruise the leaves," he joked. "We just massage them." A fuller fermentation than most oolongs receive follows, and then a gap firing. The leaves are allowed to cool after a gentle first firing that doesn't fully arrest the fermentation (the remainder of fermentation then proceeds slowly) before getting a hot and quick blast to finish it off. "It gives the tea a finesse, a delicate touch."

Sanjay tried making this oolong with the leaves from the first two flushes, he explained in November as he began to tinker with the year's new batch, "but only in autumn did I find those delicate floral notes with very mellow cups and basically fruity undertones—not like fresh fruit but moistened dried apricots, maybe raisins—and, in the dry leaf, hints of chocolate."

But Glenburn has recently found their biggest critical international success in a specialty tea called Silver Needle (always singular; never *needles*), the finest and most delicate white tea, which is made solely with buds plucked when they are about to unfold. Silver Needle is a traditional but rare style from China's Fujian province, where it is known as Bai Hao Yin Zhen. Its namesake color comes from the fine pubescence that coats the underside of each leaf bud. Once dried, the long, slender swordlike buds have a characteristic silvery hue. Made only in midsummer, and only from select fields planted out with cultivars that produce large, succulent buds, processing is delicate. Standing in the well-lit factory, Sharma held out a flexible, white tasting card with a handful of recently dried buds, an inch long and as erect as spikes. The plucked buds get a gentle wither, to reduce the moisture content gradually and avoid sudden shrinkage of the leaf cells, and then are dried. No rolling. No fermentation.

"It's a very delicate cup with a hint of astringency and mildly green and zesty," he explained. The liquor is superlight, pale, almost silvery white in the cup, and carries subtle, clean flavors with a crisp, short finish and a touch of dryness. "If it's oxidized, it'd go flat. Every cup needs a little astringency to stimulate the palate."

His exceptional handicraft was awarded first place in the white-tea category at the 2013 North American Tea Championship in Las Vegas, a significant achievement from Darjeeling, which is very much a new kid on the white-tea arena. The 2013 harvest of Silver Needle was selling from Glenburn direct for $460—at the summer's exchange rate, not far under Rs 30,000—per kilo.

While expensive, it is so exclusive and labor-intensive to produce that even Glenburn's most productive pluckers can gather only enough Silver Needle for about *ten* cups in an entire working day.

The synonym in Darjeeling for these specialty teas is *fancy teas*, which can have something of a fey ring to it. They are upstarts, somehow apart from the classic Darjeeling flushes. But they have become important members of the Darjeeling tea family. A poster in the tasting room of Rohini shows a dozen of the specialty teas that Rohini and its higher-elevation sister garden Gopaldhara offer. Across the bottom it reads, "Join the table—It's absolutely Darjeeling."

CHAPTER 16

Soil

A cup of tea might be made from leaves, but the flavors begin in the earth. One of the most encouraging signs of change in Darjeeling is the improving health of the soil. Gardens have taken aggressive measures to reverse decades of harmful agricultural techniques and have restored more traditional, natural tea-farming methods lost during the postindependence surge in chemical inputs.

Makaibari has been one of the estates at the forefront of soil-level change. It's the most famous garden in the hills, producing the most famous Darjeeling tea in the world, due largely to the passions of one man, Rajah Banerjee. Farming tea is part of his makeup, his lineage. Makaibari has been run, almost since its unconventional, mid-nineteenth century establishment, by the Banerjee family. His ancestors also managed some of Darjeeling's other best-known gardens.

Yet Rajah's entry into the family business was anything but assured. In the mid–1960s, he went to England to study mechanical engineering at Imperial College London. After four years he returned for a holiday on Makaibari. He was keen to get back as soon as possible to his urban life in Europe. But, as he frequently repeats, "Man proposes and God disposes."

His father bought him a gun and a retired thoroughbred named Invitation and told him, Ride and hunt, son, enjoy your holidays. On the afternoon of August 21, 1970, as he cantered along the steep pitches and precarious bridle paths of pluckers' trails that weave throughout the estate, a wild boar bolted in front of the horse. The startled horse reared up and threw Rajah. That moment changed everything for the young heir.

"In the split second that I fell, I perceived a brilliant band of white light, connecting me to the trees in the forests around me," he wrote in his book on Makaibari. He fell slowly to earth in a suspended moment that he considers an out-of-body experience because he wasn't unconscious. "The woods sang out melancholically in an incredible concerto, 'Save us! Save us!' "[1] Elsewhere he recalled, "I was in a timeless, spaceless zone. A tunnel of light with an incredible intensity and clarity."[2]

"It took me about ten years to be able to talk about it," Rajah said in the spacious, rambling hilltop home (humbly referred to as a bungalow) that has been home to generations of Banerjees. He wore a sweat suit with a SILVER TIPS T-shirt pulled over the zippered jacket top. "Now I can talk about it rationally. They would have found me certifiably crazy."

He knew he wasn't mad that August day forty-five years ago. Although he didn't fully understand the experience yet, Rajah knew instantly that he had to spend the rest of his life on Makaibari. At dinner that night he told his parents that he was staying and would become a tea planter. He didn't explain what had made him suddenly change his mind. They were puzzled, but happily accepted his decision.

Rajah's well-honed stories, studded with bits of original wisdom, retold for visitors who arrive almost daily from around the globe, come across not so much fresh and spontaneous as original and sincere. In particular, hearing his anecdote of being thrown from the horse, almost verbatim to how he has recorded it elsewhere, remains, like a Greek drama whose story is known but masterfully handled onstage, a riveting experience. Fittingly, details of the fall lend it the essence of a fable, including the animal that startled the horse and set the event into motion. In the Indian tradition, one of Lord Vishnu's reincarnations was as Varaha, a boar whose rooting around in the earth and turning over soil showed him how to till and plow, teaching man cultivation. Today the Indian wild boar (*Sus scrofa cristatus*; *suar* in Hindi, *varaha* in Sanskrit) remains a sacred animal associated with agriculture[3] and also fertility, due to its digging deep in the earth to allow for the growth of shoots.[4]

Rajah is a master raconteur. He loves to talk, to educate, to be listened to. *Pontificate* might be the best word. (He keeps to the first person, although there would be little surprise if he switched, from time to time, to the third.) He is brilliant and aggrandizing, curious, arrogant but generous, preachy but unique, with flair, charm, and rare magnetism. Had he not taken up tea planting, he could have become one of those legendary teachers, the kind at boarding school who inspire student rebellions and at university that pack lecture halls and have, year after year, a loyal following of not just the curious or needy but also the most brilliant. Instead, he remains in his rural, isolated tea garden tending to its daily needs. "The world comes to you. Look: you came," he said. Rajah's vocabulary is rich, colorful, and precise, laid out not so much the way a jeweler displays his fanciest wares, but the way a butcher wields his tools to work, in order to provoke and persuade. Or maybe the way a jester handles his props: puns and intricate allusions come quickly. His sense of humor is ripe and, not infrequently, cutting. Guests are challenged and interrogated. ("Come on! What do you taste? You're a *gourmand. You* should know this!") Ideas, offered with a brawny, combative intellectual persuasiveness, are original, iconoclastic, and often bewildering. Too frequently, guests are muted and can only nod into their cups of tea. While he speaks in polished paragraphs and dislikes being interrupted, he is genuinely interested and inquisitive, with little patience for trivialities. The effort to reach Makaibari is too great, and his time too limited. Guests should listen but respond, clearly and specifically; they should be clever and preferably confident—or come with a skin as thick as that of buffaloes, whose heads are hung on the wall of the sitting room and outside his office.

Once deciding to stay on Makaibari, he wanted to do more than simply maintain the long-running traditions of the estate as handed down by his ancestors. To respond to the plea from the forest, the farm needed to evolve into a place more in sync with nature's rhythms.

By balancing the five internal senses together with external forces, you have harmony. "If you are in harmony, and you are a farmer, then you have healthy soil," Rajah said in the quiet house. He slurped his tea. From the first flush, it had been recently fired, locking in the fresh greenness of the young buds, the aroma of the hills. The liquor shone whisky gold in the cup. "I decided then to dedicate myself to healthy soil."

So began what he calls the greatest voyage of his life. He would not only make some of the finest vintages of Darjeeling tea ever produced, set a world record at auction—"I don't care about records," he says, but rarely fails to mention this one—and get some of the highest prices for tea anywhere, but also unravel the three critical questions that he believes assail us all, questions we hope remain dormant: Where do we come from? What are we doing here? Where are we going?

"I was seeking the flavor in the balance sheet of life," he said, repeating one of his favorite phrases.

• • •

Rajah's father, Pasupati Nath (P. N.) Banerjee, possessed a deep passion for hunting—and a notoriously accurate shot. Both are evident in the airy sitting room of the Makaibari bungalow. Surrounding a photograph of P. N. standing erect in his Sam Browne belt and wide-brimmed hat is a dusty menagerie of stuffed trophies: tigers squatting nonchalantly on their haunches with yawning, fang-filled mouths; a matching pair of stuffed leopards and the skin of a third stretching across a wall; a heavy rack of deer antlers. The opaque, amber-colored eyes of an enormous buffalo head mounted on the wall gaze out over the room.

Hunting in the estate's forests one day as a young man, not long after taking over from his father, P. N. was engulfed in a sudden seasonal rain-storm. Waiting it out at the edge of the forest, he noticed that water running off the planted sections of the garden was murky with sediment. The estate's wealth—its nutrient-rich topsoil—was being washed away in the rain. Yet rivulets of water flowing out of the woods ran clear. Seeing how the fallen leaves from the trees offered a barrier that was preventing erosion, he realized the need for a similar solution for the tea bushes.[5]

He began searching, and in 1945 workers started mulching. They spread loppings and cuttings from various grasses and plants on the estate like an insulating blanket across the ground between the bases of bushes.

Mulching accomplishes numerous things. It absorbs the area's heavy rain, from the short, powerful bursts before the monsoon through the steady downpours during the rainy season itself. This prevents soil erosion as well, helping the moisture to be absorbed into the earth rather than just running off it. The mulch layer protects the soil against evaporation during the dry season and periods of drought. Underneath, the loamy earth is rich in humus and decomposition. Mulching also prevents weeds by depriving them of light and acts as a gentle buffer between soil and air, allowing earthworms to flourish and work in the topmost layer of soil, churning and better aerating the earth. And it helps build topsoil.

Something more profound was going on here, too, Rajah explained. "With the mulching, the tea became part of the woodlands."

This was the first step in Makaibari's organic journey. However, P. N. continued to use chemical applications. Later, Rajah worried that the spraying was killing the rich organisms that were flourishing from the mulching and even giving animals insecticide poisoning. While Rajah was keen to stop the practice, his father was still in charge of Makaibari. Workers called P. N. *burra sahib*, big boss, and Rajah *chota sahib*, little boss. (Most of those living in Makaibari's villages still refer to him as *chota sahib*, at least when talking *about* him. It is used on the garden not unaffectionately.)

In a hidden corner of the estate, on a steep slope of tea among a heavily wooded section that was rarely visited, even by his father, Rajah and two of Makaibari's most senior workers secretly tended a patch of bushes. Manuring at night, it took the men nearly a month to carry organic compost from a nearby village on Makaibari and spread it around the site. Rajah was able to have the tea plucked and processed apart, and as he tells it in his book, his father frequently commented on the exceptional quality of the leaves during the batch tastings, probing the production manager for their specific source. Rajah managed to kept the secret for the whole harvest year before finally revealing his stealthy, organic undertaking.[6]

Once party to the subterfuge and having tasted the difference, P. N. supported his son's idea. P. N. provided cows for manure, workers learned composting techniques, and the estate began converting away from chemical applications.

But the end of using chemicals wouldn't come until Rajah took over Makaibari. In the early 1980s, India's tea industry struggled severely. National taxes and labor costs rose sharply, exports to the UK plummeted, and Kenyan and Sri Lankan teas offered stiff competition on the global market. Prices dropped. Profit margins dwindled. Dozens of estates in Darjeeling were abandoned; the remainder strained to survive. Rajah's father retired to Calcutta and thrust the running of the garden onto his son. The *chota sahib* had nothing to lose and launched fully into realizing his organic vision. Rajah doesn't see it that way, though, and bristles at the notion. "I didn't take over anything. How can you take over change? I was merely a conduit," he insists.

Occupying one end of the upper floor of a small, two-story building fronting the factory with its green roof and corrugated, silver siding, Rajah's office has a worn, green-and-white-patterned carpet and pale yellow walls, a pair of frayed wicker chairs, and a large desk covered with a leather mat and stacks of papers. A long, glass-fronted bookcase runs across one end of the room. Trophies, awards, and plaques crowd its top; inside, shelves overflow with books on birds and animals, generators and income-tax law, and tomes such as Will Durant's *The Age of Louis XIV* and *The Life of Greece*. The doors to a small terrace are always thrown open to the hum of the factory and the smell of freshly fired tea. A *shankha*, a large conch shell associated with Hinduism, sits in a corner.

The path to organic farming began with his father, and Rajah, he finally conceded, continued to drive it forward. "I was on a mission. It was a process of slowly moving. We moved ahead a little each day."

For buyers and consumers, being an organic farm means being a *certified* one. The idea for Makaibari's getting certification was instigated by a chance meeting in 1987 with Kiran Tawadey, an elegant woman who owns Hampstead Tea, a brand of organic and Fairtrade teas that gets exported to seventeen countries. "She said, 'There's big bucks in it,' but I told her, 'I'm not in it for the bucks,'" Rajah explained.

Tawadey, then in her late twenties and just starting out in the business, was not easily dissuaded. She began introducing Rajah to the broader organic community and asked him to host an inspector on the estate. He agreed. (Why? "I can't say no to anybody.")

Makaibari convincingly satisfied the criteria during the inspection, and in 1988 Makaibari was duly certified organic, the first tea estate in India to be so. Rajah is deeply proud of it, although he tends to underplay it. "I became certified because a buyer wanted it," he said in a deadpan tone.

The transition to organic was not an easy time. "All my neighbors thought I was some sort of a witch, doing witchcraft in tea, and stayed away from it, from the crazy man," he explained in the Makaibari documentary. "It was very, very lonely the first few years."[7] Organic isolation didn't last long. "The moment the whole garden started prospering, proving the point that eco-agriculture could be economically viable, everybody has started jumping in the bandwagon," he said with a jaunty, upward lilt to in his voice.[8] When Makaibari started achieving record prices, the bandwagon became even more popular. "I was astonishingly propelled from laughingstock to pioneer," he wrote in his book.[9]

What a change in a quarter century. According to the Darjeeling Tea Association, by the end of the 2013 harvest, fifty-eight of Darjeeling's tea gardens—an astonishing two-thirds—were certified organic with a number more in the conversion.*

---

*A number of gardens became "organic by default." Having been unsustainable during the tough years of the 1980s and 1990s, they were closed and fell into disuse. When snapped up by buyers after 2000, they had been years without chemical inputs, and the new owners did not need to go through the three-year process to make them organic.

Converting comes with significant consequences. "It is a costly affair," said Jay Neogi at Ambootia, the flagship and namesake of the group with eleven organic Darjeeling gardens. Certification is expensive, organic materials cost more, and organic cow manure is in short supply in the hills.

But these are largely secondary concerns. Far more important, yields plummet. Ambootia saw its production drop from 200,000 kilograms (440,000 pounds) to 120,000 kilograms (about 265,000 pounds); it has now stabilized at 150,000 kilograms (331,000 pounds), or down 25 percent from previous amounts.

This is standard. Chamong Tee's thirteen Darjeeling gardens all converted to organic production and generally experienced drops around 25 to 30 percent. Some were even higher. Marybong has been typical. The historic estate of the Wernickes and Louis Mandelli began the three-year process of moving from conventional to organic in 2007, the year Vijay Dhancholia took over as manager. Production went from 165,000 kilograms (375,000 pounds) to 102,000 kilograms (about 225,000 pounds) in 2012, a 40 percent loss. According to Dhancholia, a hailstorm during the first flush that year contributed to the slashed numbers, and with excellent weather conditions, he sees the garden capable of hitting 140,000 kilograms. But even that optimistic amount would still mean a 15 percent drop from the days of its conventional farming. In 2013 Marybong did significantly better but still missed that target by 10 percent, producing 126,000 kilograms, down a quarter from preconversion times.

With crop losses compounded on the accountant's balance sheet by increased production costs, why turn organic?

"Market," said Satish Mantri, the manager of Singbulli, a garden that stretches fourteen miles end to end through the Mirik Valley, with a conceding shrug. Singbulli completed its first fully organic year in 2013. It was a change for the garden—and Mantri. He has been a manager for nearly three decades. Neither had a choice.

"Organic is not a luxury anymore, but a necessity," Sujoy Sengupta explained over lunch at Chamong Tee's fifth-floor offices in a downtown-Kolkata office block called Sagar Estate. Oversize portraits hung on the walls of the empty conference room. Each had a smudge of vermilion pressed against the glass to the forehead. A marigold wreath dangled across one of the gilt frames.

Back in the late 1980s and 1990s, Sengupta explained, being organic meant something on the market. "Then, organic was more like adding an extra edge to your product." Not now. Because so many gardens have converted, he said, "now just being organic is no longer a huge marketing advantage."

A morning shower had drenched the city, but within an hour, the sun had come out and the humidity rose to unbearable levels. Under the loud, cyclical whir of the boxy air-conditioning unit, Sengupta mused about Marybong, a garden he knows well. After a stint in the Dooars, he had his first posting in Darjeeling at Glenburn, where he was a young assistant manager with Sanjay Sharma, then spent five years on Lingia and four on Marybong before coming to the head office in Kolkata as a tea taster and blender. Middays he is particularly distracted. Kolkata straddles the time zones of his customers in Japan, India, and Europe, and a constant cacophony of e-mails arrive on his open laptop, with messages pinging on his BlackBerry and the telephone ringing. His lunch that day went neglected as he took calls, typed quick messages, and repeatedly left the room in search of documents or numbers.

The first Chamong garden to convert was Tumsong, back in 1988. Yields fell 25 percent. The drop upon conversion is at first steep and then levels off. In theory, or at least in hope, yields should recover as the tea bushes grow stronger and build their natural resistance. But that hasn't been the case on Tumsong or elsewhere in Darjeeling. "If it hasn't come back in twenty-five years," Sengupta said in a resigned tone, "it won't."

Contributing to the decline from conversion is the climate, but also more selective plucking, Sengupta said. "The market is demanding finer plucking." By his calculation, though, this has accounted for only up to a 5 percent loss of yield.

The drop in output worries more than just a garden's stakeholders. "Going organic means a loss of volume," Sanjay Kapur said in his Delhi office. "Some estates have had a perceptive drop in *quality.*" The urge to bump up amounts can be great. "They want to make the one hundred thousand kilograms, not eighty thousand. So they make it up with leaf weight. Pick a bit later, pick larger leaves." This isn't across the board, Kapur was keen to stress, and many gardens remain rigorous in their plucking standards.

"We never compromise on quality," said Sengupta over lunch. That can't change. At its heart, Darjeeling is about offering a superior product. It will never be able to compete on volume or price. "They have to keep quality," Vijay Sarda of Nathmulls in Darjeeling warned rather gravely. "The moment they lack quality, the industry will go down."

To offset lower yields, the tea should get a price push in having the certified-organic label, as well as new options for sales to previously inaccessible clients, though Girish Sarda at Nathmulls cautioned, "Only if you know your market." Gardens need to have importers lined up to buy their invoices, he stressed, namely ones from Germany, France, the UK, and Japan. "If not, you will be selling at the same price as conventional teas."

No local market exists for organic teas: buyers in India are not willing to pay a premium for that certificate. The indifference to organic teas seems in stark contrast to the clamor for green teas almost exclusively because of their health properties. Indian consumers have no similar association with organic teas.

Just how much rise in price a tea gets by being organic remains an unknown variable, said Sengupta. There is no exact—or rough—calculation.

Even the Darjeeling tea auctioneer, Anindyo Choudhury, at J. Thomas & Co. finds it difficult to estimate. "First, is it an established garden?" he asked. "And second, who are you selling to? To packeteers and blenders—then it doesn't matter." They will blend with conventional teas. It must be, he stressed, "exporters selling to the niche market." If the garden has an established name and is selling to exporters of that niche market, then it will see an increase, he said. Pushed on a number, he reluctantly and hesitantly agreed to somewhere around 5 or 10 percent.

Because, if there is no financial compensation, what's the point? he asked. "It's a huge expense. There needs to be a benefit." For Singbulli, the change immediately brought up the price of its lower-end teas.

Not all gardens in Darjeeling have had successful conversions. Namring Tea Estate is an example of what Sarda cautions against. This lovely garden runs down from the eastern slopes of Tiger Hill to the Teesta River. Teas, labeled Upper Namring, from its highest section are considered some of the finest in the district. In 1997, Namring turned organic. Yields fell 35 percent. "We couldn't get a market," said H. R. Chaudhary, running his hand over his close-cropped, silver hair. "Marketing is a big thing." The losses were untenable, and in 2004 the garden returned to conventional production.

For some, it isn't only about price. The drop is offset by other gains. "If you want to make your farm sustainable, you must sacrifice something," Tukvar's young manager, Rajesh Pareek, observed. Solidly built and broad shouldered, he would not look out of place in a Venice Beach gym. Tukvar, among the first Darjeeling gardens planted out—and the first to top Rs 10,000 at auction (Rs 10,001, at J. Thomas & Co. in Kolkata in 1992), briefly holding the world record—saw a 20 to 25 percent drop from its recent organic conversion. Still, they are producing up to 300,000 kilograms, or 660,000 pounds, of tea a year, making it one of the largest estates in Darjeeling. While the garden, which sells under the name Puttabong, sacrificed yield, they are conserving the farm's soil and protecting the environment and wildlife, Pareek said.

One of the Chamong properties that suffered steep declines was Ging Tea Estate, down the Lebong Road on the backside of Darjeeling. In autumn, trees with pink blossoms lined the switchbacks down to the factory. Across the Rangili Valley, the tea-covered slopes of Glenburn and Tukdah estates radiated green in the morning sun. Relaxing on the shady verandah of the manager's bungalow with a cup of tea, Mukul Chowdhury, the senior assistant manager, said Ging's output tumbled from 180,000 kilograms (400,000 pounds) to 96,000 kilograms (about 212,000 pounds) with 2006 certification, although it has now stabilized at around 120,000 kilograms (about 265,000 pounds), a loss of one third. Chowdhury, a tall, middle-age Bengali from a landowning family, came to these Himalayan foothills two decades ago. The flower gardens around the solid, gray-stone bungalow buzzed with honeybees. Butterflies and small sunbirds skimmed around in the morning autumn sun that lit up in butterscotch yellows the marigolds studding the hedges along the fields of tea. Look around, he seemed to say with a wave of his hand at the surroundings, *this* is the trade-off.

That night, on Makaibari, Rajah Banerjee said, "Healthy soil is healthy mankind."

Not all are convinced that going organic is the best move for their garden. Castleton, Margaret's Hope, Gopaldhara, and Namring are four marquee estates that produce some of the most sought-after and expensive Darjeeling teas, and they remain conventional. So does Glenburn.

Why to turn organic was answered in a single word. Why *not* took Sanjay Sharma an afternoon.

"It's pure soil science," Sanjay began, dropping down one of Glenburn's steep garden roads from the manager's bungalow in his ranger-green Maruti Gypsy. It was July. Rain had been falling in starts and stops all day, and a late break finally allowed him to take the sturdy but roofless jeep down to look over a lower field. A Scottish tea company had started the estate in 1859 and named it Glenburn, "a river valley" in Scottish. With 40 percent of the estate bordered by rivers, the name is particularly fitting. The Rangeet River marks the northeastern boundary of the garden and separates it from Sikkim.

The monsoon rains had washed out chunks of the precarious track, and stones, some the size of dinner plates, had been set in the deep ruts and along the crumbling edges. Sanjay brought the jeep to a stop and then inched it around a tight hairpin switchback before easing out the clutch. The road passed a mobile weighment station where pluckers were hanging their conical wicker baskets on a scale before dumping the tea leaves out on a tarp. A large, blue plastic sheet covered in leaves stretched across the wet ground behind the open bed of a pickup with bald tires and metal grates over the taillights. A couple of men were packing the leaves into large mesh bags and heaving them into the pickup's bed. Sanjay got out for a moment and spoke to the group in Nepali.

"The tea tree is a bonsai," he said, continuing to drive down the uneven gravel road. "You have stunted it with pruning and plucking. It's creating new foliage to sustain itself. It's a *tree*. And left alone it grows high. Naturally there would be a little new foliage in spring." He maneuvered through a corner so sharp that it took a four-point turn to complete. "But we are plucking it thirty to forty times a year, every five to seven days. The plant is trying to survive. The most important thing for it is nitrogen."

Nitrogen forms the triptych of primary nutrients for a tea plant, along with potassium and phosphorous. Potassium, or potash, works largely on root development, while phosphorus focuses on fruit, flower, and seed development. Nitrogen is the prime ingredient responsible for the tea plant's growth and leaf development and is an essential part of chlorophyll, which creates the brilliant green pigments and causes photosynthesis to take place. As tea is a leaf crop, nitrogen is essential for good yields. It's generally added by a fertilizer application or, on organic gardens, using manures, composts, and cover crops. "The old planter's adage says that every fifty kilos of green leaf needs one kilo of available nitrogen," Sanjay said. "How do you put it back? The best compost has half a percent available nitrogen. A good producing field might produce five thousand kilos of green leaf. That'd be twenty thousand kilos of compost. You'd have to *bury* the plants in it."

At the bottom of the estate along the river, the land flattened out. Narrow drainage ditches for runoff had been dug and created a herringbone pattern across a section of tea that had been planted out in spring. The river sits at eight hundred feet above sea level, some twenty-four hundred feet lower than the bungalow, and it ran fast and milky from the monsoon rains. Golden *mahseer* carp migrate from the Ganges up through the river during the rainy season. In winter, when the water runs lower and clear, Sanjay fly-fishes for Himalayan trout. A pair of crested serpent eagles floated across the river to perch on a tangle of branches on a cliff above the water. He named them and then unclipped the phone on his belt, opened a birding app, and flipped through screens until he found the species with its distinctive white band across the tail to confirm his identification.

"Conventional teas are safe," he said later in an exasperated tone, after checking the field and grinding back up the steep track in the lowest gear toward the bungalow. "They are not hazardous to health. How about Japan? China? Taiwan?" He was referring to three great tea-producing countries where customers are not insisting on organic teas. "Organic teas don't *taste* different."*

Glenburn's use of chemical inputs is slight, and maximum residue limits (MRLs) are within what the EU, Japan, and the USA permit. "The conventional practices we follow need to be very judicious," he said, "how we go about it. We're not polluting the environment with huge chemical loads and deadly pesticides." He laughed at the often unambiguous view of conventional gardens all being awash with toxins. "We take the best from conventional and the best from organic and play it by ear and see what the tree needs."

While it will be sprayed if an infestation of red spider mites gives the bushes a telltale rusted appearance, Glenburn uses eight hundred thousand kilograms (1.7 million pounds) of organic manure a year, which he buys from farmers on a nearby organic tea estate—"My neighbor hates me," Sanjay joked with a schoolboy grin, as Glenburn can pay more—and has an active program of vegetative composting and vermicomposting, which uses earthworms to convert the organic waste into fertilizer. Three or four times a year, men harvest Guatemala grass, a robust, broad-bladed perennial that grows on parts of Glenburn, and haul it around the garden for mulching and rehabilitating uprooted soil. Sanjay instigated a

---

*Or necessarily better. For instance Steven Smith buys mostly—but not exclusively—organic for his bespoke line of fine teas, one of finest and most respected in the United States. "It's about quality first, and that's what we buy."

massive planting of marigolds. They die off and self-seed, coming up the following year. "Self-generating mulch." He introduced them for aesthetics, too. When they flower in October and November, Glenburn's vibrant green tea fields are interwoven with rows of brilliant yellowish-orange buds.

Such a hybrid approach is not uncommon in Darjeeling. Other conventional estates have significantly cut their use of chemical fertilizers and pesticides. "Conventional—but minimal," said Namring's Chaudhary. "Practically organic. Or near-organic." Rohini's B. B. Singh said, "I use only when the pests and insects come." It is for treatment rather than prevention. "It's like if you have fever—you take pill."

For Glenburn, instead of organic, Sanjay Sharma opted for what he calls "an integrated approach" that looks at the larger picture. "The whole thing: land, people, plants, tea," he explained in the jeep on the way back up to the bungalow. He does what is best for *all*, not just one. "The teas, the environment, people in every aspect, we need to do good by them. People have different needs. The future must be secure. Sustainable. Security will only come if production is up and the teas are selling. The trade-off with organic is losing production."

Three Indian peafowl—better known as peacocks—crossed the road in front of the Gypsy. A lesser yellow-neck woodpecker (as Sanjay's app confirmed) urgently knocked on a tall shade tree with leaves dulled like antique coins. Wild boar and Indian muntjac—generally called barking deer, a small, tawny-colored animal with short antlers partially covered in fur and a doglike "bark" that sounds more like a husky cough—roamed the underbrush, unseen in the swiftly failing light.

"It's not about organic, but sustainability. I have five thousand mouths to feed," Sharma said, referring to the large community living on Glenburn. The manager has an enormous responsibility not just to the estate's owners in Kolkata, but to the nearly nine hundred full-time employees working on the garden and their dependents, who risk rolling into a downward spiral of poverty. His decisions affect everyone.

Sharma had little desire to put into jeopardy his relatively small yield—125,000 kilograms (275,000 pounds) a year or so to support thousands of people—and thin profit margin that is continually being teased by the vagaries of weather and politics. Glenburn's teas are well respected, sell in shops from the luxury home-furnishing chain Good Earth in India's most exclusive retail enclaves to two hundred small tea shops in the United States; at auction, they are popular not only with exporters but also blenders, who particularly like their high-quality monsoon flush. It's doubtful that Glenburn could get enough of a price push to compensate for production declines if it went organic.

But something else was also behind his reluctance to turn organic: Sanjay remains skeptical about the motivations of those who insist on organic teas when their lifestyles don't necessarily follow suit. "I don't want to go organic just to make someone *feel* good by drinking my tea. Why? So some guy can feel better—and I can starve my own people?

"We don't make organic teas," he said emphatically. "But we sure as hell make responsible teas."

At least for now, one of Darjeeling's premier gardens has decided to undertake both conventional and organic production. On steep slopes near Mirik, west of Darjeeling along the Nepal border, and watered by the Mechi and Rangbang Rivers, Thurbo, part of the Goodricke Group, produces 240,000 kilograms (530,000 pounds) of tea a year, with roughly 70 percent conventional and 30 percent organic.

One of its autumn teas, an FTGFOP1 Moonlight, in Sale No. 51, the penultimate sale of the calendar year, achieved the highest price for 2013 at J. Thomas & Co.'s wholesale auction, selling for Rs 5,700 per kilogram (not far under $100).

It was a conventional—rather than organic—batch.

But even with that, the future resides in that smaller, lower-producing organic portion of Thurbo that experienced a sharp drop upon conversion and has stabilized around 20–25 percent below previous yields, according to Suman Das, Thurbo's assistant manager.

"It will all go organic," Das said in the garden's wood-paneled tasting room. "That is the future."

Most people working with Darjeeling tea agree. Even with production loss, the organic trend shows little sign of abating. While organic teas do not fetch more from buyers for the local Indian market than conventional ones, nonorganic ones are becoming more difficult to export to Europe, Darjeeling tea's most important market. The trend in Europe for organic teas is growing stronger. "In the next seven to ten years," said the DTA's Sandeep Mukherjee at the end of the 2013 season, "I think Darjeeling will be one hundred percent organic."

CHAPTER 17

Celestial Influences

As an engineering student in London, Rajah Banerjee attended lectures outside his own degree course and, in an Imperial College hall, first encountered the ideas of the Austrian philosopher Rudolf Steiner (1861–1925), whose writings on education and child pedagogy (the Waldorf Schools), medicine, arts, and sciences remain influential. Steiner developed a philosophy called anthroposophy that he defined as "a path of knowledge whose objective is to guide the spiritual in man to the spiritual in the universe."[1]

Not long before Steiner's death, a group of farmers from Silesia (a region today largely in Poland with pieces in the Czech Republic and Germany) approached the eminent philosopher. Their seed strains were deteriorating, they told him, their plants losing vitality. Animals were becoming barren. Pests and diseases were taking larger and larger tolls on their crops. Their fields, filled with chemicals from the First World War, were infertile. Deeply concerned with the degeneration of their soil, they wanted a way forward to heal the land.

In response, Steiner gave a series of eight lectures in June 1924 at the country estate of Count Carl von Keyserlingk at Koberwitz (then in Germany; now Kobierzyce, in western Poland). Together called *Agriculture Course*, they offered a doctrine that elevated planting and harvesting beyond a strictly material level and endowed it with a mystical dimension. Essentially, Steiner took farming from the dirt and embraced a wider view that incorporated an archetypal rhythm following the celestial cycles. The lectures formed the basis of biodynamic farming (from *bios*, "life" in Greek, and *dynamis*, "energy").

Years after his first brush with Steiner in London, Rajah, living on Makaibari and immersed in organic agriculture, came back to the philosopher's oeuvre. Steiner's holistic vision of farming deeply interested him. "And since it concerns not only the earth but the denizens beyond it and the sun, moons, and stars of the universe as a whole, it was literally my cup of tea," he said in the Makaibari documentary. "I personally felt that it was the highest form of organics."[2]

"Insects and diseases are combated by the use of nature's own remedies (ladybugs, trichogramma, wasps, lace wings, preying mantises, garlic and pepper sprays, etc.)," wrote Wolf Storl of the organic method. "Biodynamics is also ecologically orientated, but takes a much wider scope into account, including the sun, the moon, planets and subterranean features, in its effort to understand the totality of all factors."[3]

Another way to sum up the difference is, in Storl's words, "putting one's energies into supporting the good, rather than into fighting the bad."[4] That means, according to journalist Katherine Cole, biodynamic agriculture is about bolstering the health of the farm rather than treating its sickness. In her book on biodynamic wine growers in Oregon, she lays out the tenets of the approach in a series of ageless maxims: "Time farming decisions according to the movements of the moon and stars in the sky. Use the raw materials on your property to nourish your crops. Protect nature, which in return will protect your harvest. And, in doing all these things, harness the spiritual forces of the heavens."[5]

Across India, Steiner's biodynamic method has found fertile ground, with more than five hundred farms implementing its procedures—dairy farms, farms that grow cotton, grapes, mangoes, vanilla, cardamom and peppers and various vegetables, a handful of coffee plantations in the south, and tea estates in Darjeeling, Assam, and Kerala.[6] This is in part because its theories lie close to many of the agricultural practices described in the ancient Hindu scriptures, namely the collection of four books known as the Vedas. Passed down orally for millennia, they offer a comprehensive body of knowledge on the natural world, from the mundane and practical to the spiritual. Steiner's profound engagement with these scriptures generated two lecture series that formed a book called *The Bhagavad Gita and the West* and later deeply informed his agricultural treatise.

Biodynamic farming in India is, in many respects, more than three thousand years old.

"Many of the essential principles of bio-dynamic agriculture mesh seamlessly with Vedic agricultural practices," wrote a journalist in the

Hindu, one of India's most widely read English-language newspapers. "Our farmers respond instinctively to the concept of the 'planting calendar'; following the almanac, and knowledge of planetary and cosmic rhythms and their influence on plants is used to plan agricultural activities."[7]

A key to the Vedic teachings is the harmony of the five elements (*pancha bhuta*) which make up everything in the universe. The first four—*vayu* (wind or air), *apa* (water), *agi* (fire), and *prithvi* (earth)—are empirical. But these are infused with a fifth, *akasha* (sometimes translated as "ether"), the opposite of matter. It's what fills the gaps between the elements, keeps the cosmos in order, and the celestial bodies moving in a disciplined manner. This is the unexplainable element. "The living being must always be permeated by an *ethereal*—for the ethereal is the true bearer of life," Steiner said in his third lecture in *Agriculture Course*.[8]

Steiner wasn't only an ideas guy, a theoretician recycling Vedic agricultural wisdom from a time when farming was closely linked with the heavens. He also laid the framework for a series of practical applications centered around nine "preparations." This part of biodynamics, more than its underlying philosophy, makes it an easy target to mock and to dismiss as "voodoo farming" or "muck and magic."

Numbered today (somewhat arbitrarily) 500 through 508, these preparations enliven the soil and surrounding environment. In Preparation 500 cow horns are packed with fresh cow dung (ideally from lactating cows), buried underground in autumn with the tips pointing upward, and then dug up six months later in spring. "This is the period when the earth is breathing in and cosmic earth forces are most active (winter)," the Bio-Dynamic Association of India (BDAI) informs farmers on its Web site. A pea-size pinch of this rich humus is added to a bucket of lukewarm rainwater, then stirred for one hour before being sprayed so that it falls in a gentle mist over the tea plants. "Apply when the dew is falling (the earth breathes in) i.e. late afternoon or evening—descending Moon."[9] According to Demeter, the German-based company that is the main certifying body of biodynamics as well as a trademark and label for products that carry its certification, "The horn manure preparation (500) works on plant root development, plant form and its vitality, promotes plant growth, the soil micro-life which is active in the humus fraction and the Ego component of our cultivated plants."[10]

Preparation 501 includes crushed silica quartz crystal (silicon dioxide). Steiner recommends first grinding it down in a mortar with an iron pestle and then on a glass surface until very fine. This hazardous powder (inhaling it can cause silicosis, a lung disease) is moistened with springwater or rainwater into a paste, packed into the horns, and buried—again tips pointing up—from the spring equinox until the autumn one. As the BDAI instructs, "This is the period when the earth is breathing out and the cosmic light energy is most active (summer)." A small amount—"enough to cover the small fingernail"—scraped from inside gets stirred into warm water and sprayed onto the fields. "Apply when the dew is rising (the earth breathes out)."[11] The quantity of quartz is minute, even homeopathic, and acts as an energizer, drawing in warmth and cosmic properties.

The remaining preparations consist of involved formulas using yarrow, chamomile, dandelion, and other natural ingredients to enhance composting. Stuffing yarrow blossoms into a stag's bladder, hanging it in the sun for the summer, and then burying it for the winter before unearthing is the gist of Preparation 502. Preparation 505 calls for putting oak bark into the brain cavity of a cow, sheep, or goat skull, interring it in a swampy expanse in autumn, and lifting it in springtime. It is then dried until the potent odor has dissipated. A small ball of these preparations is placed within composting heaps. They marshal the cosmos's forces to encourage rich soil life in the clay-humus.[12]

Key to preparations 500 and 501 is the stirring of the mixtures into water before applying. Ideally using a whisk or clutching a handful of straw, stirring begins clockwise to create a vortex in the slurry, reverses directions until another vortex reaches the bottom of the pail, and so on. Stirring takes about an hour and activates and energizes the solution.

When a farmer at Steiner's lecture asked about using a mechanical stirrer, the philosopher argued that it needed to be done by hand. "When you stir manually, all the delicate movements of your hand will come into the stirring. Even the feelings you have may then come into it."[13] Steiner offered an analogy of being treated by a machine versus by a doctor, who transmits enthusiasm through human touch. "Light has a strong effect on the remedies; why not enthusiasm? Enthusiasm mediates; it can have a great effect. Enthusiastic doctors of to-day can achieve great results."[14]

At the heart of Steiner's point is that it needs to be done consciously. For Steiner, this was also a way of developing a personal relationship between the farmer and the land.

● ● ●

In 1993, Makaibari became the first tea estate in the world to be certified biodynamic. The certificate only lasts six months. Demeter has renewed it biannually since.

Makaibari's holistic approach to farming seeks a harmony between those living on the estate and the soil, microorganisms, plants, and animals, with tea playing a nurturing role in a tightly linked ecological web.

The estate sits just below Kurseong, known as the Land of White Orchids, about halfway to Darjeeling from Siliguri. It's a fifteen-minute walk down Pankhabari Road to the factory on an upper section of the garden, passing first the Castleton Tea Estate, Darjeeling Tea Research & Development Center, Cochrane Place Hotel, and the turnoff for Ambootia Tea Estate before entering Makaibari land. Black-and-orange butterflies flutter above the shrubby trees that line the narrow, windy road, brilliantly plumed birds flit about, and triangular, green-and-white Gorkhaland flags snap in the breeze. Steep pitches covered in emerald foliage fall down from the road's shoulder; quiet contours of tea bushes are broken by pockets of scrub and overlooked by tall neems, Persian lilacs, *shirish* (East Indian walnut) with irregular fissures on their yellow-gray bark, and stout fig trees.

Spread along the four ridges of the estate are seven villages, tight clusters of brick houses painted in blues or greens or reds with tin roofs. "Living in these villages are 1,558 people," Rajah said in the first days of July, adding, with a smile, "The last one was born ten days ago." He takes pride in knowing each by name.

Over half of Makaibari's land is under a cover of forest where wild things thrive. Above the canopy of green tea bushes rise the soft calls of birds. The trees and skies bustle with a plethora of large and small birds, colorful and drab. Most impressive are the great pied hornbills, black-and-white, vulture-size birds with five-foot wingspans and heavy, yellow-orange, concave-topped casques. They eat small rodents and reptiles but prefer feeding on fruit trees. Wild figs are a favorite; they can devour 150 in a single meal. Their loud barking call, at times more of a retch, reverberates across Makaibari.

Inside the estate's forests are troops of rhesus and Assamese macaque monkeys, cobras, boar, barking deer, wild goats, and large cats. "There is just one tiger—but plenty of leopards," said a resident in the village closest to the factory. The animals, with their distinctive black spots and black-tipped ears, hunt around the tea estate villages on occasion, he said, skulking at night after a pye-dog, goat, or even cow.

But no creature on Makaibari makes a bigger stir than a bug that sits easily in the palm of a hand. In 1991, a strange green insect that looked exactly like a tea leaf appeared on Makaibari. Rajah Banerjee christened it Tea Deva—"God of Tea"—after the class of deities from the Vedas. Entomologists identified it as a member of the Phillidae family, an insect highly adept at mimicry. Sometimes called a walking leaf, it can impersonate leaves, sticks, and branches.

The insect is rare enough that an extremely generous bounty of Rs 5,000 ($90) goes to anyone who finds one. For a plucker, that's equivalent to fifty-five days of wages. "The one who has luck will get that bug," a field supervisor said during a sunny first flush day, as she watched over a dozen pluckers working a section below Lower Makaibari. As the women moved through the bushes, rapidly gathering shoots and tossing them into their baskets, they kept an eye out for a moving leaf. Each year, pluckers find a couple of Tea Devas.

Why Banerjee is so keen on finding them, and willing to pay so much, is a matter for debate. "To show to foreigners," answered one of the pluckers in the group. She was in her fifties, with red rubber boots, a golden stud in her nose, and a folded towel on her head where the thick strap of her basket rested.

It's part of the legend of the farm. Or, as some cynics say, one of its gimmicks. The manager of another Darjeeling estate, when asked if he had seen any Tea Devas on his farm, wryly remarked, "I thought Rajah Banerjee had a monopoly on those."

"If the farm is purely organic, then the tea bug will come," said the plucking supervisor. "It proves the organicness of the leaf."

Rajah Banerjee goes further. In his book he wrote, "As Rudolf Steiner—the father of biodynamic agriculture—has stated, if all agriculture practices are truly holistic, then the principal crop will be reflected in mimicry."[15]

The notion is perfect for the legend and near-mythical status of Makaibari. Perhaps too perfect. Malcolm Gardner, biodynamic research expert at the Rudolf Steiner Library of the Anthroposophical Society in America and editor and cotranslator of Steiner's agriculture lectures, exclaimed when asked, "In my thirty years of studying everything related to Steiner's agriculture, I have never come across this quote or anything close to it."

Many in the West remain dubious about biodynamic farming despite its recent popularity. (It is practiced across the world in various sectors, perhaps most famously in the United States in viticulture.) Evidence for the results for biodynamic farming tends to be more anecdotal than scientific. As anecdotes go, Makaibari is biodynamic farming's greatest success story. Even if the Tea Deva doesn't convince Rajah Banerjee's skeptics, the price tag on his world-record-setting Silver Tips Imperial and the discerning clients it attracts should.

Silver Tips Imperial sits at the top of Makaibari's selection of vintages. The delicate tea has a satiny floralness that's soothingly subtle. "This is the dynamic one," Rajah said one spring morning, sipping a cup of it in the Makaibari tasting room. By that he meant the energized one, the one produced by forces of nature not completely understood by science.

Made with silvery, unfurled buds, it has—unlike Glenburn's Silver Needle—a degree of fermentation and a extremely light roll. It is not a white tea, Rajah insists, even if some retailers market it as such. "It is exceptional handiwork," he said. Beyond that, he is recalcitrant. He has spent thirty years perfecting it and remains evasive on manufacturing specifics. "Don't ask any questions about Silver Tips Imperial and you won't get any lies," he said. "Isn't that right?" he called out to his wife across the sitting room of the bungalow one evening, then turned with a wide, tight-lipped grin that bunched up his cheeks around his eyes and brought to a halt any further discussion on producing the illustrious tea.

Another difference from Glenburn's Silver Needle is that the leaves of Makaibari's Silver Tips Imperial are energized by cosmic forces and plucked around the full moon. According to Demeter, "The moon and planets influence the growth of roots, leaves, flowers and fruit, just like moon phases have an influence on sea tides."[16] The highest tides of the month are when the moon is the fullest. A tea plant is made up largely of water—the green leaves contain around 78 percent moisture—so it's hardly unthinkable that the moon could have an influence.

During this period, the elements of the earth are drawn upward by cosmic forces, explained Makaibari's production manager, Sanjoy Mukherjee, a young man with a wispy mustache and a broad smile. "The taste and aroma levels are very high." Holding a Nike baseball hat in his hand and waiting to begin the morning batch tasting, he added, "This is the magic of the universe." (The opposite happens with the new moon, when the water is falling to the roots. Then, he advised, harvest potatoes and carrots.)

Production of Silver Tips Imperial is limited: only 120 kilograms (265 pounds) in 2013, according to Mukherjee. The first of five pluckings took place at the end of March, just as the first flush had got under way. It had a special resonance, as it was Holi, the Hindu spring festival of colors.

"It is a fusion of external forces . . . spirit-soul . . . which can never die," Rajah said in the tasting room, trying to explain its uniqueness. "It is a reflection of past, present, and future in one teacup."

But it costs dearly to sample a tea that at bedtime can, according to Rajah, "cull one to celestial slumber." While Makaibari significantly bettered its 2003 auction benchmark, selling Silver Tips Imperial a few years later in a tea expo in Beijing for Rs 54,000 a kilo[17] (then about $1,315), even such princely sums pale next to what Banerjee gets for his best vintages through private sales. The highly respected English-language Indian newsmagazine *Outlook* reported in 2005 that the British royal family was paying Rs 200,000 (about $4,500) per kilo for Silver Tips Imperial, and the sultan of Brunei even more, some Rs 250,000 (about $5,700) for that same amount.[18]

Commoners can get the celestial leaves, too. Craft House shops in Delhi sell twenty-five-gram (about three-quarter-ounce) packets for Rs 2,600 (about $50). That amount weighs less than thirteen playing cards—a single suit in a deck—and will brew just ten cups of tea. But at Rs 104,000 ($1,900) per kilo, it's significantly less than the queen and sultan pay.

Makaibari is not the only biodynamic estate in Darjeeling.

Originally planted out in 1861, the year of Rudolf Steiner's birth, Ambootia stretches from twelve hundred to forty-two hundred feet, and occupies some 966 hectares (2,400 acres) with just 350 hectares of those under tea. The garden is divided into sixty sections, with about two dozen reserved for the German organic-tea company Lebensbaum. The high, northeast corner of Ambootia abuts Kurseong (and neighbors Makaibari and Castleton estates), and to reach the factory requires thirty minutes of aggressive driving down the curvy, bumpy drive lined by a hedge of *Lantana camara*, with small clusters of yellow and pink florets.

In early October 1968, unusually heavy rains fell across Darjeeling and Sikkim, causing hundreds of landslides. Ambootia received thirty-five inches of rain in just fifty to sixty hours. The saturated soil in the southern section of the estate fell away in what is said to be the largest landslide in South Asia. It carried off 150 hectares (370 acres) of Ambootia, taking two villages and some three hundred homes with it. For the next decade or so, the slide continued to expand.[19] Today, it's carpeted over in green, but standing on its abrupt edge feels like being on the rim of a sweeping waterfall chasm void of water.

This catastrophe remained deeply imprinted on the mind of Sanjay Bansal when he took over the garden from his father in 1992. "For the new owner this was one of the pinching proofs that the increasing use of chemicals (pesticides and fertilizers) in tea gardens had a huge negative effect on the soil structure," wrote the newsletter by Soil & More, a Dutch soil and sustainable-farming consulting company. "Chemicals, especially the salt in fertilizers, destroy the microbial life which normally holds together the soil particles. This leads to a loss of soil structure causing either leakage of water or floods due to water logging."[20] Alongside the aggressive reforesting program, Bansal transitioned the garden to organic farming in 1993, and the following year introduced biodynamic practices.

The move from conventional farming meant the garden lost about a quarter of its yield, but it helped stabilize the land while being able to produce teas for the most exclusive names in Europe: Harrods, Fortnum & Mason, Simon Lévelt, Alnatura, Lebensbaum, and Schwarzsee. Mariage Frères in Paris stocks more than fifty Darjeeling teas from thirty-plus gardens. A hundred-gram (3.5-ounce) packet of Ambootia's second flush Brumes d'Himalaya—"Himalayan Mists"—made especially for the French boutique, sells for 120 euros ($170), the most expensive tea in the shop.

Bansal actively champions the organic and biodynamic movements, but on the ground, the garden's manager, Jay Neogi, is more prosaic about its esoteric theories. Driving around Ambootia, he said, "I don't see any pests." Why not? "It's ecologically balanced." At being pushed for a fuller reason, he simply shrugged and smiled. "Seeing the effects but not necessarily seeing the cause."

The fields were vibrant green, the bushes healthy looking. There was no barren earth. Herbs and mulching covered the ground between tea bushes. Spiderwebs stretched across bushes, dragonflies buzzed about, and even ladybugs, as featured in the Ambootia logo, crawled on tea leaves—all signs of a naturally healthy garden.

And a healthy place to work. "I feel different when I enter the garden," said one of Ambootia's field managers, a young Bihari who has worked on the estate for four years. In charge of one of the four divisions, he has a dozen field supervisors and 220 pluckers under him. "I don't have words to describe it. But I feel totally different. The air, the water."

"Why do we believe?" Neogi asked. "Because the product is good. The outcome." He considered this idea thoughtfully. "As long as the outcome is good, then we are satisfied."

That satisfaction has influenced the entire Ambootia group, which has converted all of its gardens to biodynamic farming. Along with Ambootia, the group's other ten Darjeeling gardens—Chongtong, Happy Valley, Monteviot, Moondakotee, Mullootar, Nagri, Nurbong, Sepoydhoorah (Chamling), Sivitar, and Aloobari—have also become certified biodynamic. According to the group's precise general manager, Krishnendu Chatterjee, their eleven properties, spread over a total of 4,302.57 hectares (10,631.87 acres) containing 2,284.56 hectares (5,645.27 acres) of tea, are producing more than 12 percent of Darjeeling's total output under Demeter's strict biodynamic guidelines.*

To this list of biodynamic gardens is added another, Selimbong Tea Estate in the Mirik Valley near Gopaldhara and Chamong. The smallish garden, just 307 hectares (759 acres) and half that under tea, produces around 50,000 kilograms (110,000 pounds) of tea. It has held Demeter certification since 1997.

Biodynamically speaking, probably no other place in the world nor any other single product can match what is being produced by Darjeeling's tea gardens. Around two-thirds of Darjeeling's tea is organic. That is comprehensible. But that about 15 percent of its total tea can be called voodoo vintages is highly surprising, especially as the area does not market itself as such.

But does biodynamic tea actually *taste* better? Does planting according to the moon's orbit and the position of the constellations make a difference

---

*In August 2014, Ambootia's factory, built in 1920 and completely updated and modernized in 2009, burnt to the ground. The fire started around nine P.M., quickly engulfed the building, and by the time the fire brigade made it from Kurseong, all was lost. Plucking resumed the following day while the embers still smoldered. Until the new factory can be rebuilt, the green leaves will be processed at one of the group's other gardens. After the factory at Monteviot burned down in 2004, the same year it was acquired by Ambootia, its green leaf was sent to Ambootia. Now, with Ambootia's, it will get trucked to Moondakotee and Nagri tea estates for processing until the factory can be rebuilt.

in that final judgment of a tea when it's sipped from the cup? Does spraying the leaves with ground silica crystals that have been buried in cow horns give deeper muscatel flavors? A more nuanced body?

While some argue passionately that indeed biodynamic tea does taste better—and can point to stellar client lists as proof—this is, in many ways, not the main object. Rather, biodynamic farming seeks more than merely *taste*. "Biodynamics is a human service to the earth and its creatures, not just a method for increasing production or for providing healthy food," wrote Storl.[21] Or flavorful teas. "The ultimate goal of farming is not the growing of crops, but the cultivation and perfection of human beings,"[22] wrote the legendary Japanese philosopher and farmer Masanobu Fukuoka, who visited Makaibari when he was ninety years old, in his manifesto on natural farming, *The One-Straw Revolution*. Approvingly, Rajah Banerjee quotes this line in his own book.

As Steiner's comment about stirring slurry reflects, biodynamic farming is done consciously. The passion is what matters, the reverential feelings that the farmer has for his crops and the land. "Whatever we do," said the young Bihari field manager on Ambootia, "it is about nature."

Such feelings toward nature have a long lineage in India. "Hindus, with their reverence for sacred rivers, mountains, forests and animals, have always been close to nature," wrote Ranchor Prime in *Hinduism and Ecology*.[23] Trees, Prime noted, have an important status: the great forests that once sheltered Lord Rama and his beautiful wife during their years of exile, and Krishna and his flute as he danced with friends and herded cows; the big shade trees—"silent symbols of India's spiritual roots"[24]—under which travelers rested from the heat and gurus passed on wisdom to disciples. "O King of trees! I bow before you. Brahma is in your roots, Vishnu is in your body, Shiva is in your branches. In every one of your leaves there is a heavenly being," claims an ancient verse quoted by Prime.[25] This early Vedic tradition of placing a high value on trees was passed down.[26] Two thousand years ago the ancient Roman historian Quintus Curtius Rufus took note: "To anything they have started to cultivate they give divine status, especially to trees, violating which constitutes a capital offense."[27]

"Most people farm for profits," Rajah Banerjee said in the Makaibari documentary. "They're looking for the flavor in their balance sheet. When we talk about the flavor and balance sheet of life, we are talking about healing the land and the tea and creating an environment whereby man becomes a rhythm of nature. We are not protecting or conserving forests.

It's the reverse process. Man becomes a rhythm, a part of the forest, an extension of the forest."

In his bungalow's sitting room Rajah proclaimed, "The creature who wins against nature destroys itself."*

Farming isn't a battle against nature, but a partnership with it. It is respecting the basics of nature in action and ensuring that they continue.

We do not live nor farm in a void. There is a "connection between our environment and our way of life," wrote Prime. "A way of life does not exist in a vacuum. It is based on a way of thinking: a philosophy of life."[28]

Over a cup of freshly processed first flush tea, Rajah said, "When you eat or drink something, it becomes a material part of your being."

---

*This echoes a line by the celebrated American environmental campaigner Rachel Carson: "Man is a part of nature, and his war against nature is inevitably a war against himself."

CHAPTER 18

Initiatives

For Darjeeling tea to keep its position on the top shelf of the world's most distinguished products—or even, perhaps, for it to merely survive—the industry must go beyond simply turning 100 percent organic, offering new varieties of teas, opening new markets, or interesting more tea drinkers within India. The challenge is less in the soil, bushes, or leaves themselves than with the people who reside on the estates. A tea garden needs to be not just a sustainable, self-sufficient farm, but a sustainable, self-sufficient community. It's not merely about creating well-made teas but also having a stable workforce. While Darjeeling's celebrated flavor stems from leaves, its future rests in the people who pluck them. If you can't get the leaves off the bush and processed, everything else becomes irrelevant.

The rapid rise of staggeringly high worker absenteeism in the last few years has moved this to the forefront of urgent threats. Of the major hurdles ahead, the gardens can—and need to—be proactive in immediately tackling this one.

"We know where they are going," said Sanjay Sharma about Glenburn's disappearing workforce, whose absenteeism has suddenly and swiftly climbed to around 30 percent. "We have to head off and head back workers. The only way is being able to offer them better employment, better quality of life. It's a hard one. It's easier said than done."

To put the critical challenge in the simplest of terms: the future of Darjeeling depends on motivating a marginalized, low-paid labor force to continue working on the estates. This is particularly challenging when a single kilo of tea can sell for more than they make in the entire year, an especially stark notion at blue-chip gardens. Makaibari might get record prices, but workers receive the same daily wages as on every other garden in the district.

Tea gardens are based on a Raj-era system that remains largely in place. "The colonial foundation is not working," Rajah Banerjee said in autumn. "It's broken." A fundamental change in the serflike structure needs to evolve, to include more worker involvement, even ownership, to make them a dynamic, integrated part of the estate—and a party to its successes. "We need to look out an alternative window," he said.

"It's about partnership, not ownership," insists Rajah. He refuses to call those who work on Makaibari *laborers* or even *workers* and instead refers to them as *community activists* or *participants*. This isn't only about semantics, but, rather, deeply invested involvement. "They are not workers but a community. It's their home. The key is in community participation."

The 1991 creation of the Makaibari Joint Body (MBJB) was one initiative to encourage this. The committee, comprised of elected members from the estate's seven villages, is mostly women. Elections take place every three years; the only permanent member is Rajah. The committee makes decisions about the garden and on microloans for projects such as homestay constructions. It runs a nursery and, in 2012, opened a small library with books to lend and Wi-Fi-connected computers to use. While three of the four computers were not working by autumn 2013, it was still offering free computer lessons to people on Makaibari. Even with class sizes of twenty, the continual waiting list reflects the program's popularity.

Sometimes partnership comes in subtle forms. "Encouragement is partnership," Rajah said one cold night in the spacious drawing room of the Makaibari bungalow. "Empowerment is partnership. What do marginalized women that have been empowered invest in?" He mimed jiggling an old-fashioned waist belt heavy with coins. "They invest in the best primary education. That creates awareness." As he spoke, he made slow loops around the room. "Then they invest in the best secondary school. This builds capacity." He stopped for a moment near his wife, Srirupa, who huddled close to an electric heater that reflected glowing orange in the lenses of her eyeglasses. "With awareness and capacity you create character, and if you have character, you can succeed at anything." He smiled, then said emphatically, "*That's* what you get when you empower the ladies!"

Estates across Darjeeling are trying various initiatives that range from reforesting—giving out varieties of trees, including bamboo, which has a multitude of uses—to harvesting rainwater and buying vehicles to ply the roads as taxis. But the ancient cow has been the base for the most inspired schemes.

"A thoroughly healthy farm should be able to produce within itself all that it needs," Rudolf Steiner stated in his second agricultural lecture.[1] At the center of the farm and its health is the cow, both in traditional Vedic practice as well as in organic and biodynamic farming.

The cow has long been sacred in India, valued but also protected. In ancient India, killing one was a serious crime tantamount to killing a Brahman and punishable by death.[2] The animal has an elemental mother-liness, with its milk replacing that of a baby's mother. Cows can convert grasses and roughage that are inedible and indigestible to humans into milk, which in turn can become butter and ghee (clarified butter), yogurt, and cheese, excellent sources of protein but also some of the most important offerings for the gods. The cow was also key to rural life by providing manure for fertilizer as well as fuel. Their leather could be used for sandals, garments, and receptacles, and they could be trained to pull plows and carts.[3] As a large poster hanging in Ambootia's tasting room titled "The Cow Story" illustrates, it was the most useful of all domesticated animals.

The cow's importance remains so on many of Darjeeling's tea estates, especially as the number of organic gardens has dramatically increased in the last decade. Gardens generally do not own the cows; rather, they belong to those living in the estate's villages, who sell the manure for organic fertilizer to the garden while keeping the milk to drink or to sell at the market.

Always a pioneer, Rajah went a step further in utilizing cow dung on Makaibari decades ago. Inspired by Gandhi's notion of *swadeshi*—self-sufficiency or self-reliance—Rajah used a component from the Mahatma's bucolic vision and offered a way to turn the dung into a clean and renewable fuel. Biogas is created from a slurry of cow manure and water via anaerobic digestion. The organic matter breaks down in a biogas plant (also called a digester), and a hood traps the methane created. This can be stored and then burned as fuel, generally for cooking.

One of the biggest advantages of biogas is that it reduces the need to cut firewood from the surrounding hillsides to use for cooking fuel. Cutting fewer trees shores up the soil of Darjeeling's fragile hillsides against erosion, slows the spread of deforestation, and helps stop land-slides that claw away at the slopes. In additon, homes become healthier by the cutting of smoke from the kitchens, and this can improve the quality of life—and often the economic circumstances of the family. Collecting firewood was considered a woman's job, and for many women was their single most time-consuming task, taking three or more hours a day. Being free of this provides a significant amount of time to dedicate to other pursuits, including ones that generate income. It created what Rajah calls "grassroots entrepreneurs," who began selling their organic milk, planting and tending patches of vegetables (to eat at home or sell in the market), making paper, brewing millet wine, and opening homestays. This "income away from tea," as he calls it, complements a household's wages from the estate.

Such dynamic programs on Makaibari have not been without missteps. Rajah's first foray into biogas used a community-size unit that failed within months. He revisited the idea in spring of 1988 with individual digesters. With people more personally responsible, it worked better. But visits throughout the 2013 harvest to Makaibari showed few signs of cows, and the hoods of all seven biogas digesters in Upper Makaibari were cracked and out of use.

"Maintenance is always a problem," agreed a small group of men living in different villages around the estate. They spoke of having cows a handful of years ago—"in the years of biogas." One said, "But it was too much work cutting grass for them." It was easier in the beginning when they could find fodder closer. One of the men, who lives in Upper Makaibari near the factory, estimated that his village had just four or five cows, with perhaps forty to fifty in all of Makaibari. And not from any garden program. "Bought with their own money," he said. They sell the cow dung to the garden.

While Rajah's bucolic biogas dream remains unrealized, most homes now have gas stoves that run on propane cylinders bought in the small shops around the garden. Cooking with wood, though, has not disappeared. Gas is expensive and generally reserved for the midday meal, when time is limited. Most families still use wood to cook morning and evening meals. To warm their homes on winter evenings, they burn tea-garden prunings. No one, the men said, has heating.

Still, Rajah offers what he has done on Makaibari as a framework. "We've been part of creating something that could bring dynamic change," he said in his office. "It has turned into a movement." He was referring not only to the natural methods of farming, but also something deeper. "When you come into Makaibari, you feel a part of it."

• • •

Darjeeling is a favorite for visitors, and recent spells of political stability have seen numbers in town shoot up with both Indian and foreign guests. The 2010–11 season saw 135,000 domestic tourists. That number climbed to 430,000 for 2011–12 and to 730,000 for 2012–13.[4]

Often affectionately calling the city Darj, Indian visitors stroll the Chowrasta (and let their kids be led around it on scruffy ponies), browse the vintage photos in Das Studio, and sit on Keventer's roof terrace, where, in Anurag Basu's 2012 Bollywood blockbuster *Barfi!*, Ranbir Kapoor unsuccessfully proposed to Ileana D'Cruz, then climbed the nearby clock tower to turn back the time fifteen minutes, as if it had never happened. Families jam the Hasty Tasty for familiar Indian dishes, buy knitted woolen hats with tassels in the bazaar for the cold evenings, and pick up packets of tea at Nathmulls to take home as gifts.

Darjeeling's tea and tea gardens are clearly a draw, the gardens' lazy carpeting of green across the area a scenic attraction. But tea tourism is one initiative that remains largely untested, yet is full of promise. While West Bengal's chief minister, Mamata Banerjee, is keen on the concept, complaints remain about the convoluted nature of converting land from agricultural to tourism use. The gardens, who lease their land from the state government, can only transform a mere fraction of their estates to dedicated tourism usage: just five acres (two hectares), with actual construction limited to a single acre (the remaining four acres are for landscaping and beautifying the property).[5]

So far, just a handful of gardens have tapped into the concept and allowed people to be guests on a working estate. Each has taken a different approach.

To offer some of the many visitors who turn up at Makaibari a place to stay, the estate instigated a homestay program in 2005. According to Nayan Lama, its young coordinator, twenty-two families are engaged in the program, fifteen in the village near the factory and another seven in Phoolbari (Flower Village), on the lower reaches of Makaibari. Using microloans from the Makaibari Joint Body, each host family has constructed a separate room for guests and an outdoor Western-style toilet. For Rs 600 (about $10) per person, visitors get a room, three meals, visits to the tea fields and factory, tastings, and plenty of tea to drink. Primarily European and North American college-age students are attracted, but

Indian tourists have begun staying, too. While accommodations can be rustic at best and susceptible to power outages and water shortages, the opportunity to experience a tea estate at ground level is unique and especially tantalizing at one as well-known and innovative as Makaibari.

"Should you plan to interact positively with our working philosophy and get the true pulse and insouciance of the Makaibari spirit," Rajah Banerjee replied after an initial inquiry, "then a homestay with one of our community members is recommended."

The money for these, Rajah likes to point out, "goes to the woman of the house." Clearly he trusts women more than men with fiscal diligence. While he helped get it off the ground, "now it runs itself," he said proudly. "I don't keep a penny."

One of the families involved is that of Maya Davi Chettrini, the first female field supervisor, and her husband, a stocky forest ranger who helps guard the estate's woodlands. The guest room is painted ocher red and lime green and has a pair of beds, a tall stack of soft blankets, and views down over the tea-covered valley. Dinner in the front room one spring night included dal and a tangy stewed-chicken dish with plenty of aromatic long-grain white rice, which was eaten by candlelight during an hours-long electrical outage.

Homestay mornings start not long after sunrise, with the chickens crowing and general movement among the small but dense village of Upper Makaibari. A typical breakfast includes a masala omelet (with minced tomatoes, onions, and green chilies from one of the pots alongside the house), *aloo dum* (spicy potatoes) dabbed with heady mango pickle, and plenty of freshly fried *parathas* (unleavened bread).

While guests have a second cup of Makaibari tea from an ample thermos and begin planning out their day on the garden, Maya shoulders a small cloth carryall with a bottle of water, takes from a hook outside the door her red umbrella, bleached and tattered by the elements, and heads to the fields to work.

Glenburn Tea Estate (and now Boutique Hotel) has staked out the opposite end of the tea-garden experience. Whereas Makaibari offers A Day in the Life of a Tea Plucker, Glenburn's luxurious experience is A Day in the Life of a Tea Planter.

It's also at the other end of the price range. Compared to Makaibari's Rs 600 a day, an all-inclusive single at Glenburn runs around Rs 18,000 (over $300). *All-inclusive* means everything from the washing and darning of clothes to a jeep and driver at the disposal of every guest—from pick-up until drop-off. There are four-course meals, riverside picnics, and visits to the tea factory, guided walks with experts on traditional medical plants or birdlife, and hikes down to the 110-year-old Manjitar Suspension Bridge, which dangles one hundred feet above the Rangeet River as it crosses over to Sikkim. The day begins with a light tap on the door and a "bed tea"—a tray of freshly brewed tea and a few biscuits—and ends with sophisticated dishes that use tea and tea leaves as ingredients.

Husna-Tara Prakash was largely responsible for getting the hotel element of Glenburn operating. Raised in England, she attended boarding school in India at the elite Welham Girls' School in Dehradun, then did her undergraduate and postgraduate work in the natural sciences in England at Cambridge. She married a man whose family owns Glenburn and ended up back in India. Visiting the estate the first time, she saw its potential as a special place to stay. After a major refurbishment, the first four rooms opened in 2002, followed by another four in 2008.

Standing on an upper balcony of the beefy, imposing redbrick Victorian mansion in Kolkata where Glenburn has an office, she explained that the hotel component wasn't just something else to do along with producing tea. The key, she stressed, was to give the hospitality part of the garden full attention—from a packed picnic hamper with chicken-and-mint sandwiches, apple cake, and hot tea to unwrap at a scenic viewpoint on the long drive up to Glenburn from Bagdogra Airport to specially designed tea-patterned fabrics that decorate the rooms. Though there are only eight of them, they command a staff of fifty—all from Glenburn's tea families.

The keys to the success of this concept were offering access to Glenburn's charismatic resident tea planter, manager, tea maker, and snake catcher Sanjay Sharma, and making them feel like personal guests rather than paying clients. That meant showing them around the estate, leading tastings of Glenburn's range of teas, and offering a glimpse of a planter's working life. At the day's end, Sanjay joined them for drinks on the verandah of the sprawling and elegantly refurbished century-old *burra* bungalow where he could hold court and tell well-honed anecdotes explaining cultural details of the garden or relate his latest snake-catching caper. Like Rajah Banerjee, he is a splendid storyteller, although his anecdotes lack the mystical platitudes so present in Rajah's. Sanjay's tend to be light and never preachy, rarely long, and studded with caustic, self-deprecating zingers. He tends to stop at a good line, and the remainder of the story needs to be coaxed from him.

On one muggy summer evening, the guests eventually moved to the large, oval table in the dining room with Sanjay at its head as seasoned host but also head chef. He had developed many of the kitchen's signature dishes, mostly original takes on international classics (tea-marbled deviled eggs) or European accents on Indian ones. Sanjay's *plat de résistance* is succulent tea-smoked chicken breasts served on a bed of wilted spinach leaves and moistened with a tea jus aromatized by star anise, cinnamon, bay leaves, and peppercorns. While somewhat inspired by episodes of *MasterChef Australia* he catches on YouTube, it is also influenced by Sanjay's mother, who comes from the far-northeastern Indian region bordering Burma called Nagaland, where slow-smoking is an important way of preserving. The dinner finished with Glenburn's "chai dessert," a thick "tea" spiced with cinnamon, ginger, bay leaf, nutmeg, and vanilla seeds scraped from a leathery pod with the tip of a sharp knife and whisked as it comes to a boil to give it the consistency of a frothy cappuccino.

Glenburn is rated number one out of all of the TripAdvisor hotels listed in Darjeeling, and it's generally booked solid. "We also make tea," Sanjay sarcastically quipped, spooning up the last of his dessert. The guests laughed. Had Glenburn not been producing some of the finest teas in Darjeeling, it wouldn't have been funny.*

Tourism, however, remains at the mercy of politics, as was demonstrated even before 2013's monsoon had cleared.

After the beginning of a staggeringly good tourist season, the GJM called a strictly enforced *bandh* on the last day of July that shut down the hills. A month later, an Indian newspaper reported, "The unusually deserted look of the popular mall road of Darjeeling is a testimony to [its

---

*Having dreamt of life under wide African skies as a kid, and more recently of new challenges after twenty years in the Darjeeling hills, nearly all of them on Glenburn, Sanjay defied both conventional wisdom and the expectations that he would forever remain in Darjeeling. He was courted for a number of years by his original employer and during the 2014 harvest finally accepted a position managing a particularly pictur-esque tea estate in western Uganda with a desire not just to make great teas but also to eventually open the kind of guest house that operates on Glenburn.

effect on tourism]. Only two of the about seven hundred hotels are partially operating, where media persons are the only inhabitants."[6]

The *bandh* was rescinded the day after the piece ran, but the damage for the busy autumn festival season ahead had already been done. Peak tourist season in the hills is during the Puja and Diwali holidays of late October and early November. Most visitors had already canceled.

KANCHENJUNGHA IN VIEW, NO VIEWERS read a newspaper headline of the famously elusive mountain obscured by clouds much of the year. "The glistening white Kanchenjungha under an azure [sky] was in view today but there was hardly any tourist to marvel it," the piece opened. "Chowrastha, Darjeeling's famous promenade that is chock full in the Puja season, was deserted—the ripple effect of nearly a month of agitation that has kept visitors away."[7]

Such lack of stability is also keeping investors away from larger tea-tourism projects and potentially scuttling, or at least delaying, those in the making. Perhaps that isn't fully a bad thing. "We also make tea" would be an unfortunate and unworthy tagline for Darjeeling.

Cows, joint councils, and planters' bungalows redone as boutique hotels may all prove to be stopgaps as much as trucking in day labor for absentee workers, measures that merely delay, or soften, the playing out of Darjeeling's labor endgame. The solution needs to be far more radical— perhaps something along the lines that Rajah Banerjee floated a decade ago. While he has been at the forefront of many of the area's most significant movements that eventually found a wide following from other gardens, this potential scheme could be the one that no one would dare implement.

"Nobody wants to be a farmer anywhere," he said in the 2005 documentary on Makaibari. "But there's a solution. The only way out. If it's your cow, you're going to look after it very well. If it's your own farm, you're going to look after it very well." It's about motivation through partnership, though this time through ownership. "In ten years' time, the lands of Makaibari will be distributed to the 550 householders in Makaibari, to the ladies only, as stakeholders. The land goes back to the people. As opposed to the land that was taken away from the people in my great-grandfather's epoch."[8]

He reiterated the idea around the same time, telling *Outlook* agazine, "In about ten years' time, I want to parcel out the entire tea garden area (except the forests) to the workers. After all, they're the rightful owners of this land since they've worked on it for generations. I'll purchase the tea leaves and run the factory."[9]

"Maybe it's utopian, it's idealistic," he said in the documentary, "but that's the way I feel now." He smiled widely on-screen, like an amazed child. "The colonial style of hierarchical management is over."[10]

By the summer of 2013, the project appeared stalled. It was moving ahead in fits and starts, Rajah said in his office. "But [it] may not happen within my lifetime." He seemed downcast. Or maybe just realistic. He would be risking everything that he had built up over the last forty-five years. Other estate managers in Darjeeling saw his plan as completely impossible without a well-established, cooperative system already in place. "Makaibari wouldn't last six months," said one.

A year later the idea had been completely discarded. In June 2014, Rajah Banerjee sold a nearly 90 percent stake in Makaibari to the Kolkata-based Luxmi Group. The *Times of India* valued the much coveted (and highly secretive) deal "in excess of Rs 20 crore" (Rs 200 million, about $3.5 million).[11] He is in his mid-sixties; his sons seemed little inclined to take over; he felt that a decision on the garden's future needed to be taken. Banerjee, who created and enshrined the legend of Makaibari, will remain at the helm as its face and chairman until he retires.

The Luxmi Group owns seventeen tea estates in Assam and the northeast of India that produce 15 million kilograms of tea a year, more then double all of Darjeeling. These will no doubt benefit from their association with Makaibari and its first-rate reputation. The group is heavily into real estate development and owns Obeetee, the largest manufacturer and exporter of handmade carpets in India. The new owner's financial soundness will help Makaibari weather the current situation in the hills, while an injection of cash to strengthen brand awareness and increased distribution will bring its teas to more customers. In September, it privately sold a twenty-kilogram lot of Silver Tips Imperial plucked during the June 2013 full-moon night just before the summer solstice for $1,850 a kilogram (Rs 1.1 lakh) to a trio of specialty Makaibari retailers in the United States, the United Kingdom, and Japan. It was an auspicious start. But while the new owners inherited Makaibari's iconic status, they have also taken over the challenges of getting workers into the fields to pluck the celebrated leaves.

Others in the hills continue to believe that the 150-year-old structure of Darjeeling's tea gardens needs to be completely overhauled. Something must urgently be done, argues Rishi Saria, whose family owns and runs two Darjeeling estates. "I don't see many gardens surviving in current form."

While some management would be open to implementing an entire new system for compensating workers, they often complain that the mind-set in the Darjeeling hills is entrenched and not open to large changes. Any move would need the workers' agreement and the government's approval. These are often overlapping. Labor and politics here are deeply intertwined: "Those who rule the tea gardens, rule the hills," goes a local maxim. "They'd rather see eighteen, twenty gardens shut than make any changes," said a tea executive.

From a proprietor's point of view, two main issues stand out: the heavy substructure of the estate, with a large number of workers who have little accountability; and having to provide rations. "We are a modern society now," said one Darjeeling planter. "Why should we be giving them rations? They should be buying in ration shops. The British had to because there was no food. But nothing has moved on." Even monetizing this part of the compensation continues to be highly controversial. Many garden workers see any discussion of this during labor negotiations as a way for the estate to pay them less. "They take away the rations and there will be revolution," Rajah Banerjee warned.

Saria sees the employee-owned-and-run Kanan Devan Hills Plantation (KDHP) in southern India's Western Ghats as a successful example of looking through Banerjee's "alternative window." Allowing workers to be shareholders party to an estate's decisions and rewards might be the only way out of Darjeeling's labor crisis.

KDHP consists of seven large gardens that cover twenty-four thousand hectares (sixty thousand acres) and produce over 23 million kilograms (50 million pounds) of CTC (nearly three-fourths of the total), orthodox, green, and organic teas. Planted out in the 1870s, it runs across the picturesque hills around Munnar in Kerala. After the Foreign Exchange Regulation Act was enacted in the 1970s and restricted foreigner ownership, the British proprietors partnered with the Tata family, who eventually acquired the plantation fully in 1983. By 2000, though, it was a losing venture, and after four consecutive years in the red, Tata decided to reduce its exposure in the plantations themselves and focus on the marketing and selling of their branded teas.[12]

But Tata didn't want to close the plantation outright. When a three-month trial of a cooperative system on one of the estates showed little promise—management was turned over to a group of employees who were completely in charge of the decision making process—an employee buyout was proposed, and the board accepted it. Skeptics saw it as a clever ploy by Tata to pass off a loss-making plantation.[13]

On April 1, 2005, the Kanan Devan Hills Plantation Company was formed. Nearly all of the 12,700 employees became shareholders in a 69 percent ownership of the company. Tata retained an 18 percent stake, with the remaining shares held by a welfare trust and ex-Tata employees. There is a professional management team and board of directors, with employee involvement coming through numerous committees. These range from those on the grassroots level and those dealing in operational details to others being active in decision making and as members of the board. Each year, the best worker and the best staff member are appointed to the board of directors. When the top plucker was tapped, she became the first woman employee to sit on the board.

The change was immediate. Productivity shot up 24 percent in the first quarter alone, which the managing director and mastermind of KDHP, T. V. Alexander, attributed to the perfect combination of restructuring, good weather, and worker enthusiasm.[14] Even once the initial excitement had faded, productivity continued to climb, from 33.3 kilograms per worker per day at the time of the handover to 52.6 by 2009–10. In 2014 it was 49.7 kilograms, an impressive number given the climatic conditions that prevailed that year.

"This feeling that the company belongs to them has brought a greater sense of commitment and responsibility," Alexander said in 2010.[15] Workers tend to keep an eye on their fellows and look for ways to cut costs and boost profits. While Darjeeling was suffering unauthorized absenteeism of over 30 percent, at KDHP it was only 10.88 percent for 2013.

The new venture also turned a surprisingly quick profit. When the plantation changed hands, it was running an 8 crore loss (Rs 80 million, or $1.8 million). In 2008–09 there was a net profit of 12.5 crore (Rs 125 million, just under $3 million), and for 2009–10 a profit of 40.48 crore (just over Rs 400 million, about $9 million). For 2013–14 the profit was Rs 15.55 crore (about $3 million).

Such profits have meant strong bonuses, capital appreciation of the shares (the Rs 10 shares are now worth about Rs 50), and dividends, which paid 14 percent in 2005–6, 25 percent in 2008–9, and 50 percent in 2009–10.[16] (From 2005–2006 through 2012–2013, there was a total of 159 percent pay out.) Within just three years, the original investors had a quick return on their money.

Since the plantation's reboot, social services have been a key part of the KDHP mission—from the three hundred Self Help Groups comprised of over five thousand women employees to offering aid in generating additional income to rice purchased in bulk directly from mills and offered at cost to the workers—along with sustainable farming practices. These efforts were rewarded in April 2014 with a coveted certificate from the New York–based Rainforest Alliance, with its green-frog seal, for following ten principals that range from social management to soil conservation and integrated waste management.

Perhaps the clearest sign of the plantation's success came in July 2013 when Tata bought just over 10 percent of KDHP shares, taking its stake up to 28 percent.[17]

While KDHP is very much on a macro scale—it produces almost three times the tea of all Darjeeling—Saria sees the model of workers owning 70 percent of the estate as viable in Darjeeling, even for individual gardens that produce a mere fraction of that amount of tea. The biggest issue at the moment on Darjeeling's estates is the workers. "Their end needs to be sorted out more than anything else." Offering them an ownership stake would fulfill a long-held dream of generations of workers and would also ensure the continued quality of Darjeeling tea. "If you want quality, you can't have workers not involved. And why buy Darjeeling if you are not getting quality?"

More double-hedge plantings of high-quality cultivars, better soil, and a motivated team thoroughly invested in the success of the estate could double production from roughly four hundred kilograms (nine hundred pounds) a hectare, which is the area's current norm, to eight hundred kilograms, Saria believes. By having to deal less with the day-to-day running of the factory and fields of Gopaldhara and Rohini, including continual labor issues, he and his father could focus on marketing and giving more energy to what he calls the "value chain" that stretches from production to distribution, bringing up the per kilogram value of their teas. He figures that revenue could triple. "If revenues go up, so can wages."

KDHP find their system of employee ownership promising and see no reason why, with some slight tailoring, it cannot be put into practice elsewhere. "Implementation of such a model is the most challenging part," according to Sanjith Raju, KDHP's deputy manager of Human Resources. "There has to be a continued commitment and willingness by the top management." KDHP carried out an unprecedented effort to educate every one of its massive workforce in the benefits of the new ownership model. "Each employee had to understand the proposed model and put their trust in this experiment that had been the first of its kind in the tea industry." That required a willingness to invest their own money in the new company. For workers who required it, management helped secure loans from various financial institutions. Today, 99.8 percent of the workers own shares. Each holds at least three hundred shares.

"Transparent business operations and employee relations has been the cornerstone for sustaining this successful venture," Raju said. The continuing investment in KDHP by both workers as well as Tata reflects the success of their model that remains based heavily on trust.

Any change to the structure of Darjeeling's gardens needs to be bold. Merely tinkering with the details will make little lasting difference. Employee ownership would be a fight to implement. But a big fight might be the only long-term solution to dealing with the labor crisis. "You have to take a great leap forward," Saria said. "You can't be fighting over pennies when pounds are at stake."

CHAPTER 19

Back down the Hill

Tea estate factories close during the Hindu festival of Diwali, the five-day "festival of lights" that takes place in autumn. Over the following few weeks, the remaining tea is picked off the trees and processed, packed into tin-rimmed wooden boxes or flat, hand-stenciled paper sacks, and loaded into the back of snub-nosed trucks and Mahindra Pik-Ups for the plains.

Along Hill Cart Road, the narrow-gauge Darjeeling Himalayan Railway runs alongside and, in places, right on the roadway itself. Shops sit so close that shiny foil packets of *chaat* can be plucked off the shelves by passengers, or oranges that have just arrived from orchards in the Mirik Valley. Between the scattered roadside villages, overhanging trees tunnel the road in a lattice of branches. Rays of light, as though filtered through the high, broken windows of a deserted mill, whiten the road in spots. All around, on the steep hillsides, the smooth sprawl of tea is offset by thatches of impenetrable scrub, deep forest, and sheer drops. Small groups of half-hidden pluckers move imperceptibly on the distant hillsides.

At Kurseong, the serpentine traffic turns onto the Rohini Road, curling around a series of switchbacks like a cycling peloton. The view stretches down to the flat, brown plains with a slivery flash of river in the distance. Small groups of skinny men with scarves pulled around their mouths stand beside pots of burning tar: road crews repairing damage from the recent monsoon. Fist-size stones outline eaten-away patches of asphalt. Vehicles shunt around the tight corners, slowing to a stop in places to yield to trucks laboring up the narrow road. Ears pop from the change of pressure. Autumnal shadows angle across the tarmac. At the corners where streams pass under the road, trucks with large, open tanks have returned to siphon water to sell to villagers. A troop of monkeys sit across a web of branches like ornaments.

Eventually the road descends through tiered terraces of rice paddies. Sun catches the golden stalks, bending under the weight of the ripe, purple-tipped grains just a few weeks from being harvested. A pair of water buffalo with shiny backs, silvery as sealskins in the sun, amble along a narrow path. Triangular traffic signs bordered in red warn of elephants crossing the road. The plains. The air has lost its sharpness. Dust seems to gather and hang, giving a buttery hue to the light. Below a bridge over the Balasan River, a dozen women from a settlement of stone-breakers spread their colorful, laundered saris across the rocky riverbed to dry. At the T-junction near Siliguri, the traffic forms a tailback, then stutters ahead.

In Siliguri the tea gets transferred to railcars or hefty, highly decorated lorries—colorful vehicles adorned with painted frescoes of gods and mythical landscapes, and the ubiquitous HORN PLEASE across the tailgate, to which drivers happily respond—destined for Kolkata warehouses before going to buyers or the auction house.

The end of the year. The daily struggle of getting tea in, processed, and out to customers begins to fade—at least for a few months. Questions bubble to the forefront about the future, about Darjeeling's precarious future.

Even if it can counter, or at least adapt to, the changes in weather, endure Gorkhaland's frequently disruptive statehood aspirations, and stem the exodus of workers—that is, navigate environmental, political, and social change—and continue to make exquisite teas, will Darjeeling keep its place among the finest artisanal goods on the globe? Even if more Indians begin to drink Darjeeling's tea, can it sustain relevancy in India, or its collective cultural heritage? For global consumers, how can Darjeeling's gardens break from their hilltop isolation and share with an audience beyond a coterie of aficionados what makes their tea so unique—not only in flavor, but history, methods, and culture? How can they demonstrate the importance of its continuing?

Most growers seem content to produce fine teas, but not necessarily to offer the language with them that will seduce buyers. Planters are rarely successful in sharing their deep passion for the leaf or in offering a unique drinking experience to accompany their exquisitely handcrafted products. They have not been able to share what makes their teas so special—so utterly unique, with such a compelling story—that people should spend a significant amount more for Darjeeling tea than just about anything else on the shelf of a tea shop. That remains, more often than not, trapped up in the hills.

"The Indian grower is not interested in a beautiful aroma and how to poetically describe it—which is what a wine taster does. What he's interested in is the size of the leaf and the strength of the liquor, whether the infusion is coppery or greenish or reddish, whether the liquor is clear or cloudy," a Mirik Valley–based packager and importer of high-end teas from India grumbled in an interview with a trade journal. "The Indian tea industry is selling a product, a commodity—tea could be anything. What they need to be focused on is selling a dream, an idea, a hope."[1]

For that, Darjeeling should be looking not at the wine but the coffee industry, because that is precisely what European- and American-style coffee *culture* in India is doing so successfully right now. Costa Coffee, the Coffee Bean & Tea Leaf, Barista Lavazza, and the ubiquitous Café Coffee Day—generally reduced to the initials CCD—with more than sixteen hundred branches across India, are having a huge cultural impact. A CCD outlet even sits smack on Darjeeling's most iconic spot, the Chowrasta.

In Delhi's trendy Hauz Khas Village, establishments all sport foreign names: Amour, Amici Café, Maison des Desserts, and Café Out of the Box (OTB), plus the curiously named bar-café He Said, She Said (open "since Adam 'n' Eve" and graced with a motto based on Las Vegas's: "What Happens in There Stays in There"). Amici prepares cappuccinos, ristrettos, lattes, macchiatos, mochas, affogatos, americanos, and its Rs 99 espressos with illy coffee beans using, the menu proudly notes, a Cimbali machine ("an Italian masterpiece").

In Khan Market, a two-square-block enclave of shops in Delhi with the highest retail rent in India, chain cafés such as CCD and OTB are offset by lovely one-offs such as Café Turtle, reached by climbing up through the well-stocked Full Circle Bookstore and then a final flight of stairs. In Mumbai, Bangalore, Thiruvananthapuram, Ajmer, Jammu, Hyderabad, and Guwahati, the coffee culture is taking hold.

The coffee goliath Starbucks recently established a partnership with Tata Global Beverages, a unit of India's largest business group, to open an untold number of branches in India—at the press conference announcing the joint venture, a Tata executive speculated as many as three thousand.[2] The inaugural location launched in Mumbai in October 2012, and the first Starbucks opened on the inner circle of New Delhi's Connaught Place the following February. With thirty-five hundred square feet of space spread over two floors and a staff of forty,[3] the Delhi branch is neither a small coffee cart, nor another carbon copy of those bland, inter-changeable Starbucks branches found from Spokane to Barcelona and Tokyo. Rather, it's a unique outlet with brutalist-style exposed-concrete interior walls, handwoven jute ropes that hang in a loose webbing below the ceiling, and stools made from hefty lengths of logs right out of a back-woods campsite. In another enviable touch, baristas prepare drinks with coffee beans nationally sourced from the hills of South India. Single-origin Indian estate blends are now among the offerings.

"Best coffee? No way," the *Guardian* quoted one skeptic on social media in Mumbai just after the opening. "It's all about feeling foreign and upper class."[4] "People come for the ambience," a young, energetic cashier clad in a baseball cap and still-stiff apron said on a busy spring morning in the Connaught Place branch. Jazz music covered the muffled chatter of customers engulfed by the vast space. "And the coffee, too," she added as something of an afterthought. "The Java Chip Frappuccino is our most popular."

And expensive. A venti (large) costs around Rs 210 with tax, or a bit under $4. Even the smallest-size, basic, black, filter coffee costs about Rs 110 ($2)—more than a Darjeeling tea plucker's daily take-home. That's steep for most living in Delhi, where the average monthly per capita income is around $250, the highest in India and more than three times the national average. A cup of chai on the street costs just Rs 5; when drunk inside a simple café, it's perhaps double that.

"It's a fashion," said Girish Sarda at Nathmulls in Darjeeling of the country's current coffee culture, "with style value"—a way to go out and meet friends with a bit of flair. "It is the hip-hop generation swayed by ads," Sandeep Mukherjee at the DTA puts it, "swayed by the swankiness."

It's not about the drink, but the moment, the experience with the drink. CCD, Starbucks, and others are offering the dream that accom-panies the beverage. The bottom of the Starbucks receipt reads, "To inspire and nurture the human spirit . . . One person, one cup and one neighborhood at a time!" Even if that's vague and esoteric, clearly coffee's role goes beyond that of a simple beverage. The slogan running across the front of every Café Coffee Day branch sums it up more directly: "A lot can happen over coffee." CCD's longer advertisement offers a grander vision of the image they are fostering:

> You could do it to start a movement,
> To make a friend, or to enjoy your coffee.
> You could do it with a friend,
> A stranger, or your professor.
> You could do it for love, for peace,
> Or for your bum.
> No matter who you are, or what you do,
> Great things happen when you just
> Sit down,
> Because a lot can happen over coffee.

Yet no one in India so far, points out Nathmulls's Sarda, is preparing coffee at home—at least not quality coffee. If they do, then it's usually just a spoonful of Nescafé stirred into hot milk or water.

At the moment in India, Starbucks-style café culture dedicated to *tea* is almost nonexistent. Rare exceptions are Cha Bars located in various Oxford Bookstores, the iconic chain established in 1919 on Kolkata's Park Street. The first tea bar opened in 2000 and then expanded to other branches. Around the same time Starbucks arrived in New Delhi, the bookshop's Connaught Place store moved to a new location with a contemporary-edged, overwhelmingly white, and well-lit Cha Bar. It offers more than 150 varieties of tea, including a dozen Darjeeling options. The most popular choice, though, is the classic *dhaba* (roadside eatery) masala chai served in small, thick glasses. The drink has a zestiness with the flavor of spice dominating that of the tea. The back of the throat gets an even sharper snap from Truck Driver's 100 Mile Ki Chai, with plenty of black pepper in the masala blend.

The Cha Bar's menu quotes a verse from Bengal's most famous poet (and Nobel Prize winner), Rabindranath Tagore, that could be the call for such lush and lusty drinks: "Come oh come ye tea-thirsty restless ones, the kettle boils, bubbles and sings, musically."

As one heads out of the hills among the loads of autumn teas to catch an afternoon flight from Bagdogra, the final views in the wing mirror of the high slopes are, simply, breathtaking. Coffee in India might have the moment, but Darjeeling tea has romance—not in the colonial vestiges of how a tea estate is structured, but in the green hills, in Darjeeling and its backdrop of majestic, icy Himalayan peaks, in the pure mountain air and vintage Raj-era bungalows with peaked tin roofs and latticed eaves.

The romance is also in the teas themselves: struggling artisans in the truest sense, individually producing teas using methods and tools that have changed little in a century, against odds so improbably stacked against them that the very survival of their industry is in peril.

That romance comes into the cup at home, too. It begins in the process, the ritual and routine of preparing. First, take the opposite experience—making a sweet, milky masala chai with brisk CTC tea from Assam: fussing with the spices to find a balance between the lingering cool of cloves, the peppery bite of ginger, the warmth of cinnamon, and the hot masculinity of cardamom pods crushed like bubble wrap between thumb and forefinger, stirring until tiny bubbles wheel up the sides of the pot, then dashing the tea between a pair of glasses to blend. The bouncy hecticness of the Indian street is present in masala chai.

Darjeeling tea is different. Soft-spoken rather than brash. Simplicity over baroque flamboyance. Contemplative more than energetic, with little sense of urgency or heavy-handedness. The same is true when preparing it. Putting the kettle to boil. Springing the lid open on a tin of Darjeeling tea—that immediate aroma: the grassy floralness of a spring tea, the mellower, spiced notes of an autumn one—and spooning some dry leaves into the pot, or plucking a tea bag from a metal tin whose original logo has begun to flake. Watching as tight bubbles form on the bottom of the kettle and drift unsteadily to the surface, then pouring the hot water over the leaves. The reaction is immediate, the interaction with the leaves. "No other drink is so engaging," said Steven Smith in Portland about a pinch of second flush Darjeeling leaves beginning to come alive in the cup. The leaves breathe and stretch in the pot as sand streams through the wasp's waist of an hourglass timer marking the minutes, the muscatel flavors bloom, and the color of the liquor turns to shimmering brass or copper. And then, finally, pouring through the strainer into a favorite teacup to sip.

The personalities of Darjeeling are reflected in each cup. They change from garden to garden, day to day. Sanjay Sharma calls ones from Glenburn "Glenburn in a cup." The manager of each Darjeeling estate could say the same. A unique set of conditions make it not just *a* Darjeeling tea but one from a particular garden. Nothing is added, no flavors, no scents, no secrets. Just natural Darjeeling. Uniquely so.

"So many factors to produce an act of nature. You can't repeat it. It's like a human face," Sanjay Kapur said in his Delhi workshop. "That's what makes the tea so dynamic—and addicting."

Where will Darjeeling tea be in twenty years? In late autumn, the season nearly finished, Sanjay Sharma stood on a large boulder along the Rangeet River at the bottom edge of Glenburn's property and looked out over the water that had just begun to run clear in the last few days after unusually late rains. He considered the question, turning around to face a field of young tea shrubs. They had been brought up in the nursery from Glenburn's own seeds and planted out as saplings only in spring.

"I'm an optimist," he finally said, looking over the healthy plants. "You have to be. You look at the mud, put a hole in it, plant something . . ." He let the sentence fade. A tight smile spread slowly across his face as he turned back to the river that he could soon start fishing.

"The level of passion would surprise you," Anindyo Choudhury said of planters, owners, and managers in Darjeeling. "Despite the hardships they are going through now, they remain passionate."

The Darjeeling tea industry continues to move ahead, slowly. Healthier soil, new plantings, fine vintages, excellent green and white teas, higher prices, a wider public. Movement, as required, as the twelfth-century Indian saint Basavanna intoned to Shiva a thousand years ago:

> Listen, O lord of the meeting rivers,
> things standing shall fall,
> but the moving ever shall stay.[5]

It is moving ahead, though not in step with the highest technology with which India has lately become famous, or chemical-driven concoctions, or genetically modified superstock. But it is staying true to its hands-and-nose approach to making crafted teas using century-old machines and honed skills—new varieties and styles, perhaps, but using ancestral methods passed down from tea planter to tea planter, crafting teas that reflect both a specific place and a specific season one batch at a time in ways nearly unchanged since Darjeeling started making tea. "Darjeeling tea is not an industry," Rajah Banerjee once said. "It is a handicraft, a very specialized art."[6]

Can that handicraft survive? There is no replacement if it does not, no place to outsource its unique flavors, no hills that will yield up such delicate aromas and subtle body. Nowhere else can duplicate its set of contributing influences nor its elusive taste.

Those begin in the steep hills and fertile soil of Darjeeling and grow upward toward the cycling cosmos. Two leaves and a bud at a time.

Recipes

PERFECT CUPS OF TEA

Darjeeling Tea
Masala Chai
Chennai Chai
Tibetan Tea with Salt and Butter
Fresh Passion-Fruit Chai

BEGINNINGS TO A DARJEELING DAY

Aloo Dum
Puri
Masala Omelet
Porridge

TO ACCOMPANY AFTERNOON TEA

The Ritz of London's Afternoon Tea Scones
Afternoon Tea Pound Cake
Onion Pakoras (Spicy Onion Fritters)
Timeless Cucumber Sandwiches
Glenburn's Chicken-and-Fresh-Mint Hamper Sandwiches
Delhi Sandwiches

LOCAL FAVORITES

Tea Garden Momos
Thukpa
Chili Oil (Tsu-La-Tsu)
Spiced Chicken Cutlet

TEA SPECIALS

Tea-Marbled Deviled Eggs
Darjeeling Tea Sorbet

PERFECT CUPS OF TEA

DARJEELING TEA

Steeping the perfect cup of Darjeeling tea is simple but exacting.

Bring a kettle of freshly drawn (or bottled) water to a boil. Rinse out a teapot and quickly discard the water. Add 1 level teaspoon—about $\frac{1}{12}$ ounce or 2.5 grams—of pure long-leaf Darjeeling tea per cup to the teapot. Pour the water over the leaves, cover the pot, and steep for 3 to 3 ½ minutes, letting the leaves breathe and stretch. Strain into warmed teacups.

Darjeeling's nuanced flavor is best appreciated without milk, sugar, or, because of its slight natural astringency, lemon. But if it is impossible to drink it straight, increase steeping time to 4 minutes for adding sugar and to 5 minutes for milk.

MASALA CHAI

Indian spiced tea—properly called masala chai—can include any number of spices, though cardamom pods, fresh ginger, cloves, black peppercorns, and a piece of cinnamon stick are the most common. Some also include fennel seeds, poppy seeds, coriander seeds, and even bay leaves.

Makes 4 glasses:

4 cardamom pods
2 cloves
4 whole black peppercorns
1-inch/2.5-cm piece cinnamon stick
2 cups/480 ml whole milk
1-inch/2.5-cm piece fresh ginger, grated or chopped
3 Tbsp sugar, or more to taste
2 Tbsp loose, strong black tea leaves or 2 tea bags

In a mortar, crush the cardamom, cloves, peppercorns, and cinnamon stick.

In a heavy-bottomed saucepan, add the milk and 2 cups/480 ml water, the crushed spices, and the ginger. Bring to a boil, reduce the heat to low, allow the foam to subside. Stir in the sugar and tea and simmer for 3 to 5 minutes, depending on desired strength of tea, stirring from time to time and watching that it does not boil over.

Strain into 4 tea glasses.

CHENNAI CHAI

Call this version from Chennai—established by the East India Company in 1639 and known as Madras until 1996—masala chai light. Or at least *lighter*. Instead of boiling the spices in the milky liquid, the ginger and cardamom are placed in a droopy cloth strainer and the tea is poured through them. (While the cardamom here is for the flavor, the ginger is largely for health.) You make this at home but also get it on the street, where the strainers are stained and stretched from use.

Makes 2 glasses:

1 Tbsp strong black tea leaves or 1 tea bag
½ cup/120 ml whole milk
2 Tbsp sugar or to taste
2 cardamom pods
½-inch/1.25-cm piece of fresh ginger, peeled

In a saucepan, bring 1½ cups/360 ml water to a boil, add the tea, and boil for 4 minutes. Add the milk, return to a boil, and boil for 1 minute. Stir in the sugar.

Meanwhile, in a mortar, crush the cardamom pods with a pestle. Add the ginger and give it a firm smack. Transfer to a strainer.

Slowly pour the tea through the strainer into 2 tea glasses.

TIBETAN TEA WITH SALT AND BUTTER

"Tea is a favourite beverage, the black sort brought from China in large cakes being that preferred," wrote Dr. Archibald Campbell, Darjeeling's first superintendent and the area's original tea planter, of the Lepchas. "It is prepared by boiling, after which the decoction is churned up in a chunga, with butter and salt; milk is never taken with tea."[1]

Visitors to Darjeeling today still find similar salty butter teas—though usually with the addition of milk—prepared by the Tibetan community. In 1959, the fourteenth Dalai Lama, then a teenager, and about 80,000 of his followers fled China over the Himalayas into India after an abortive uprising. Today 150,000 Tibetan refugees live in India, including many in Darjeeling.

This recipe is adapted from Kunga's, a decades-old-favorite, family-run Tibetan place in the center of Darjeeling just below the Planters' Club. "Yak's milk is best," the owner advises. "But if you don't have yak's milk, then use Amul Gold." For those that can't find that popular brand of Indian milk, any other whole milk or even half-and-half works well.

It's a warm, caloric, and energy-supplying drink, great for cold weather and mountainous climates.

Makes 4 glasses:

2 heaped Tbsp loose black tea or 2 tea bags
½ cup/120 ml whole milk or half-and-half, either cow, goat, or yak
1 heaped Tbsp butter, preferably salted, and ideally from yak milk
Generous pinch salt (more if using unsalted butter)

In a saucepan, bring 3½ cups/800 ml water to a boil, add the tea, remove from the heat, and let steep for 5 minutes. Strain the tea, and discard the leaves.

Transfer to a blender. Add the milk, butter, and salt. Cover the blender tightly and blend for 2 to 3 minutes until frothy.

Return the liquid to the saucepan and bring to a boil. Pour into tea glasses, and serve scalding hot.

FRESH PASSION-FRUIT CHAI

The restaurant of the quirky and efficient Cochrane Place Hotel in Kurseong is aptly named Chai Country Café as it sits within minutes of Ambootia, Castleton, and Makaibari estates, with another dozen gardens visible from its terraces. The bar has a resident tea master and mixologist, a young Bengali named Laltu Purkait, who prepares highly original drinks that range from Paan Chai, which recalls *paan*—betel leaf filled with areca nut, lime paste, spices, and all sorts of other ingredients and chewed after a meal—to an even more exotically spiced Tandoori Chai, which uses almonds and rosewater to balance its heady, savory spice blend and offer floral notes to the flickering hints of fire.

This recipe is Laltu's specialty during the monsoon, when passion fruit are in season. Brilliant, cloudy orange in color, with high tangy notes, a certain sweet freshness, and nonaggressive bite of pepper. Don't discard the seeds. They are good for digestion, Laltu insists.

Per glass:

1½ tsp Darjeeling or another orthodox long-leaf tea
Pulp of ½ fresh passion fruit, with all juices and seeds, about 1½ Tbsp

1 Tbsp sugar

1 generous pinch freshly ground black pepper

In a stove-top teapot or saucepan, bring 1 cup/240 ml freshly drawn water to a boil. Remove from the heat. Add the tea, cover the teapot, and let infuse for 4 minutes.

Meanwhile, in a tall tea glass, add the passion fruit pulp, juice and seeds, sugar, and black pepper, and whisk well.

Strain the tea into the tea glass. Serve hot.

BEGINNINGS TO A DARJEELING DAY

ALOO DUM

This classic potato dish, popular across much of India, is a breakfast favorite in Darjeeling. Often including tomatoes and a thicker "gravy," this version is the kind of quick and simple one found on many tea gardens and takes its inspiration from Prem, the family cook on Goomtee Tea Estate. At the center of the estate is the factory, and up a couple dozen meandering rockery steps through flower gardens, is the red-roofed manager's bungalow, with its varnished wood floors and walls, airy rooms, and long, enclosed verandah, built by the India-born, British tea pioneer Henry Montgomery Lennox for his family.

Serve the *aloo dum* with hot puri (following recipe) as Prem does.

Serves 4 to 6:

2 pounds/910 g small or medium white potatoes

Salt

6 garlic cloves, roughly chopped

1 heaped Tbsp freshly grated fresh ginger

3 Tbsp sunflower or canola oil

1 heaped tsp cumin seeds

2 generous pinches turmeric

½ tsp chili flakes

Finely chopped, fresh cilantro (coriander leaves), for garnishing

Scrub the potatoes but do not peel. Place them in a pot, cover with water, and bring to a boil over high heat. Add a generous pinch of salt, reduce the heat to medium low, partly cover the pot, and gently boil until tender (but not mushy) and the tip of a knife penetrates with little resistance, 20 to 25 minutes. Drain. Once the potatoes are cool enough to handle, peel and cut into pieces just bigger than bite-size.

Meanwhile, mash the garlic to a paste in a mortar with the ginger.

In a large sauté pan, skillet, or wok, heat the oil over medium heat and add the cumin seeds. When they begin to jump, stir in the garlic-ginger paste. Cook until aromatic, about 30 seconds. Stir in the turmeric and chili flakes, season with salt, and immediately add the potatoes. Add 2 to 3 Tbsp water and turn to coat the potatoes in the sauce well. Reduce the heat to low, loosely cover the pan, and cook for 3 to 5 minutes until hot and cooked through. Garnish with cilantro and serve.

PURI

Puri—fried flatbread that puffs up like a bellows—is a favorite companion to *aloo dum* (previous recipe) on Darjeeling gardens, especially for guests or on special occasions. (Chapatis and *parathas* are other daily options.) Puri is also a classic snack combo in the north of the country with a glass of masala chai. Puri never tastes better than when eaten on an Indian railway platform during—or better, after—a long train journey.

Makes about 12 puri:

2 cups/250 g atta flour or an equal blend of whole-wheat flour and all-purpose flour (see note below)
½ tsp salt
1 Tbsp vegetable oil plus more for deep-frying

Put the flour and salt in a mixing bowl and work in the 1 Tbsp of oil. Gradually work in ⅔ cup/150 ml lukewarm water to form a firm dough. On a lightly floured surface, knead until soft, about 10 minutes. Lightly oil, cover, and let rest for 30 minutes.

Roll out the dough with the hands to a thick rope and divide into 12 pieces each about the size of a walnut. Until ready to roll, cover with a damp towel or piece of plastic wrap to keep from drying out.

In a deep skillet or wok, heat 2 inches/5 cm of oil over medium-high heat. The oil is the right temperature when a small piece of dough floats and vigorously bubbles.

One by one, press down the balls of dough and roll out, working in different directions to keep it round, into thin disks about 5 to 6 inches/12.5 to 15 cm in diameter. Carefully pull up the puri and slide it into the hot oil. Lightly force down with a back of a large, slotted spoon and keep it submerged with gentle taps until it begins to puff up and turn a golden brown, 10 to 15 seconds. Gently turn it over. (Do not turn again.) Fry until deep golden brown, another 10 to 15 seconds. Transfer with the slotted spoon to paper towels to drain. Serve hot.

Note: Atta flour is stone-ground, semihard wheat flour. It is sometimes sold as *chapati flour*. A good substitute is a one-to-one blend of whole-wheat and all-purpose flours.

MASALA OMELET

Another breakfast staple around Darjeeling, feisty and flavorful masala omelets are best kept thin and prepared either individually or for two people.

This recipe serves two. Individual omelets can be prepared without folding in half; simply cook until set and then slide off the pan and onto a plate.

4 large eggs
Salt and freshly ground pepper
1 small red onion, finely chopped, about ¼ cup
1 plum tomato, finely chopped, about ¼ cup
1 small green chili, deseeded and minced
2 tsp sunflower, canola, or light olive oil
Finely chopped fresh cilantro (coriander leaves), for garnishing

In a mixing bowl, whisk the eggs until spongy. Season with salt and pepper. Fold in the onion, tomato, and chili.

In a 10-inch/25-cm nonstick skillet, heat the oil over medium-high heat.

Pour the egg mixture into the pan. Immediately swirl the pan to evenly spread the mixture and to keep the egg from sticking as it begins to set. Without stirring, let the egg firm up, 1 to 2 minutes. Loosen the omelet with a thin spatula, and fold the omelet in half. Let cook for another 2 minutes or so until done but still moist in the middle, turning it over toward the end.

Slide the omelet onto a plate, generously scatter cilantro over the top, and serve immediately.

PORRIDGE

Included in *The Englishwoman in India* and published anonymously by "A Lady Resident" in 1864, this porridge recipe still familiar in Darjeeling:

> Put as many cups of water, or milk, as you require porridge, into a large saucepan: when it boils fast throw in some salt, and shake the oatmeal in with one hand, stirring all the time with the other. Use a stick and not a spoon. Pour it into a deep dish when thick enough, and send a jug of milk to table with it.[2]

Surely early British settlers in Darjeeling found this dish—slow to digest, slow to release its energy—a perfect way to begin the area's cold and damp mornings.

It's no surprise that the Windamere Hotel, which began its life as a boardinghouse for English and Scottish planters, still serves the best in town. Made with Indian-grown oats and served every morning, the flavor is bold, and its texture, far from gooey or clumpy, is fine without being too chewy. While some traditionalists in Scotland demand that just oats, water, and a pinch of salt be used, in the high altitudes around Darjeeling, milk is added, too.

This recipe calls for traditional, noninstant, non-quick-cooking oats. Serves 4:

1 cup/110 g medium steel-cut or Scottish or Irish oats (noninstant)
1 cup/240 ml whole milk
Salt
Small jug milk, hot or cold as desired, for serving
Brown sugar, for serving

In a medium saucepan, bring 2 cups/480 ml water to a boil. Add the oats and the milk, and stir with the handle of a wooden spoon. Return to a boil over medium-high heat, reduce the heat to low, and simmer uncovered until the consistency is thick and the oats tender but still chewy, about 45 minutes, stirring from time to time. Add in a touch more water or milk if needed.

Remove the pan from the heat, stir in a couple pinches of salt, cover, and let sit for 5 to 10 minutes. Stir again.

Serve in bowls with the jug of milk on the side to pour generously over the top as desired as well as brown sugar to stir in to sweeten to taste.

TO ACCOMPANY AFTERNOON TEA

THE RITZ OF LONDON'S AFTERNOON TEA SCONES

These divine scones are adapted from *The London Ritz Book of Afternoon Tea*. While the author calls them "austere little cakes, perfect vehicles for jam and cream,"[3] do not overwhelm them with such sweet toppings, as the scones themselves have a delicate and delightful flavor.

Makes about 12 scones:

1½ cups/225 g all-purpose flour plus more for dusting
2 tsp baking powder
1 tsp cream of tartar
½ tsp baking soda
¼ tsp salt or slightly less
3 Tbsp unsalted butter, cut into small pieces, plus more for greasing pan
⅔ cup/160 ml whole milk or buttermilk

Preheat the oven to 425°F/220°C/gas mark 7.

Sift the flour into a large mixing bowl. Add the baking powder, cream of tartar, baking soda, and salt. Work in the butter with the fingertips until the mixture has the consistency of large, flaky crumbs. Stir in the milk using a spatula until the dough is soft.

On a floured surface, roll out the dough to a ½-inch (1.25-cm) thickness. Using a pastry cutter 2 to 2½ inches (5 to 6.5 cm) in diameter or a water glass, press out rounds. (Do not to twist when pressing out, or the scones are likely to bake unevenly.)

Lightly grease a baking sheet with butter. Arrange the rounds on the sheet. Lightly dust their faces with flour.

Bake until they have risen and turned golden, 10 to 15 minutes.

Remove from the oven. Serve warm.

AFTERNOON TEA POUND CAKE

So named for its use of a pound each of its quartet of ingredients—flour, sugar, eggs, and butter—this loaf endures as a favorite for afternoon tea. As the author of an Anglo-Indian cookbook remarked, "A pound cake is a pound cake, as solid and dependable as the British Empire in its heyday."[4] This version has baking powder to give the cake a slightly fluffier note and some vanilla extract to offer a fragrant hint of warmth.

Serves 6 to 8:

1½ cup/150 g all-purpose flour
1 tsp baking powder
Generous pinch of salt
⅔ cup/150 g butter, at room temperature
¾ cup/150 g granulated sugar
1 tsp pure vanilla extract
3 large eggs, at room temperature

Preheat the oven to 350°F/180°C/gas mark 4.

Line the bottom of an 8- or 9-inch/20- or 23-cm loaf pan with parchment paper. Sift the flour together with the baking powder and salt.

In a mixing bowl, cream the butter and sugar together for at least 2 or 3 minutes until pale, light, and fluffy. Add the vanilla extract and then the eggs, one by one, scraping down the mixing bowl after each. Beat until smooth and silky. While beating over low speed, gradually add in the dry ingredients until incorporated.

Pour the batter into the loaf pan. Smooth down the surface with a spatula. Tap down to settle.

Place in the oven and bake until golden, about 35 minutes. When its done, the top should be springy and a toothpick inserted into the middle should come out clean.

Let cool after taking from the oven, then remove the cake from the pan. Cut into thin slices and serve.

ONION PAKORAS (SPICY ONION FRITTERS)

Bought on a railway platform during a stop of the Darjeeling Mail on its journey north from Kolkata to NJP station outside Siliguri, in one of the roadside tea shops on the curvy and much-patched road up into the hills, or for afternoon tea in Darjeeling itself, crispy, deep-fried *pakoras*—also known as *bhajia*—are a favorite snack with tea. The Elgin serves its delectable *pakoras* with trio of chutneys and some sweet tomato-chili sauce. They make a perfect snack while dinner slow-cooks.

Or just to nibble on to pass a rainy day. On one such drizzly June day in Darjeeling, the city was brimming with Indian visitors escaping the searing the heat of the plains. "But none of the tourists ventured out today," one hotel manager lamented to the *Calcutta Telegraph* correspondent. "They watched TV and ordered unending rounds of tea and *pakora*."[5]

Makes about 10 to 12 pakoras:

1 cup/125 g gram (chickpea) flour
¼ tsp turmeric
¼ tsp black onion seeds (optional)
⅓ cup loosely packed chopped cilantro (coriander leaves)
1 to 2 small, fresh green chilies, deseeded and finely chopped
½ tsp salt
2 medium yellow onions, thinly sliced
Vegetable oil for frying

Preheat to the oven to 200°F/95°C.

Place the flour in a mixing bowl and work in about ½ cup/120 ml warm water. The batter should be pasty and silky and just thicker than pancake batter. Add in a touch more water, or flour, if needed. Whisk in the turmeric, black onion seeds, cilantro, green chilies, and salt. Add the onions and blend well with the hands, separating the segments and slightly crunching them down against the bottom of the bowl. The batter should coat the onions but not be clumpy.

In a deep skillet or sauté pan, heat at least 1 inch/2.5 cm of oil to 375°F/190°C. When the oil is hot enough, a small amount of batter should float and vigorously bubble.

Working in small batches that don't crowd the pan or bring the temperature of the oil below 350°F/180°C, drop spoonful-size globs of the mixture with a pair of soupspoons into the oil, flatten out slightly, and fry until crispy and a rich, deep golden brown, 3 to 5 minutes.

Remove with a slotted spoon, and place on absorbent paper towels to drain. Transfer to a baking sheet and place in the oven to keep warm until all of the *pakoras* have been fried.

Remove any solid bits from the oil before adding the next batch of *pakoras*. Fry the remaining batter, being sure that the oil has returned to 350°F/180°C before adding the next batch. Serve hot.

TIMELESS CUCUMBER SANDWICHES

Few items on the tea tray are more unappealing than a poorly made cucumber sandwich with soggy bread. But when done well, nothing makes a better companion for an afternoon cup of Darjeeling tea: small, crustless, and prepared using thin slices of bread and cucumbers sliced so thin that they are transparent. Cut into rectangles—properly called fingers—they might seem a touch dainty, but they won't (unlike scones or pound cake) spoil one's appetite for dinner. More important, their delicate, fresh flavors won't overpower even the subtlest first flush Darjeeling tea.

Spreading the butter evenly but not thickly is key, as it makes a sealing layer to keep bread from getting moist. Prepare only at the last moment so that both bread and filling are at their freshest.

Makes 12 finger sandwiches:

1 firm medium garden cucumber
Salt
8 thin slices fresh white or brown bread
Unsalted butter for spreading, at room temperature

Scrub the cucumber and remove any wax. Slice crosswise as thinly as possibly, ideally with a mandoline. Place in a colander and lightly salt. Let the cucumbers sweat and draw out the flavors for 15 minutes. Place on paper towels and pat dry.

Lay out 4 slices of the bread and on one side, spread a thin, even coat of butter from crust to crust. Arrange the cucumbers in 2 or 3 layers. Butter one side of the remaining 4 slices of bread in a thin, even coat from crust to crust, and lay on top.

Gently press down with the palm and trim the crusts with a serrated knife. Cut each sandwich into three even rectangles. Neatly arrange on a platter and serve immediately.

GLENBURN'S CHICKEN-AND-FRESH-MINT HAMPER SANDWICHES

Flights into Bagdogra Airport—Darjeeling's closest access point by air—all land just after lunch. For guests staying at Glenburn Tea Estate, the four-hour journey up to the garden is broken with a stop on a knoll below Kurseong. The driver unpacks a picnic hamper that includes a thermos of tea—shockingly good, considering it was prepared in the morning—slices of cake, fruit, and some sandwiches, including this delicious Glenburn classic.

Makes 3 sandwiches:

2 bone-in, skin-on whole chicken legs, about 1 pound/450 g total
¼ cup/60 ml mayonnaise, preferably Hellmann's
¾ tsp Dijon mustard
2 Tbsp finely chopped, fresh mint
6 slices white bread

Place the chicken in saucepan, cover with water, and bring to a simmer. Reduce the heat to low, cover, and simmer until tender, 30 to 40 minutes. Remove from the heat, uncover, and let legs cool in the water. Remove and discard the skin, and debone the chicken. Hand-shred the pieces. There should be about 1½ cups/175 g of loosely packed chicken meat.

In a mixing bowl, whisk the mayonnaise with the mustard and mint. Fold in the chicken.

Spread the filling on 3 slices of the bread. Cover with the remaining slices. Trim the crusts. Cut the sandwiches diagonally. Wrap in wax paper.

DELHI SANDWICHES

During the Raj era, some of the only fish found in hill stations such as Darjeeling—or even landlocked places such as Delhi—were tinned anchovies, sardines, and salted fish. Cooks sometimes got creative with their use in recipes. Michael Smith, culinary advisor to *Upstairs, Downstairs* and *The Duchess of Duke Street* television miniseries, offers the Delhi Sandwich ("Straight from the Days of the Raj is this one!") in *The Afternoon Tea Book*.[6] I have adapted it only slightly. Smith recommends spreading this between slices of brown bread or hot over buttered toast or over split, toasted English muffins.

Makes 5 or 6 sandwiches:

6 anchovy fillets
6 ounces/170 g skinned and deboned tinned sardines, about 1¼ loosely packed cup of fillets
1 tsp mild chutney
1 medium egg
¾ tsp mild curry powder

Salt (optional)
2 to 3 dashes of Tabasco or 1 pinch cayenne pepper
10 to 12 slices brown bread

In a blender, add all of the filling ingredients and blend to a paste. Transfer to a saucepan.

Over low heat, cook until the paste has firmed slightly and cohered, about 5 minutes. Spoon into a bowl and let cool.

Spread the filling on 5 or 6 slices of the bread. Cover with the remaining slices. Trim the crusts. Cut the sandwiches diagonally.

Arrange on a platter and serve.

LOCAL FAVORITES

TEA GARDEN MOMOS

Much beloved by locals, Himalayan steamed dumplings, filled with meats or vegetables and known as *momos*, is the dish more associated with Darjeeling. While cooks here roll out the dough from scratch before stuffing, using readily available dumpling or wonton wrappers make these easy to prepare. Cold *momos* can be reheated in a frying pan with a small amount of oil.

Makes about one dozen *momos*, serves 2:

1 packed cup/100 g finely chopped green cabbage
1 medium onion, finely chopped
1 medium-small carrot, grated
2 garlic cloves, finely chopped
½ Tbsp minced fresh ginger
¼ tsp ground cumin
¼ tsp ground coriander seeds
½ fresh red chili, diced
Salt
2 Tbsp vegetable or canola oil
¼ tsp turmeric powder
Broth for filling steamer, preferably beef bone or chicken, or water
12 to 14 dumpling or wonton wrappers

In a mixing bowl, add the cabbage, onion, carrot, garlic, ginger, cumin, coriander, and chili, and season with salt. Blend well.

In a large saucepan or wok, heat the oil over medium heat and add the vegetable mix and about 2 Tbsp water. Cook, stirring frequently, until the cabbage and onions have softened and the carrots turned a yellowish orange, about 10 minutes. Remove from the heat and stir in the turmeric powder. Return to the mixing bowl, and let cool. There should be about 1 cup/175 g.

Remove the rack(s) from the steamer. Fill the bottom of the steamer with at least 1½ inches/4 cm of broth. Cover with a lid and bring to a boil. Reduce the heat and keep hot. Meanwhile, rub the steaming rack(s) with oil and set aside.

Fill a small bowl with water. Place a wrapper on the open palm of a hand, rub a touch of water around the top edges, then place a generous tablespoon or so of the mixture in the center. Fold into a semicircle, and working around the edges, pinch into pleats forming a slight crescent-shaped curl. Be sure the edges are well closed. Place on the steaming rack perpendicular to the edge with the pinched pleat facing upward.

Repeat with the remaining wrappers. Arrange the *momos* close but not touching in the steaming pan following the curl of the *momos* in a pinwheel formation.

Carefully place the rack(s) in the steamer, cover, and steam over high heat until tender to the touch, 15 to 20 minutes. Serve hot.

THUKPA

This favorite Darjeeling noodle dish is perfect for those cold, clammy evenings around the tea-covered hills.

The recipe make four generous, hearty bowls with plenty of warming broth. Serve with a spoonful of piquant chili oil (following recipe).

Salt
12 oz/360 g dried egg noodles
6 cups/1.6 L Light chicken, beef, or vegetable stock
3 Tbsp vegetable oil
1 large onion, finely sliced
Salt
1 medium carrot, grated
1 small turnip, peeled and grated
2 garlic cloves, finely chopped
10 oz/300 g thinly sliced or ground beef or pork
Finely chopped, fresh coriander (cilantro) for garnishing

In a large pot bring 4 quarts/4 L water to a boil. Generously salt and then add the noodles. Boil until tender, 2 to 4 minutes, but follow the directions on the package. Drain and rinse with cold water to keep them from clumping together. Divide among 4 deep soup bowls.

Meanwhile, bring the stock to a simmer. Cover and keep very hot.

In a deep frying pan or wok, heat the oil over high heat. Add the onions and a pinch of salt and cook until they begin to turn transparent, about 5 minutes. Add the carrots and turnips and cook until they have softened and changed color, about 5 minutes. Add the garlic, cook for about 1 minute until aromatic, while stirring continuously. Season the beef with salt and add, cook, stirring continuously until browned, 2 to 4 minutes. Stir in a spoonful or two of the simmering stock to moisten and remove from the heat.

Arrange the mixture on top of the noodles.

Ladle in the stock, adding it to the side of the bowls so that the meat stays in place on the top of the noodles. Generously garnish with the cilantro and serve immediately.

CHILI OIL (TSU-LA-TSU)

A spoonful of this piquant and deeply flavorful oil gives a stunning jolt to a bowl of *thukpa* (page 245). It also makes an excellent dip for *momos* (page 244). This recipe is adapted from a small, locally produced book by the Inner Wheel Club of Darjeeling, published nearly twenty-five years ago and sold exclusively at the Oxford Book & Stationery Co. on Darjeeling's Chowrasta. With its deep-scarlet cloth cover glued over cardboard, faded gold letters, and landscape shape, it can be mistaken on the shelf for an album of antique panoramic photos of the Himalayas.

Makes about 1 cup/240 ml:

2 tsp minced, fresh ginger
5 or 6 spring onions (scallions), trimmed and minced (or chopped cilantro)
3 garlic cloves, minced, about 1½ tsp
1 Tbsp chili flakes or ground red, dried chilies
¼ tsp salt
1 scant cup/200 ml peanut oil

Place the ginger, onions, and garlic in a sturdy, heatproof bowl that can comfortably hold the ingredients and oil. Add the chili flakes and season with salt.

In a small saucepan, heat the oil to boiling, then carefully pour the oil over the ingredients. Stir and let cool.

To store, cover and refrigerate.

SPICED CHICKEN CUTLET

The firmest, and perhaps finest, piece of advice that Rajah Banerjee gave on a visit to Makaibari Tea Estate was to allow enough time in the Bagdogra Airport when flying back to Delhi to try the legendary chicken cutlets in the terminal restaurant owned by its employees and run as a cooperative.

"The great fault of Indian cooks in regard to cutlets is over-handling," sternly warned the 1898 edition of *The Complete Indian Housekeeper and Cook*. "They beat, chop, and season the meat out of all distinctive taste. Now, a plain cutlet should simply be *cut* and trimmed, dipped in the yolks of eggs, bread-crumbed, and fried a light golden brown."[7]

Happily, cooks in the eastern Himalayas today rarely prepare *plain* chicken cutlets. Instead, as in the Bagdogra Airport restaurant, they rub the chicken with ginger, garlic, cilantro, and chilies before breading and frying. A delicious treat.

Serves 4:

4 boneless chicken breasts, about 1¾ lb/800 g
3 garlic cloves, peeled
1½-inch/4-cm piece fresh ginger, peeled
1 medium-small onion, finely chopped
½ to 1 small, green chili, minced
2 heaped Tbsp minced fresh cilantro (coriander leaves)
Salt
Freshly ground white pepper
2 large eggs
All-purpose flour for dusting
1 cup/140 g fine, dry bread crumbs
Sunflower, canola, or light olive oil for frying

Thinly slice the chicken on the flat into 3 or 4 pieces. If desired, gently pound with a meat tenderizer or mallet until flattened.

In a mortar, mash the garlic, ginger, and onion together into a paste. Blend in the chili and cilantro. Rub the paste over both sides of the chicken slices. Season with salt and white pepper.

In a wide bowl, whisk the egg. Place the flour in a bowl and the bread crumbs in another.

Generously coat the bottom of a large sauté pan or skillet with oil and heat over medium-high heat until the surface shimmers. Reduce the heat to medium.

Working in small batches that won't crowd the pan nor bring down the temperature of the oil, lightly flour the cutlets, dip them in the egg mixture, then evenly coat with bread crumbs. Fry until golden brown on the outside and cooked through on the inside, 1 to 2 minutes per batch. Place on absorbent paper, and fry the remaining cutlets. Serve hot.

TEA SPECIALS

TEA-MARBLED DEVILED EGGS

This is Sanjay Sharma's divine take on deviled eggs with an Indian twist and a nod to those ancient teahouse eggs found in China. The results give the outside of the peeled eggs a lovely brown marbling and the filling a powerful combination of balanced flavors. The use of fresh mint here is less a reflection of the traditional Darjeeling kitchen than the influence of Sanjay's mother. She loved mint's flavor and added it to many of her dishes. With a large bed of it growing beside the *burra* bungalow on Glenburn, Sanjay followed suit.

Makes 12 egg halves:

6 large eggs, at room temperature
2 heaped Tbsp loose-leaf strong black tea or 3 or 4 tea bags of black tea
2 Tbsp minced onion
2 heaped Tbsp minced, fresh mint
½ to 1 small green chili, minced
¼ cup/60 ml mayonnaise, preferably Hellmann's
Salt and freshly ground pepper

Place the eggs in a small saucepan and cover with at least 1 inch/2.5 cm water. Bring to a boil, reduce the heat to medium low, sprinkle in the tea leaves, and gently boil for 9 minutes. Remove from the heat.

Without discarding the liquid, remove the eggs with a slotted spoon, and using the back of a spoon, smack the shells to create webby veinings of cracks. Do not peel. Place in a large bowl.

Let the tea-infused water from boiling the eggs cool for a few minutes, then it pour over the eggs. Allow them to sit in the liquid until completely cooled, at least 1 to 2 hours. Turn the eggs from time to time for even marbling.

Gently peel. Slice in half lengthwise, carefully setting aside the whites. Place the yolks in a mixing bowl.

Add the onion, mint, chili, and mayonnaise to the bowl, season with salt and pepper, and blend with a fork.

Spoon a generous amount of filling into each of the egg halves and mound attractively with the inside curve of a spoon. Arrange on a platter.

DARJEELING TEA SORBET

This sorbet, loosely adapted from Anthony Wild's *The East India Company Book of Tea*, is indulgent, even festive, and shows off one of Darjeeling tea's many culinary possibilities. It can also be prepared in a sorbet or ice-cream maker. Instead of freezing and whisking with a fork as follows, pour the chilled tea mixture into the machine and churn, adding the whisked egg white toward the end of the freezing time.

Makes about 1 quart/1 liter:

3 Tbsp/10 g high-quality loose-leaf Darjeeling tea
¼ cup/50 g sugar
Juice of 1 ripe lemon, about 3 Tbsp
1 large egg white, at room temperature

Place the tea in a large, heatproof teapot. Bring 3 cups/700 ml freshly drawn water to a boil, remove from the heat, let cool for a moment, then pour over the tea. Let infuse for 5 minutes.

Pour the liquid through a fine sieve or muslin bag into a freezerproof mixing bowl. Stir in the sugar, then the lemon juice. Allow to cool.

Once the liquid has cooled completely, place in freezer and allow to freeze. Once the liquid begins to freeze, start frequently scraping the edges of the bowl with a fork or spoon and stirring.

Meanwhile, in a clean bowl, beat the egg white with a mixer over medium speed to soft peaks that are opaque and still moist.

When the liquid is nearly frozen, fold in the egg white and whisk with a fork. Keep in the freezer until ready to serve.

Serve in chilled sorbet glasses.

Store, tightly covered, in the freezer and use within 1 week.

Author's Note and Acknowledgments

Upon finishing university in the early 1990s, I flew to London and attempted to travel overland to Cape Town. I didn't make it, and that planned year on the road morphed into four of backpacking around Africa and Asia before I settled down in London to do graduate work. In a litany of exotic places, I discovered the disparate world of tea, learned that it was far more than just a hot drink, and that, in the diverse manners of its preparation and service, it played an integral part in the daily life of many cultures. Perhaps more than anything else those years, I was sustained by numerous daily cups of tea—generally milky, always sweet, often spiced.

I had been on the road for a couple of years when I traveled to Darjeeling and tasted *tea* itself for the first time: pure and fresh, no sugar, no milk, no lemon, no cardamom or ginger, no black pepper. It was winter, and that week, huddled near an ineffective coal fire in my room at the Planters' Club, a pot of autumn flush under a knitted tea cozy with fraying threads on a side table, tea warmed me after lengthy strolls around the surrounding tea-covered hillsides (glimpsing, briefly but memorably, Kanchenjunga). The liquor seemed just as bright and fresh as the mountain air.

While over the years I have visited many of the world's tea-producing areas, none managed to seduce or intrigue me like Darjeeling—the tea itself, the hills, the industry's history, a garden's archaic structure, the warmth of the people. I long wondered exactly how and why the tea grown here is, simply, the finest, and why it could not be replicated elsewhere.

To find out, it took closely following an entire harvesting year and spending time on Darjeeling's gardens during each of the year's four flushes, from the opening first flush in March to the end of the autumn one in November, watching the tea change with the seasons—and *tasting* those changes in the cup.

While the book is supported by broad reading and research, the secrets of Darjeeling's uniqueness were ultimately revealed by hanging out with industry experts in Kolkata and Delhi and, most important, with tea planters, supervisors, pluckers, and tea-factory workers on sixteen Darjeeling estates (and as an anonymous interloper on many others). Accompanying them in the fields among bushes they know intimately, checking tea fermenting on long beds, and joining the ritual of daily batch tastings, I came to appreciate the handicraft nature of Darjeeling tea. But I also learned of the deep and urgent challenges the storied industry is battling.

In researching this book in India I relied heavily on the generosity of others, quite often strangers. I was treated with surprising openness in the secluded, generally private, and often secretive world of Darjeeling tea, welcomed with *chaat* and biscuits, *momos*, and full lunches, as countless people generously shared their experience and knowledge. And, of course, tea. There were many hundreds of cups of tea not only in tasting rooms but also to leisurely drink on the verandahs of managers' bungalows. Afterward, I was inevitably sent on my way with bulging foil packets of tea leaves from the day's choicest batch, just fired and barely yet cooled, to sustain me between visits.

I would particularly like to thank the following, beginning with people on the estates: Jay Neogi, Krishnendu Chatterjee, and Sumit Jha (Ambootia); Sumit Kumar (Bannockburn); Parminder Singh Bhoi (Castleton); Mukul Chowdhury (Ging); Sanjay Sharma, Husna-Tara Prakash, Jenni Bolton, Darlene Khan, and staff (Glenburn); Ashok Kumar, Prem, and staff (Goomtee); Rishi Saria (Gopaldhara); B. N. Mudgal, S. K. Choudhary, and Shantanu Kejriwal (Jungpana); Shankar Lal Chaudhury (Lingia); Rajah Banerjee, Kuldip Basu, Indrey Sarki, Sanjoy Mukherjee, Nayan Lama, and Maya Chettrini and family (Makaibari); Vijay Dhancholia and Normal Chhetri (Marybong); H. R. Chaudhary (Namring); B. B. Singh and Shiv Saria (Rohini); Satish Mantri (Singbulli); Suman Das (Thurbo); and Rajesh Pareek (Tukvar).

In Darjeeling, special thanks go to Sandeep Mukherjee at the DTA; Girish Sarda, Vijay Sarda, and Sailesh Sarda at Nathmulls; Elizabeth

Clarke, Tinduf-La, and staff at the Windamere Hotel; the staff of the Elgin Hotel; Shabnam Bhutia and staff at the Planters' Club; Maya Primlani and staff at the Oxford Book & Stationery Co.; the family at Kunga's restaurant; and R. N. Chatterjee. In Kurseong, thanks to Ravindra Kang, Laltu Purkait, and staff at the Cochrane Place Hotel. In Kolkata, thanks to Anindyo Choudhury, Sabyasachi Choudhury, Karanvir Singh Chadda, Kavi Seth at J. Thomas & Co.; Sujoy Sengupta at Chamong Tee; and Vinita Mansata at Earthcare Books. In Delhi, deep appreciation to Sanjay Kapur and assistants at Aap Ki Pasand, and Vikram Mittal and assistants at Mittal Stores. And in Munnar, Kerala, Sanjith Raju at KDHP.

A special thanks to those in India who patiently answered my many follow-up questions on the phone and by e-mail, checked details for me, and dug up statistics: Anindyo Choudhury, Vijay Dhancholia, Ravindra Kang, Vikram Mittal, Jay Neogi, Girish Sarda, Rishi Saria, and Sanjay Sharma. Much appreciated!

Outside of India, thanks to Steven Smith of Steven Smith Teamaker, Malcolm Gardner and Judith Kiely at the Rudolf Steiner Library of the Anthroposophical Society in America, Kiran Tawady of Hampstead Teas in London, and Salvador Sans at Sans & Sans in Barcelona.

For all of those friends who have shared pots of tea over the years (and all over the globe), many thanks for teaching me how much the drink can mean.

Deep appreciation goes to my agent, Doe Coover, who has been integral to this book from its inception.

At Bloomsbury USA, I wish to wholeheartedly thank George Gibson for his early enthusiasm, strong guidance, and keen editing. Also thanks to Rob Galloway, Nathaniel Knaebel, Laura Phillips, Gleni Bartels, and eagle-eyed copyeditor Steve Boldt. At Bloomsbury UK, Michael Fishwick, Oliver Holden-Rea, and Anna Simpson. At Bloomsbury India, special warm-hearted thanks to Diya Kar Hazra for her insight and enthusiasm. Also to the rest of the crew office. And also to Anurima Roy, Yogesh Sharma, and the rest of the Delhi team. And those at Bloomsbury Australia.

And finally to my parents, Bill and Joanne and in-laws Tomàs and Rosa, for their help while I was researching the book. And to Eva, Alba, and Maia for their patience at my lengthy absences as I disappeared into the Darjeeling hills and then, once back home, my office.

Notes

TWO LEAVES AND A BUD

1. Main sources for details on the auction are the Fall 2003 *Upton Tea Newsletter*; various contemporary newspaper articles; and a piece from the July 28, 2003, issue of *Outlook*, J. Thomas & Co. records; and an interview with the auctioneer at the time, Kavi Seth.
2. Singh, "Makaibari Tea Estate."
3. Statistics from J. Thomas & Co.
4. Pratt, "Darjeeling—Part 3."
5. "2003 Makaibari Silvertips."
6. O'Connor, "Starbucks Opens Its First Tea Bar."
7. Indian Tea Association Web site, "Chronology."
8. Gandhi, *Key to Health*, 24.

CHAPTER 1: INTO THE HILLS

1. Forster, *Passage to India*, 96.
2. Ali, *Field Guide to the Birds of the Eastern Himalayas*, xi.
3. Twain, *Following the Equator*, 529.
4. Hooker, *Himalayan Journals*, 101.
5. Ibid., 103.
6. Ghosh, *Hungry Tide*, 6.
7. O'Malley, *Bengal District Gazetteer: Darjeeling*, 73.

CHAPTER 2: JOURNEY FROM THE EAST

1. Heiss and Heiss, *Story of Tea*, 4.
2. Ibid., 6.
3. Ibid., 7.
4. Hohenegger, *Liquid Jade*, 72.
5. Fisher, *Way of Tea*, 64.

6. Yü, *Classic of Tea*, 107.

7. Ibid., 111.

8. Sōshitsu, *Japanese Way of Tea*, 10.

9. Ibid.

10. Watts, *Way of Zen*, 86.

11. Ibid., 190.

12. Ibid.

13. Okakura, *Book of Tea*, 1.

14. Ibid.

15. Ibid., 64.

16. Ibid., 35.

17. Ibid., 11.

18. Ukers, *All About Tea*, 1:38.

19. Okakura, *Book of Tea*, 7.

20. Ukers, *All About Tea*, 1:23.

21. Ibid., 1:24–25.

22. Moxham, *Tea*, 27.

23. Wheeler, *Early Records of British India*, 22.

24. Illustration in Ukers, *All About Tea*, 2:294.

25. Ibid.

26. Cowper, *Selected Poems*, 40.

27. Ukers, *All About Tea*, 1:27.

28. Churchill, *Poetical Works of Charles Churchill*, 20.

29. Johnson, "Review of *A Journal of Eight Days' Journey*."

30. Illustration in Ukers, *All About Tea*, 2:294.

31. Pettigrew and Richardson, *New Tea Companion*, 12.

32. Yü, *Classic of Tea*, 50.

CHAPTER 3: THE COMPANY

1. "Tea," *Asiatic Journal*, 775.

2. Keay, *Honourable Company*, 24.

3. Ibid., 25.

4. Robins, *Corporation That Changed the World*, 43.

5. Keay, *Honourable Company*, 111.

6. Ibid., 81.

7. Robins, *Corporation That Changed the World*, 44.

8. Keay, *Honourable Company*, 78.

9. Robins, *Corporation That Changed the World*, 46.

10. Ali, *Twilight in Delhi*, x.

11. Robins, *Corporation That Changed the World*, 68.

12. Cavendish, "Black Hole of Calcutta."

13. James, *Raj*, 30.

14. Robins, *Corporation That Changed the World*, 3.

15. Ibid., 73.

16. Ibid., 143.

17. Ali, *Twilight in Delhi*, x.

18. Ukers, *All About Tea*, 1:44.
19. Ibid., 1:73.
20. Ibid., 1:99.
21. Ibid.
22. Moxham, *Tea*, 27.
23. Robins, *Corporation That Changed the World*, 109.
24. Ukers, *All About Tea*, 2:130.
25. "History and View of the Tea Trade," 345.
26. "Tea," *Asiatic Journal*, 775.
27. Griffiths, *Tea*, 96.
28. Keay, *Honourable Company*, 430.
29. Ibid., 431.
30. Hanes and Sanello, *Opium Wars*, 19.
31. Keay, *Honourable Company*, 431.
32. Boorstin, *Discoverers*, 176.
33. Chopra, *Indigenous Drugs of India*, 205.
34. Watt, *Papaver Somniferum*, 19.
35. Dormandy, *Opium*, 64.
36. Watt, *Papaver Somniferum*, 19.
37. Martin, *Statistics of the Colonies*, 366.
38. Fay, *Opium War*, 14.
39. Griffiths, *Tea*, 242.
40. Trocki, *Opium, Empire*, 32.
41. Robins, *Corporation That Changed the World*, 157.
42. Trocki, *Opium, Empire*, 71.
43. Keay, *Honourable Company*, 452.
44. Fay, *Opium War*, 18.
45. Haines and Sanello, *Opium Wars*, 37.
46. Ibid., 55.
47. Dormandy, *Opium*, 139.
48. Ukers, *All About Tea*, 1:7.
49. Hanes and Sanello, *Opium Wars*, 156.
50. Griffiths, *Tea*, 95.
51. Dormandy, *Opium*, 151.

CHAPTER 4: AN INDIAN TEA INDUSTRY

1. Barua, *Urban History*, 47.
2. Ukers, *All About Tea*, 1:135.
3. Barua, *Urban History*, 47.
4. Ibid.
5. Griffiths, *History of the Indian Tea Industry*, 36.
6. *Original Correspondence of Sir Joseph Banks*, 8.
7. Kew Gardens Web site, "About Nathaniel Wallich."
8. Arnold, "Plant Capitalism," 917.
9. Ibid.
10. Ibid.

11. Ibid., 918.

12. Ibid., 917.

13. Mann, *Early History of the Tea Industry*, 6.

14. Ferguson, *Empire*, 142.

15. Ukers, *All About Tea*, 1:138.

16. Griffiths, *History of the Indian Tea Industry*, 41.

17. Dormandy, *Opium*, 130.

18. Griffiths, *History of the Indian Tea Industry*, 40.

19. Ibid., 41.

20. Ibid.

21. "Copy of Papers Received from India," 99.

22. Ibid.

23. Mann, *Early History of the Tea Industry*, 12.

24. Griffiths, *History of the Indian Tea Industry*, 47.

25. Ukers, *All About Tea,* 2:145.

26. Bruce, *Account of the Manufacture*, 16.

27. Griffiths, *History of the Indian Tea Industry*, 45.

28. Ukers, *All About Tea,* 2:145.

29. Moxham, *Tea*, 99.

30. Scott, *Great Tea Venture*, 160.

31. Ibid, 2:99.

32. Bruce, *Account of the Manufacture*, 7.

33. Ibid., 8.

34. Ibid., 15.

35. Griffith, *Journals of Travels in Assam*, 15.

36. Griffiths, *History of the Indian Tea Industry*, 51.

37. Ibid.

38. "First Public Sale of the Newly Discovered Assam Tea," 339.

39. Ukers, *All About Tea*, 1:147

40. Griffiths, *History of the Indian Tea Industry*, 69.

41. Mann, *Early History of the Tea Industry*, 30.

42. Ibid., 13.

43. Ibid., 36.

44. Griffiths, *History of the Indian Tea Industry*, 58.

45. "Tea in India."

46. Moxham, *Tea*, 114.

47. Roy, *Historical Review of Growth*, 168.

48. Griffiths, *History of the Indian Tea Industry*, 127.

49. Ibid., 129.

50. Ibid., 144.

51. Paul, *Story of Tea*, 67.

CHAPTER 5: CHINA LEAF

1. Dunse History Society Web site, "Robert Fortune."

2. Rose, *For All the Tea in China*, 8.

3. Fortune, *Journey to the Tea Countries of China*, 165.

4. Ibid., 355.
5. Ibid., 414.
6. Ibid., 356.
7. Ibid.
8. Rose, *For All the Tea in China*, 198.
9. Harcourt, *Flagships of Imperialism*, 100.
10. Kipling, *Land and Sea Tales*, 35.
11. Keay, *India Discovered*, 21.
12. Fortune, *Journey to the Tea Countries of China*, 358.
13. Ibid., 362.
14. Ibid., 363.
15. Ibid.
16. Ibid.
17. Ibid., 398.
18. Ibid.

CHAPTER 6: DARJEELING

1. Hooker, *Himalayan Journals*, 106.
2. Lamb, *British India and Tibet*, 68–69.
3. Hooker, *Himalayan Journals*, 113.
4. Lamb, *British India and Tibet*, 69.
5. Ibid., 70.
6. O'Malley, *Bengal District Gazetteer: Darjeeling*, 21.
7. Pinn, *Darjeeling Pioneers*, 35.
8. Banerjee and Banerjee, *Darjeeling Tea*, 4.
9. Pinn, *Road of Destiny*, 35.
10. Hooker, *Himalayan Journals*, 137.
11. Ibid., 120n.
12. Campbell, "Note on the Lepchas of Sikkim," 383.
13. Hooker, *Himalayan Journals*. 121.
14. Ibid.
15. Lepcha, "Indigenous Lepchas," 81.
16. Ibid., 78.
17. Lingdamo, "Philosophy of the Lepcha Religion," 59.
18. Sarkar, "Lepcha Community in Darjeeling Hills."
19. Lama, *Story of Darjeeling*, 49.
20. Pinn, *Road of Destiny*, 269.
21. Moon, *British Conquest of India*, 724.
22. Malleson, *History of the Indian Mutiny*, 84.
23. Pinn, *Road of Destiny*, 281.
24. Ibid., 178.
25. Darjeeling District Web site, "History."
26. Darjeeling District Web site, "Time Capsule."
27. Pinn, *Road of Destiny*, 275.
28. *Journal of the Anthropological Institute*, 379.
29. Ibid., 391.

30. Pinn, *Road of Destiny*, 274.
31. *Journal of the Anthropological Institute*, 391.
32. O'Malley, *Bengal District Gazetteer: Darjeeling*, 22.
33. Ibid., 32.
34. Ghosh, *Tea Gardens of West Bengal*, 22.
35. Ibid.
36. Ibid.
37. *Nest & Wings Guide to Darjeeling*, 49
38. Hooker, *Flora of British India*, vi.
39. Lamb, *British India and Tibet*, 75.
40. Hooker, *Himalayan Journals*, 91.
41. Ibid., 92.
42. Lama, *Story of Darjeeling*, 40–41.
43. See the lenghty 1846 memorandum by Under Secretary to the Government of India titled "On the Connection of the Sikkim Rajah with the British Government, and Dr. Campbell's Reports of the Rajah's Unfriendliness," reproduced in Fred Pinn's *The Road to Destiny* (282–297), for the complete and tangled history of the transaction.
44. Darjeeling District Web site, "History."
45. *Journal of the Anthropological Institute*, 385.
46. Griffiths, *History of the Indian Tea Industry*, 88.
47. Dash, *Bengal District Gazetteer*, 113.
48. Ghosh, *Tea Gardens of West Bengal*, 27.
49. Dash, *Bengal District Gazetteer*, 114.

CHAPTER 7: TERROIR TO TEACUP

1. Banerjee and Banerjee, *Darjeeling Tea*, 323.

CHAPTER 8: A DECISION FOR THE MOUTH TO MAKE

1. *Lord of Darjeeling*.
2. Yü, *Classic of Tea*, 74.

CHAPTER 9: KNOCKING DOWN

1. Anindyo Choudhury.
2. Kumar, *Indigo Plantations and Science*, 128.
3. "J. Thomas & Company Bets on Tea Bull Run."
4. Langewiesche, "Million-Dollar Nose."
5. Sanyal, "What I'm Today Is due to Tea."
6. "Orthodox, CTC Varieties Quote Higher."
7. Priyadershini, "A Tea Time Story."
8. J. Thomas & Co. Web site, "People."
9. Burke, *Annual Register*, 154.
10. Bolton, "EU Grants Darjeeling Protected Geographical Status."

CHAPTER 10: THE RAJ IN THE HILLS ABOVE

1. Morris, *Stones of Empire*, 2.
2. Judd, *Lion and the Tiger*, 101.
3. Hastings, "How the British Did It."
4. Dalrymple, "Plain Tales from British India."
5. Ibid.
6. Ferguson, *Empire*, 39.
7. Keay, *Honourable Company*, 422.
8. Robins, *Corporation That Changed the World*, 17.
9. Dalrymple, "White Mischief."
10. Jack, "Prince William's Indian DNA Piques Interest."
11. Kipling, *Collected Poems*, 245.
12. Allen, *Plain Tales from the Raj*, 46.
13. Smith, *Afternoon Tea Book*, 29.
14. Dalrymple, "Plain Tales from British India."
15. Ukers, *All About Tea*, 2:67.
16. Scott, *Day of the Scorpion*, 256.
17. Sherman, "Viceroys and Indians."
18. Kipling, *Plain Tales from the Hills*, 171.
19. Dalrymple, "Plain Tales from British India."
20. Das, *India Unbound*, 15.
21. Morris, *Heaven's Command*, 269.
22. Moorhouse, *India Britannica*, 145.
23. Herbert, *Flora's Empire*, 61.
24. Wright, *Hill Stations of India*, 18.
25. Steel and Gardiner, *Complete Indian Housekeeper*, 190.
26. Morris, *Heaven's Command*, 269.
27. Morris, *Pax Britannica*, 262.
28. Kipling, *Collected Poems*, 81.
29. Moorhouse, *India Britannica*, 145.
30. Ibid., 146.
31. Steel and Gardiner, *Complete Indian Housekeeper*, 53.
32. Lama, *Story of Darjeeling*, 145.
33. Sannial, *History of Darjeeling*, 95.
34. Hobbes, *Imperial India*, 67. John Oliver Hobbes was the pen name for Anglo-American novelist Pearl Mary Teresa Craigie.
35. Ibid., 70.
36. Orwell, *Burmese Days*, 14.
37. Woolf, *Growing*, 135.
38. Masani, *Indian Tales of the Raj*, 52.
39. Kay, *Far Pavillions*, 146.
40. Ibid., 10.
41. Herbert, *Flora's Empire*, 22.
42. Lama, *Story of Darjeeling*, 90.
43. Ibid., 147.
44. Dozey, *Concise History of the Darjeeling*, 209.
45. Wright, *Hill Stations of India*, 263.

CHAPTER 11: NOSTALGIA

1. Lila, "Darjeeling: Tea and Sympathy."
2. Burton, *Raj at Table*, 196.
3. Ibid.
4. Ibid., 197.
5. Steel and Gardiner, *Complete Indian Housekeeper*, 58.
6. Ibid., 59.
7. Ibid., 305.
8. Ibid., 304.
9. James, *Portrait of a Lady*, 3.
10. Orwell, *Burmese Days*, 37.
11. Brennan, *Curries & Bugles*, 219.
12. Baker, *Jigger, Beaker, & Glass*, 38.
13. Fleming, *Man with the Golden Gun*, 53.
14. Greene, *Heart of the Matter*, 59.
15. Ibid., 57.
16. Ibid., 191.
17. Maugham, *Collected Short Stories*, 91.

CHAPTER 12: PLANTERS AND PLUCKERS

1. Dozey, *Concise History of Darjeeling*, 207.
2. Lama, *Story of Darjeeling*, 90.
3. Kipling, *Plain Tales from the Hills*, 35.
4. Moxham, *Tea*, 6.
5. Ibid., 227–28.
6. Lama, *Story of Darjeeling*, 86.
7. O'Malley, *Bengal District Gazetteer: Darjeeling*, 85.
8. Much of the information on these German missionaries comes from Pinn's *Darjeeling Pioneers*, which particularly focuses on the Wernicke-Stölke families.
9. Ibid., 84.
10. Ibid., 89.
11. Ibid., 95.
12. Pinn, *Louis Mandelli*, 3. Much of the information on Mandelli comes from Pinn's self-published monograph on the planter.
13. Ibid., 8.
14. O'Malley, *Bengal District Gazetteer: Darjeeling*, 84.
15. Banerjee, *Rajah of Darjeeling Organic Tea*, 1–2. Many of the details on Samler come from Banerjee's work plus stories from himself, passed on down through generations.
16. Ibid., 2–3.
17. Ibid., 3.
18. Lama, *Story of Darjeeling*, 85.
19. Pinn, *Louis Mandelli*, 8.

20. Ukers, *All About Tea*, 2:156.
21. Pinn, *Louis Mandelli*, 17.
22. Ibid., 28. Pinn's slim work is enclosed within coarse-grained, custard-yellow covers the texture of birch-tree bark. Printed in southern India on grayish mimeographed sheets, it includes cyclostyled pages that reproduce a number of Mandelli's handwritten letters. In looping, upright, and mostly unjoined cursive, Mandelli's writing is old-fashioned and measured, composed with studied steadiness in neatly spaced lines. There are no splotches or gatherings of ink from the pen pausing, no words scratched out. The lower loops of the *f*'s are narrow and pointed like Arthurian swords, the *a*'s curl around like cats' tails, and the stems of the lowercase *d*'s bend over almost horizontally, a flourish that feels less a stylish dash of verve than, even then, something antiquated.
23. Ibid., 29.
24. Ibid., 33.
25. Ibid., 29.
26. Ibid., 50.
27. Hume and Marshall, *Game Birds of India*, 83.
28. Baker, *Fauna of British India*, 241.
29. O'Malley, *Bengal District Gazetteer: Darjeeling*, 84.
30. Ibid.

CHAPTER 13: MIDNIGHT'S PLANTERS

1. Vikram Mittal.
2. Sandeep Mukherjee.
3. Sethi, "Lord of the Leaf."
4. Guha, *India After Gandhi*, 215.
5. Sandeep Mukherjee.
6. Sinha, "Changing Flavour of Tea."
7. Ibid.
8. Banerjee and Banerjee, *Darjeeling Tea*, 353.
9. Paul, *Story of Tea*, 62.
10. Banerjee and Banerjee, *Darjeeling Tea*, 374.
11. Ibid.
12. Ghosal, "China Buys 20,000 kg of Darjeeling Tea."
13. Banerjee and Banerjee, *Darjeeling Tea*, 374.
14. Moshavi, "Reading Trouble in Darjeeling's Tea Leaves."
15. Banerjee and Banerjee, *Darjeeling Tea*, 525.
16. Bera, "Simmering Discontent over Tea."
17. Griffiths, *Tea*, 349.
18. Banerjee and Banerjee, *Darjeeling Tea*, 353–54.
19. Ghosal, "Darjeeling Tea Prices Fall 50 Percent."
20. Chakrabarty, "New Champ Takes Darjeeling Cup."
21. Monna, "India Set to Sip Jungpana Darjeeling."
22. Ukers, *All About Tea*, 1:415.

CHAPTER 14: CRISES

1. Barth, "Why India Won't Be the Next China."
2. Sanyal, *Land of the Seven Rivers*, 120, citing Angus Maddison.
3. Ibid., 234, citing Angus Maddison.
4. World Bank Web site, "India Overview."
5. Indrawati, "To End Extreme Poverty."
6. Chandrasekhar, "Chronic Famishment."
7. World Bank Web site, "India Overview."
8. Ibid.
9. "TB Claims a Life Every 90 Seconds in Country."
10. "Delhi Is the Most Polluted City: WHO Study."
11. U.S. Energy Information Agency overview of India.
12. Sannial, *History of Darjeeling*, 21.
13. Lama, *Story of Darjeeling*, xvi.
14. Ibid., x.
15. Gupta, "Turmoil May Take Toll on Tea Trade."
16. Sharma, "Conversation With: Gorkha Leader Bimal Gurung."
17. "Will Not Delay Gorkhaland."
18. "GJM Reverses Decision."
19. Gazmer, "Darjeeling Cool to CM Visit."
20. National Tea and Coffee Development Board of Nepal.
21. Bolton, "European Blenders Establishing Himalayan Brand."
22. Chakrabarty, "New Champ Takes Darjeeling Cup."
23. Ghosal, "Darjeeling Tea Prices Fall 50 Percent."
24. Darjeeling District Web site, "Geography."

PART IV: AUTUMN FLUSH

1. Mariage Frères Web site, "CASTLETON, FTGFOP1."

CHAPTER 15: POSITIVE WINDS

1. Ghosal, "China Buys 20,000 kg of Darjeeling Tea."
2. Ghosal, "South Korea Imports 1,500 Tonne."
3. Ghosal, "European Trade Council."

CHAPTER 16: SOIL

1. Banerjee, *Rajah of Darjeeling Organic Tea*, 8.
2. Makaibari Tea Estate blogspot, "Makaibari, 1970."
3. Krishna, *Sacred Animals of India*, 53.
4. Ibid., 58.
5. Banerjee, *Rajah of Darjeeling Organic Tea*, 5.
6. Ibid., 14.
7. *Lord of Darjeeling*.
8. Ibid.
9. Banerjee, *Rajah of Darjeeling Organic Tea*, 28.

CHAPTER 17: CELESTIAL INFLUENCES

1. Bio-Dynamic Association of India Web site, "Rudolf Steiner & Bio-Dynamic Agriculture."
2. *Lord of Darjeeling.*
3. Storl, *Culture and Horticulture*, 36.
4. Ibid., 37.
5. Cole, *Voodoo Vintners*, 16.
6. Bio-Dynamic Association of India Web site, "Bio-Dynamic Farms in India."
7. Datta, "For That Exclusive Cuppa."
8. Steiner, *Agriculture Course*, 3.
9. Bio-Dynamic Association of India Web site, "Bio-Dynamic Farming Recipes."
10. Demeter Web site, "Biodynamic Preparations."
11. Bio-Dynamic Association of India Web site, "Bio-Dynamic Farming Recipes."
12. Demeter Web site, "Biodynamic Preparations."
13. Steiner, *Agriculture Course*, 77.
14. Ibid., 78.
15. Banerjee, *Rajah of Darjeeling Organic Tea*, 81.
16. Demeter Web site, "Particularities of Demeter."
17. Srinivasa, "Storm in a Tea Cup."
18. Mazumdar, "2-Leaf Booty."
19. Starkel, "Ambootia Landslide Valley."
20. "Ambootia—'Healthy Soils, Healthy People.' "
21. Storl, *Culture and Horticulture*, 37.
22. Fukuoka, *One-Straw Revolution*, 119.
23. Prime, *Hinduism and Ecology*, ix.
24. Ibid., 9.
25. Ibid., 80.
26. Ibid., 9.
27. Rufus, *History of Alexander*, 198.
28. Prime, *Hinduism and Ecology*, 60.

CHAPTER 18: INITIATIVES

1. Steiner, *Agriculture Course*, 29.
2. Krishna, *Sacred Animals of India*, 76.
3. Kansara, "Animal Husbandry in the Vedas," 279.
4. Basak, "Despite Challenges."
5. Ghosal, "Tea Tourism."
6. Basak, "Despite Challenges."
7. Chhetri, "Kanchenjungha in View."
8. *Lord of Darjeeling.*
9. Mazumdar, "2-Leaf Booty."
10. *Lord of Darjeeling.*
11. Niyogi, "Iconic Makaibari Tea Changes Hands."
12. Dutt, "Tata Global Buys 10.59% More in Kanan Devan."
13. Mary, "Tea Totallers."

14. Ibid.
15. Krishnakumar, "Tata Tea Handed Control."
16. Mary, "Ta-Ta to All That."
17. Dutt, "Tata Global Buys 10.59% More in Kanan Devan."

CHAPTER 19: BACK DOWN THE HILL

1. Drexler, "Look at Jaya Teas."
2. Bajaj, "After a Year of Delays."
3. O'Connor, "Starbucks Opens Its First Tea Bar."
4. Rao, "Why India's Yuppies Want Starbucks."
5. *Speaking of Siva*, 88.
6. *Lord of Darjeeling.*

RECIPES

1. Campbell, "Note on the Lepchas of Sikkim," 382–83.
2. Lady Resident, *Englishwoman in India*, 201.
3. Simpson, *London Ritz Book of Afternoon Tea*, 56.
4. Brennan, *Curries & Bugles*, 190.
5. Chhetri and Sinha, "Rain Civic Respite but Tourist Headache."
6. Smith, *Afternoon Tea Book*, 104.
7. Steel and Gardiner, *Complete Indian Housekeeper*, 252.

Bibliography

**GENERAL HISTORY OF INDIA, EMPIRE, THE RAJ,
AND TRAVELOGUES**

Allen, Charles. *Plain Tales from the Raj*. London: Abacus, 1975.

Baber, Zaheer. *The Science of Empire: Scientific Knowledge, Civilization, and Colonial Rule in India*. Albany: SUNY Press, 1996.

Boorstin, Daniel. *The Discoverers*. New York: Vintage, 1985.

Booth, Martin. *Opium: A History*. New York: St. Martin's, 1996.

Bowen, H. V. *The Business of Empire: The East India Company and Imperial Britain, 1756–1833*. Cambridge: Cambridge University Press, 2006.

Burke, Edmund. *The Annual Register; or, A View of the History, Politics, and Literature for the Year 1770*. London: J. Dodsley, 1794.

Chopra, R. N. *Chopra's Indigenous Drugs of India*. 1933 ed. Reprint, Kolkata: Academic Publisher, 2006.

Clarke, Hyde. *Colonization, Defence, and Railways in Our Indian Empire*. London: John Weale, 1857.

Dalrymple, William. *The Last Mughal: Fall of a Dynasty*. New York: Vintage, 2007.

———. *White Mughals: Love and Betrayal in Eighteenth-Century India*. London: HarperCollins, 2002.

Das, Gurcharan. *India Unbound*. New York: Anchor, 2001.

de Courcy, Anne. *Fishing Fleet: Husband-Hunting in the Raj*. London: Weidenfeld & Nicolson, 2012.

Dormandy, Thomas. *Opium: Reality's Dark Dream*. New Haven, CT: Yale University Press, 2012.

Fay, Peter Ward. *The Opium War, 1840–1842*. Chapel Hill: University of North Carolina Press, 1997.

Ferguson, Niall. *Empire: How Britain Made the Modern World*. London: Penguin, 2004.

Gribbin, Mary, and John Gribbin. *Flower Hunters*. Oxford: Oxford University Press, 2008.

Griffith, William. *Journals of Travels in Assam, Burma, Bhootan, Afghanistan and the Neighbouring Countries*. Arranged by John M'Clelland. Calcutta: Bishop's College Press, 1847.

Guha, Ramachandra. *India after Gandhi: The History of the World's Largest Democracy*. London: Macmillan, 2007.

Hanes, W. Travis, III, and Frank Sanello. *The Opium Wars: The Addiction of One Empire and the Corruption of Another*. Naperville, IL: Sourcebooks, 2002.

Harcourt, Freda. *Flagships of Imperialism: The P&O Company and the Politics of Empire from Its Origins to 1867*. Manchester: Manchester University Press, 2006.

Hobbes, John Oliver. *Imperial India: Letters from the East*. London: T. Fisher Unwin, 1903.

Hohenegger, Beatrice. *Liquid Jade: The Story of Tea from East to West*. New York: St. Martin's Press, 2007.

James, Lawrence. *Raj: The Making and Unmaking of British India*. New York: St. Martin's Griffin, 1997.

Judd, Denis. *The Lion and the Tiger: The Rise and Fall of the British Raj*. Oxford: Oxford University Press, 2010.

Keay, John. *The Honourable Company: History of the English East India Company*. London: HarperCollins, 1993.

———. *India: A History*. Rev. and expanded. New York: Grove, 2010.

———. *India Discovered*. London: Collins, 1988.

Kennedy, Dane. *The Magic Mountains: Hill Stations and the British Raj*. Berkeley: University of California Press, 1996.

Malleson, George Bruce. *History of the Indian Mutiny: 1857–1858*. Vol. 1. London: Longmans, Green, & Co., 1986.

Martin, Robert Montgomery. *Statistics of the Colonies of the British Empire in the West Indies, South America, North America, Asia, Austral-Asia, Africa, and Europe*. London: Wm. H. Allen, 1839.

Masani, Zareer. *Indian Tales of the Raj*. Berkeley: University of California Press, 1990.

Mason, Philip. *The Men Who Ruled India*. New Delhi: Rupa, 1985.

McKinsey Global Institute. *The "Bird of Gold": The Rise of India's Consumer Market*. Mumbai: McKinsey Global Institute, May 2007.

Moon, Sir Penderel. *The British Conquest and Dominion of India*. London: Gerald Duckworth, 1989.

Moorhouse, Geoffrey. *India Britannica*. New York: Harper & Row, 1983.

Morris, Jan. *Farewell the Trumpets: An Imperial Retreat*. London: Faber & Faber, 1998.

———. *Heaven's Command: An Imperial Progress*. London: Faber & Faber, 1998.

———. *Pax Britannica: The Climax of an Empire*. London: Faber & Faber, 1998.

———. *Stones of Empire: The Buildings of the Raj*. Oxford: Oxford University Press, 2005.

Oliver, F. W. *Makers of British Botany: A Collection of Biographies by Living Botanists*. Cambridge: Cambridge University Press, 1913.

Robins, Nick. *The Corporation That Changed the World*. Hyderabad, India: Orient Longman, 2006.

Rufus, Quintus Curtius. *The History of Alexander*. Translated by John Yardley. London: Penguin, 1984.

Sanyal, Sanjeev. *Land of the Seven Rivers: A Brief History of India's Geography.* New Delhi: Penguin, 2012.

Tharoor, Shashi. *India: From Midnight to the Millennium.* New York: HarperPerennial, 1998.

Trocki, Carl A. *Opium, Empire and the Global Political Economy: A Study of the Asian Opium Trade, 1750–1950.* London: Routledge, 1999.

U.S. Energy Information Agency overview of India. http://www.eia.gov/countries/country-data.cfm?fips=IN.

Watt, George. *Papaver Somniferum—Opium: An extract from the sixth volume of the Dictionary of Economic Products of India.* Calcutta: Government of India Central Printing Office, 1891.

Wheeler, J. Talboys. *Early Records of British India: History of the English Settlements in India.* Calcutta: Newman, 1878.

Wolpert, Stanley. *India.* 4th ed. Berkeley: University of California Press, 2009.

DARJEELING AND THE HIMALAYAS

Bhatt, Vikram. *Resorts of the Raj: Hill Stations of India.* Ocean City, NJ: Grantha Corporation, 1997.

Bisht, Ramesh Chandra. *International Encyclopaedia of Himalayas.* 3. New Delhi: Mittal, 2008.

Campbell, A. "Note on the Lepchas of Sikkim." *Journal of the Asiatic Society of Bengal* 9, pt. 1: 379–93. Calcutta: Bishop's College Press, 1840.

Dash, Arther Jules. *Bengal District Gazetteer: Darjeeling.* 1947 ed. Reprint. Siliguri, India: National Library, 2011.

Dozey, E. C. *A Concise History of the Darjeeling District Since 1835.* 2nd ed. 1922. Reprint, Kolkata: Bibiophil, 2012.

Fletcher, David Wilson. *Himalayan Tea Garden.* New York: Thomas Y. Crowell, 1955.

Gorer, Geoffrey. *The Lepchas of Sikkim.* Reprint, New Delhi: Gyan, 1996.

Herbert, Captain J. D. *Travelling to Darjeeling in 1830.* Edited by Fred Pinn. Bath, UK: Pagoda Tree Press, 2000.

Hooker, Joseph Dalton. *Himalayan Journals: Notes of a Naturalist.* Vol. 2. Rev. ed. London: John Murray, 1855.

Hopkirk, Peter. *Trespassers on the Roof of the World.* Oxford: Oxford University Press, 1983.

The Journal of the Anthropological Institute of Great Britain and Ireland. Vol. 7. London: Anthropological Institute of Great Britain and Ireland, 1878.

Lama, Basant B. *The Story of Darjeeling.* 2nd ed. Kurseong, India: Nilima Yonzone Lama Publications, 2009.

Lamb, Alastair. *British India and Tibet, 1766–1910.* London: Routledge & Kegan Paul, 1986.

Morris, Jan. *A Writer's World: Travels 1950–2000.* London: Faber & Faber, 2003.

Nest & Wings Guide to Darjeeling Area. 29th ed. New Delhi: Nest & Wings, 2009.

O'Malley, L. S. S. *Bengal District Gazetteer: Darjeeling.* 1907 ed. Reprint, New Delhi: Logos Press, 1999.

Pinn, Fred. *Darjeeling Pioneers: The Wernicke-Stölke Story.* 2nd rev ed. Bath. UK: Pagoda Tree Press, 2008.

———. *Louis Mandelli: Darjeeling Tea Planter and Ornithologist*. London: Fred Pinn, 1985.

———. *The Road of Destiny: Darjeeling Letters, 1839*. Calcutta: Oxford University Press, 1990.

Sannial, Hurry Mohun. *A History of Darjeeling*. 1880 ed. Translated by Gargi Gupta, Shipra Bhattacharyya, and Aditi Roy Ghatek. Bath, UK: Pagoda Tree Press, 2009.

Twain, Mark. *Following the Equator*. Washington, DC: National Geographic, 2005.

Wright, Gillian. *Hill Stations of India*. New Delhi: Penguin, 1998.

BENGAL, ASSAM, AND OTHER REGIONS OF INDIA

Barua, Deepali. *Urban History of India*. New Delhi: Mittal, 1994.

Betts, Vanessa. *Kolkata & West Bengal*. Bath, UK: Footprint, 2011.

Dutta, Krishna. *Calcutta: A Cultural and Literary History*. Updated ed. Oxford: Signal, 2009.

Moorhouse, Geoffrey. *Calcutta: The City Revealed*. London: Penguin, 1983.

TEA

Banerjee, Gangadhar, and Srijeet Banerjee. *Darjeeling Tea: The Golden Brew*. Lucknow, India: International Book Distributing, 2007.

Banerjee, Rajah. *The Rajah of Darjeeling Organic Tea: Makaibari*. New Delhi: Cambridge University Press, 2008.

Bruce, C. A. *An Account of the Manufacture of the Black Tea as Now Practised at Suddeya in Upper Assam, by the Chinamen Sent Thither for That Purpose. With Some Observations on the Culture of the Plant in China, and Its Growth in Assam*. Calcutta: G. H. Huttmann, Bengal Military Orphan Press, 1838.

"Copy of Papers Received from India Relating to the Measures Adopted for Introducing the Cultivation of the Tea Plant within the British Possessions in India." *Sessional Papers Printed by Order of the House of Lords, or Presented by Royal Command in the Session 1839*. Vol. 7. London: 1839.

Das, G. M. *Pests of Tea in North-East India and Their Control*. Jorhat, India: Tocklai Experimental Station, 1965.

"The Discovery of the Tea Plant in Assam." *Asiatic Journal and Monthly Registry for British and Foreign India, China and Australasia* 18 (September–December). London: William H. Allen, 1835.

Fisher, Aaron. *The Way of Tea*. North Clarendon, Vermont: Tuttle, 2010.

Fortune, Robert. *A Journey to the Tea Countries of China Including Sung-Lo and the Bohea Hills; with a Short Notice of the East India Company's Tea Plantations in the Himalaya Mountains*. London: John Murray, 1852.

Gait, Edward. "The Growth of the Tea Industry." In *Discovery of North-East India*. Vol. 5, edited by S. K. Sharma and Usha Sharma, 39–48. New Delhi: Mittal, 2005.

Gandhi, Mohandas K. *Key to Health*. Translated by Sushila Nayar. Ahmedabad, India: Navajivan Publishing House, 1948.

Ghosh, Tushar Kanti. *Tea Gardens of West Bengal*. Delhi: B. R. Publishing, 1987.

Griffiths, John. *Tea: A History of the Drink That Changed the World*. London: André Deutsch, 2011.

Griffiths, Sir Percival. *The History of the Indian Tea Industry*. London: Weidenfeld and Nicolson, 1967.

Harler, C. R. *The Culture and Marketing of Tea*. London: Oxford University Press, 1933.

———. *Tea Growing*. London: Oxford University Press, 1966.

Heiss, Mary Lou, and Robert J. Heiss. *The Story of Tea: A Cultural History and Drinking Guide*. Berkeley, CA: Ten Speed, 2007.

———. *The Tea Enthusiast's Handbook: A Guide to Enjoying the World's Best Teas*. Berkeley, CA: Ten Speed, 2010.

"History and View of the Tea Trade." *Monthly Repertory of English* 3:331–39. Paris: Parsons, Galignani, 1808.

Karmakar, K. G., and G. D. Banerjee. *The Tea Industry in India: A Survey*. Mumbai: National Bank for Agricultural and Rural Development, 2005.

The Lord of Darjeeling. Dir. Xavier de Lauzanne, Aloest Productions, 2005.

Mann, Harold H. *The Early History of the Tea Industry in North-East India*. Calcutta: Bengal Economic Journal, 1918.

Masset, Claire. *Tea and Tea Drinking*. Oxford: Shire, 2010.

Misra, Sib Ranjan. *Tea Industry in India*. Delhi: S. B. Nangia, 1986.

Moxham, Roy. *Tea: Addiction, Exploitation, and Empire*. Rev. ed. New York: Carroll & Graf, 2004.

Okakura, Kakuzo. *The Book of Tea*. Mineola, NY: Dover, 1964.

The Original Correspondence of Sir Joseph Banks Relating to the Foundation of the Royal Botanic Garden, Calcutta, and the Summary of the 150th Anniversary Volume of the Royal Botanic Garden, Calcutta. Edited by Kalipada Biswas. Calcutta: Royal Asiatic Society of Bengal, 1950.

Paul, E. Jaiwant. *The Story of Tea*. New Delhi: Roli, 2013.

Pettigrew, Jane, and Bruce Richardson. *The New Tea Companion: A Guide to Teas Throughout the World*. London: National Trust Enterprises, 2005.

Pratt, James Norwood. "Darjeeling—Part 3." http://www.tching.com/2009/04/darjeeling-part–3/. April 7, 2009.

Rose, Sarah. *For All the Tea in China*. New York: Penguin, 2010.

Roy, Suparna. "Historical Review of Growth of Tea Industries in India: A Study of Assam Tea." 2011 International Conference on Social Science and Humanity. *IPEDR* 5. Singapore: IACSIT Press, 2011.

Scott, J. M. *The Great Tea Venture*. New York: E. P. Dutton, 1964.

Sōshitsu XV, Sen. *The Japanese Way of Tea: From Its Origins in China to Sen Rikyū*. Translated by V. Dixon Morris. Honolulu: University of Hawai'i Press, 1998.

"Tea." *Asiatic Journal and Monthly Registry for British India and Its Dependencies* 21 (January–June 1826). London: Kingsbury, Parbury, & Allen, 1826.

Ukers, William H. *All About Tea*. 2 vols. New York: Tea and Coffee Trade Journal, 1935. Reprint, Mansfield, CT: Martino, 2007.

Upton Tea Quarterly. Quarterly newsletter. Hopkinton, MA: Fall 2006–Summer 2011.

Wild, Anthony. *The East India Company Book of Tea*. London: HarperCollins, 1994.

Wright, Gillian. *The Darjeeling Tea Book*. New Delhi: Penguin, 2011.

Yü, Lu. *The Classic of Tea*. Translated by Francis Ross Carpenter. Boston: Little, Brown, 1973.

FOOD AND DRINK

Baker, Charles. *Jigger, Beaker, & Glass*. Lanham, MD: Derrydale, 1992.

Brennan, Jennifer. *Curries & Bugles: A Memoir & Cookbook of the British Raj*. Boston: Periplus, 2000.

Brown, Patricia. *Anglo-Indian Food and Customs*. New Delhi: Penguin, 1998.

Burton, David. *The Raj at Table: A Culinary History of the British in India*. London: Faber & Faber, 1994.

DasGupta, Minakshie. *The Bengal Cookbook*. 2nd ed. New Delhi: UBS, 2012.

Inner Wheel Club of Darjeeling. *Himalayan Recipes*. Inner Wheel Club of Darjeeling, 1991.

A Lady Resident. *The Englishwoman in India*. London: Smith, Elder, 1864.

Simpson, Helen. *The London Ritz Book of Afternoon Tea*. New York: Arbor House, 1986.

Smith, Michael. *The Afternoon Tea Book*. New York: Macmillan, 1986.

Solmonson, Lesley Jacobs. *Gin: A Global History*. London: Reaktion, 2012.

Steel, Flora Annie, and Grace Gardiner. *The Complete Indian Housekeeper and Cook*. 4th ed. 1898. Reprint, Oxford: Oxford University Press, 2011.

NATURE, AGRICULTURE, FIELD GUIDES, AND GARDENS

Ali, Sálim. *Field Guide to the Birds of the Eastern Himalayas*. Delhi: Oxford University Press, 1977.

Anderson, E. B. *Camellias*. London: Blandford Press, 1961.

Arnold, David. "Plant Capitalism and Company Science: The Indian Career of Nathaniel Wallich." *Modern Asian Studies* 42, no 5 (2008): 899–928.

Axelby, Richard. "Calcutta Botanic Garden and the Colonial Re-ordering of the Indian Environment." *Archives of Natural History* 35 (2008): 150–63.

Baker, Stuart. *The Fauna of British India, Including Ceylon and Burma*. Vol. 1. London: Taylor & Francis, 1922.

Cole, Katherine. *Voodoo Vintners: Oregon's Astonishing Biodynamic Winegrowers*. Corvallis: Oregon State University Press, 2011.

Datta, Sukanya. *Social Life of Plants*. Delhi: National Book Trust, India, 2000.

Fukuoka, Masanobu. *The One-Straw Revolution*. Goa, India: Other India Press, 1992.

Herbert, Eugenia W. *Flora's Empire: British Gardens in India*. New Delhi: Allen Lane, 2013.

Hooker, Joseph Dalton. *Flora of British India*. Vol. 1. London: L. Reeve, 1872.

Hume, Allen Octavian, and Charles Marshall. *The Game Birds of India, Burmah, and Ceylon*. Vol. 2. Calcutta: A. O. Hume & Marshall, 1881.

Indian Botanic Garden Howrah. Calcutta: Botanical Survey of India, unknown year.

Kansara, N. M. "Animal Husbandry in the Vedas." In *History of Agriculture in India, up to c. 1200 A.D.*, edited by Lallanji Gopal and V. C. Srivastava, 275–306. New Delhi: Center for Studies in Civilizations, 2008.

Kumar, Prakash. *Indigo Plantations and Science in Colonial India*. New York: Cambridge University Press, 2012.

Mansata, Bharat. *The Vision of Natural Farming*. Kolkata: Earthcare, 2010.

Menon, Subhadra. *Trees of India*. New Delhi: Timeless, 2000.

Mukherjee, Pippa. *Trees of India*. Delhi: Oxford University Press, 2008.

Rangarajan, Mahesh. *India's Wildlife History*. New Delhi: Permanent Black, 2012.

Santpau, H. *Common Trees*. Delhi: National Book Trust, India, 1966.

Steiner, Rudolf. *Agriculture Course: The Birth of the Biodynamic Movement*. Forest Row, UK: Rudolf Steiner Press, 2004.

Storl, Wolf D. *Culture and Horticulture: The Classic Guide to Biodynamic and Organic Gardening*. Updated ed. Berkeley, CA: North Atlantic, 2013.

Tamsang, K. P. *Glossary of Lepcha Medicinal Plants*. 2nd ed. Darjeeling, India: Lyangsong Tamsang, 2012.

RELIGION, SPIRITUALITY, AND MYTHOLOGY

Gokhale, Namita. *The Book of Shiva*. Delhi: Penguin Ananda, 2012.

Knott, Kim. *Hinduism: A Very Short Introduction*. Oxford: Oxford University Press, 1998.

Krishna, Nanditha. *The Book of Vishnu*. New Delhi: Penguin, 2009.

———. *Sacred Animals of India*. New Delhi: Penguin, 2010.

Prime, Ranchor. *Hinduism and Ecology: Seeds of Truth*. Delhi: Motilal Banarsidass, 1994.

Speaking of Siva. Translated by A. K. Ramanujan. London: Penguin, 1973.

Watts, Alan. *The Way of Zen*. New York: Vintage, 1989.

NOVELS, STORIES, POEMS, MEMOIRS, BIOGRAPHIES, AND LITERARY CRITICISM

Ahmed, Ali. *Twilight in Delhi*. New Delhi: Rupa, 2007.

Allen, Charles. *Kipling Sahib: India and the Making of Rudyard Kipling*. New York: Pegasus, 2009.

Churchill, Charles. *The Poetical Works of Charles Churchill*. Vol. 2. London: C. & R. Baldwin, 1804.

Cowper, William. *Selected Poems*. Edited by Nick Rhodes. New York: Routledge, 2003.

Fleming, Ian. *Man with the Golden Gun*. London: Vintage, 2012.

Forester, E. M. *A Passage to India*. London: Everyman's Library, 1991.

Ghosh, Amitav. *The Hungry Tide*. London: HarperCollins, 2005.

———. *Sea of Poppies*. Delhi: Penguin, 2009.

Gilmour, David. *The Long Recessional: The Imperial Life of Rudyard Kipling*. New York: Farrar, Straus & Giroux, 2002.

Greene, Graham. *The Heart of the Matter*. London: Penguin, 1987.

James, Henry. *The Portrait of a Lady*. London: Penguin, 2011.

Kaye, M. M. *The Far Pavilions*. London: Allen Lane, 1978.

Kipling, Rudyard. *Collected Poems of Rudyard Kipling*. Ware, Hertfordshire, UK: Wordsworth, 2001.

————. *Land and Sea Tales.* Looe, Cornwall, UK: House of Stratus, 2009.

————. *Plain Tales from the Hills.* London: Penguin, 1994.

Maugham, W. Somerset. *Collected Short Stories.* Vol. 4. New York: Penguin, 1963.

Naipaul, V. S. *An Area of Darkness.* London: Penguin, 1968.

Orwell, George. *Burmese Days.* London: Penguin, 1989.

Scott, Paul. *The Day of the Scorpion.* London: Panther, 1985.

————. *A Division of the Spoils.* London: Panther, 1983.

————. *The Jewel in the Crown.* Chicago: University of Chicago Press, 1966.

————. *The Towers of Silence.* London: Granada, 1984.

Woolf, Leonard. *Growing: An Autobiography of the Years 1904 to 1911.* San Diego: Harcourt Brace Jovanovich, 1961.

CITED MAGAZINE AND NEWSPAPER ARTICLES
AND WEB SITES

"Ambootia—'Healthy Soils, Healthy People.'" *Quarterly Update of Soil & More 2* (June 2013).

Bajaj, Vikas. "After a Year of Delays, the First Starbucks Is to Open in Tea-Loving India This Fall." *New York Times*, January 30, 2012.

Barth, Chris. "Why India Won't Be the Next China . . . and That's Bullish." *Forbes*, June 6, 2012.

Basak, Probal. "Despite Challenges, Darjeeling Continues to Fight for Its Identity." *Business Standard*, September 1, 2013.

Bera, Sayantan. "Simmering Discontent over Tea." *Down to Earth*, May 15, 2011.

Bibek, Debroy. "Who Are the Middle Class in India?" *Indian Express*, March 24, 2009.

Bio-Dynamic Association of India Web site. "Bio-Dynamic Farming Recipes." http://www.biodynamics.in/Recipes.htm.

————. "Bio-Dynamic Farms in India." http://www.biodynamics.in/bdfarms.htm.

————. "Rudolf Steiner & Bio-Dynamic Agriculture." http://www.biodynamics.in/rsteiner.htm.

Bolton, Dan. "EU Grants Darjeeling Protected Geographical Status." *World Tea News*, November 2, 2011.

————. "European Blenders Establishing Himalayan Brand." *World Tea News*, July 7, 2014.

Cavendish, Richard. "The Black Hole of Calcutta." *History Today* 56, no. 6 (June 2006).

Chakrabarty, Shaoli. "A New Champ Takes Darjeeling Cup." *Calcutta Telegraph*, December 16, 2013.

Chandrasekhar, C. P. "Chronic Famishment." *Hindu*, February 19, 2012

Chhetri, Vivek. "Darjeeling Discovers Lloyd After 146 Yrs." *Calcutta Telegraph*, June 6, 2011.

————. "Kanchenjungha in View, No Viewers." *Calcutta Telegraph*, October 11, 2013.

Chhetri, Vivek, and Avijit Sinha. "Rain Civic Respite but Tourist Headache." *Calcutta Telegraph*, May 29, 2014.

Dalrymple, William. "Plain Tales from British India." *New York Review of Books* 54, no. 7 (April 26, 2007).

————. "White Mischief." *Guardian*, December 9, 2002.

Darjeeling District Web site. "Geography." http://darjeeling.gov.in/geography.html.

————. "History." http://darjeeling.gov.in/darj-hist.html.

————. "Time Capsule." http://darjeeling.gov.in/time-capsule.html.

Datta, Aparna. "For That Exclusive Cuppa." *Hindu*, August 31, 2003.

Datta, Kanika. "In the Drink." *Business Standard*, April 26, 2012.

"Delhi Is the Most Polluted City: WHO Study." *Financial Express*, May 7, 2014.

Demeter Web site, "Biodynamic Preparations." http://www.demeter.net/what-is-demeter/biodynamic-preparations.

————. "Particularities of Demeter." http://www.demeter.net/what-is-demeter/particularities-of-demeter.

Drexler, Madeline. "A Look at Jaya Teas." *Tea & Coffee Trade Journal* 178, no. 6 (June–July 2006).

Dunse History Society (Scotland) Web site. "Robert Fortune." http://www.dunse-historysociety.co.uk/robertfortune.shtml.

Dutt, Ishita Ayan. "Tata Global Buys 10.59% More in Kanan Devan." *Business Standard*, July 6, 2013.

"First Public Sale of the Newly Discovered Assam Tea." *Merchant's Magazine and Commercial Review* 2. New York: Freeman Hunt, 1840.

Gazmer, Deep. "Darjeeling Cool to CM Visit." *Times of India*, July 18, 2014.

Ghosal, Sutanuka. "China Buys 20,000 kg of Darjeeling Tea Finds Hot Fans in the Country." *Economic Times*, May 13, 2013.

————. "Darjeeling Tea Prices Fall 50 Percent on Quality Concerns Post-Rains." *Economic Times*, September 27, 2013.

————. "European Trade Council, German Tea Association Uphold Darjeeling Tea's Authenticity." *Economic Times*, September 27, 2012.

————. "South Korea Imports 1,500 Tonne of Darjeeling Tea," *Economic Times*, November 5, 2013.

————. "Tea Tourism." *Economic Times*, October 21, 2013.

"GJM Reverses Decision, Calls Indefinite Bandh in Darjeeling." *Economic Times*, August 1, 2013.

Gupta, Aparajita. "Turmoil May Take Toll on Tea Trade." *Times of India*, February 11, 2011.

Hastings, Max. "How the British Did It." Review of *The Ruling Caste* by David Gilmour, and *Sahib* by Richard Holmes. *Telegraph*, September 27, 2005.

Indian Tea Association Web site, "Chronology." http://www.indiatea.org/chronology/chronologyofIT.pdf.

Indrawati, Sri Mulyani. "To End Extreme Poverty, Learn from a Small Village in India." World Bank blog, June 4, 2013. http://blogs.worldbank.org/voices/end-extreme-poverty-learn-small-village-india?

Jack, Ian. "Prince William's Indian DNA Piques Interest, Not Innuendo. That's Progress." *Guardian*, June 21, 2013.

Johnson, Samuel. "Review of *A Journal of Eight Days' Journey*." *Literary Magazine* 2, no. 13 (1757).

"J. Thomas & Company Bets on Tea Bull Run." *Economic Times*, January 20, 2011.

J. Thomas & Co. Web site. "People." http://www.jthomasindia.com/people.aspx.

Kew Gardens Web site. "About Nathaniel Wallich." http://www.kew.org/science-conservation/collections/nathaniel-wallich/about.

Krishnakumar, P. K. "Tata Tea Handed Control of Its Tea Plantations to Workers to Make Profit." *Economic Times*, October 13, 2010.

Langewiesche, William. "The Million-Dollar Nose." *Atlantic Monthly*, December 2000.

Lepcha, Dennis. "Indigenous Lepchas: Philosophy of Life and Worldview." *Salesian Journal of Humanities & Social Sciences* 3, no. 2 (December 2012): 76–84.

Lila, Muhammad. "Darjeeling: Tea and Sympathy." *Toronto Star*, February 12, 2010.

Lingdamo, Peter. "The Philosophy of the Lepcha Religion." *Salesian Journal of Humanities & Social Sciences* 3, no. 2 (December 2012), 55–62.

Makaibari Tea Estate blogspot. "Makaibari, 1970." October 14, 2007. http://makaibari.blogspot.com.es/2007/10/makaibari–1970.html.

Maqsood, Zofeen. "Tea Trail." *Hindustan Times*, September 1, 2012.

Mariage Frères Web site. "CASTLETON, FTGFOP1." http://www.mariagefreres.com/boutique/UK/ft+darjeeling-castleton-tea-autumn-flush+T1267.html.

Mary, John. "Ta-Ta to All That." *Outlook*, October 25, 2010.

———. "Tea Totallers." *Outlook*, October 31, 2010.

Mazumdar, Jaideep. "2-Leaf Booty." *Outlook*, November 21, 2005.

Meyer, Karl E. "The Company Store." *New York Times*, February 21, 1999.

Monna, Sovon. "India Set to Sip Jungpana Darjeeling." *Times of India*, June 26, 2014.

Moshavi, Sharon. "Reading Trouble in Darjeeling's Tea Leaves." *BusinessWeek*, October 30, 1994.

Niyogi, Subhro. "Iconic Makaibari Tea Changes Hands." *Times of India*, June 11, 2014.

O'Connor, Clare. "Starbucks Opens Its First Tea Bar as CEO Schultz Bets on $90 Billion Market." *Forbes*, October 23, 2013.

"Orthodox, CTC Varieties Quote Higher at North India Tea Market." *Economic Times*, June 28, 2013.

Orwell, George. "A Nice Cup of Tea." *Evening Standard*, January 12, 1946.

Priyadershini, S. "A Tea Time Story." *Hindu*, January 27, 2012.

Rao, Kavintha. "Why India's Yuppies Want Starbucks (It's Not about the Coffee)." *Guardian*, October 30, 2012.

Roy, Shobha. "Darjeeling Tea: Weather Plays Truant." *Hindu*, March 25, 2013.

Rushdie, Salman. "Outside the Whale." *Granta* 11 (Spring 1984).

Sanyal, Santanu. "What I'm Today Is due to Tea: Ashok Batra." *Hindu Business Line*, April 11, 2013.

Sarkar, Debasis. "Lepcha Community in Darjeeling Hills to Back West Bengal CM." *Economic Times*, June 13, 2013.

Sethi, Sunil. "Lord of the Leaf." *Outlook*, March 13, 1996.

Sharma, Anuradha. "A Conversation With: Gorkha Leader Bimal Gurung." *India Ink* (blog). *New York Times*, March 27, 2012. http://india.blogs.nytimes.com/2012/03/27/a-conversation-with-gorkha-leader-bimal-gurung/.

Sherman, A. J. "Viceroys and Indians." Review of *The Ruling Caste: Imperial Lives in the Victorian Raj* by David Gilmour. *New York Times*, April 30, 2006.

Singh, Kishore. "Turning Over a New Leaf." *Outlook Business*, June 21, 2014.

Singh, Madhur. "Makaibari Tea Estate." *Time*, April 25, 2008.

Sinha, Rabindra Nath. "The Changing Flavour of Tea." *Hindu Business Line*, August 31, 2007.

———. "Darjeeling Tea Industry in Dire Straits." *Hindu Business Line*, November 25, 2011.

Srinivasa, Kavitha. "Storm in a Tea Cup." *Business World*, July 22, 2011.

Starkel, Leszek. "Ambootia Landslide Valley—Evolution, Relaxation, and Prediction (Darjeeling Himalaya)." *Studia Geomorphologica Carpatho-Balcanica* 44 (2010): 113–33.

"TB Claims a Life Every 90 Seconds in Country." *Hindu*, March 25, 2010.

"Tea in India." *Illustrated London News*, August 15, 1857.

"2003 Makaibari Silvertips." *Upton Tea Newsletter*. Hopkinton, MA: Fall 2003. http://www.uptontea.com/shopcart/information/INFOnl_V12N4_Article_page1.asp.

van der Zee, Bib. "Spirituality from the Soil." *Guardian Weekly*, July 8, 2005.

"Will Not Delay Gorkhaland: Gurung." *Hindu*, August 17, 2013.

World Bank Web site. "India Overview." http://www.worldbank.org/en/country/india/overview.

Index

A Note on the Author

Jeff Koehler is a writer, traveler, and cook, and the author of books and articles on food and culture including *Spain: Recipes and Traditions*, named one of 2013's top cookbooks by the *New York Times*; *Morocco: A Culinary Journey with Recipes*; and *La Paella: Deliciously Authentic Rice Dishes from Spain's Mediterranean Coast*. His work has appeared in *Saveur, Food & Wine*, NPR.org, the *Washington Post,* the *Los Angeles Times, Afar, Tin House,* and *Best Food Writing 2010*. He lives in Barcelona.